MASTER PIECES OF THE WORLD'S BEST LITERATURE

EDITED BY

JEANNETTE L. GILDER

CLASSIC PUBLISHING CO., New York

Copyright, 1910, by
ORSAMUS TURNER HARRIS
NEW YORK

INDEX TO AUTHORS

2

INDEX TO TITLES

3

4

EDITOR'S FOREWORD

ARE there not already anthologies enough? Why a new one? To such inquiries many answers might be made, but two will sufficiently set forth the reasons why this series is not only worth while, but why it meets an existing demand.

Most of the anthologies are costly. To own them, one must pay many dollars; not, perhaps, more dollars than they are worth, but more dollars than one may find it convenient to spare. The anthology to which this is the foreword is the least expensive work of its class. That is one of its two best reasons for being. The other is that this one differs from its predecessors in aiming less at quantity than at quality.

It is impossible to make a large anthology without including many names that are not now, and never will be recorded on Fame's eternal bead roll. Perhaps some of the authors represented in these volumes may never attain that position, but the number of such is smaller than in any similar works. The Editor's plan has been to give copious extracts from the writers of admitted eminence, rather than briefer selections from a host of the lesser lights of literature.

In many instances the authors now living have made their own selections, which gives special interest to the work. It is not always that an author knows what is his best, but the Editor is inclined to think that those who have named the selections by which they prefer to be represented here have chosen wisely, and to these authors the Editor gives sincere thanks. Thanks are also due to those who have approved of the selections made by the Editor; and thanks are due furthermore to the publishers who have graciously permitted the use of copyrighted material.

In the case of all such material the Editor has been at pains to name the publisher so that the reader whose appetite is whetted by the extracts will know just where to go for more. The reading appetite grows with what it feeds upon and it is our firm conviction that these selections from the works of the masters will do much to create a wider circle of readers for the writings from which they have been chosen.

Jeannette L. Gilder

JOSEPH ADDISON

JOSEPH ADDISON, poet, essayist and dramatist, was born at Milston, Wiltshire, England, May 1, 1672. His father, who later became Dean of Lichfield, instilled in his mind the love of literature. Young Addison attended first the famous Charter House School in London, and later matriculated at Oxford. Destined for the church, his talent for writing drew him into political life. His poem, "The Campaign," celebrating the victory of Marlborough, brought him a commissionership, and he was seldom without office until his death at Holland House, in 1719. His contributions to the "Tatler" and the "Spectator" made him the most famous essayist of his time. His writings, instructive, imbued with a cheerful philosophy, a touch of gayety here and there, and of an almost faultless diction, live as models of their kind. The papers on Milton, Sir Roger de Coverley and "The Vision of Mirza" are his most famous works.

WESTMINSTER ABBEY

(From the "Spectator")

WHEN I am in a serious humor I very often walk by myself in Westminster Abbey; where the gloominess of the place, and the use to which it is applied, with the solemnity of the building, and the condition of the people who lie in it, are apt to fill the mind with a kind of melancholy, or rather thoughtfulness, that is not disagreeable. I yesterday passed a whole afternoon in the churchyard, the cloisters, and the church, amusing myself with the tombstones and inscriptions that I met with in those several regions of the dead. Most of them recorded nothing else of the buried person but that he was born upon one day, and died upon another; the whole history of his life being comprehended in those two circumstances that are common to all mankind. I could not but look upon these registers of existence, whether of brass or marble, as a kind of satire upon the departed persons; who had left no other memorial of them but that they were born and that they died. They put me in mind of several persons mentioned in the battles of heroic poems, who have sounding names given them, for no other reason but that they may be killed, and are celebrated for nothing but being knocked on the head. . . . The life of these men is finely described in holy writ by "the path of an arrow," which is immediately closed up and lost.

Upon my going into the church I entertained myself with the digging of a grave; and saw in every shovelful of it that was thrown up the fragment of a bone or skull intermixed with a kind of fresh mouldering earth that some time or other had a place in the composition of a human body. Upon this I began to consider with myself what innumerable multitudes of people lay confused together under the pavement of that ancient cathedral: how men and women, friends and enemies, priests and soldiers, monks and prebendaries, were crumbled amongst one another, and blended together in the same common mass; how beauty, strength and youth, with old age, weakness, and deformity, lay undistinguished in the same promiscuous heap of matter. After having thus surveyed this great magazine of mortality, as it were, in the lump, I examined it more particularly by the accounts which I found on several of the monuments which are raised in every quarter of that ancient fabric. Some of them were covered with such extravagant epitaphs, that if it were possible for the dead person to be acquainted with them, he would blush at the praise which his friends have bestowed upon him. There are others so excessively modest that they deliver the character of the person departed in Greek or Hebrew, and by that means are not understood once a twelvemonth. In the poetical quarter I found there were poets who had no monuments, and monuments which had no poets. I observed, indeed, that the present war had filled the church with many of these uninhabited monuments, which had been erected to the memory of persons whose bodies were perhaps buried in the plains of Blenheim, or in the bosom of the ocean. . . .

But to return to our subject. I have left the repository of our English kings for the contemplation of another day, when I shall find my mind disposed for so serious an amusement. I know that entertainments of this nature are apt to raise dark and dismal thoughts in timorous minds and gloomy imaginations; but for my own part, though I am always serious, I do not know what it is to be melancholy; and can, therefore, take a view of nature in her deep and solemn scenes with the same pleasure as in her most gay and delightful ones. By this means I can improve myself with those objects which others consider with terror. When I look upon the tombs of the great, every emotion of envy dies in me; when I read the epitaphs of the beautiful, every inordinate desire goes out; when I meet with the grief of parents upon a tombstone, my heart melts with compassion; when I see the tomb of the parents themselves, I consider the vanity of grieving for those whom we must quickly follow. When I see kings lying by those who deposed them, when I consider rival wits placed side by side, or the holy men that divided the world with their contests and disputes, I reflect with sorrow and astonishment

9

on the little competitions, factions, and debates of mankind. When I read the several dates of the tombs, of some that died yesterday, and some six hundred years ago, I consider that great day when we shall all of us be contemporaries, and make our appearance together.

SIR ROGER AT THE PLAY

(From the "Spectator")

MY friend Sir Roger de Coverley, when we last met together at the club, told me that he had a great mind to see the new tragedy with me, assuring me at the same time that he had not been at a play these twenty years. The last I saw, said Sir Roger, was the Committee, which I should not have gone to neither, had not I been told beforehand that it was a good Church of England comedy. He then proceeded to inquire of me who this Distressed Mother was; and upon hearing that she was Hector's widow, he told me that her husband was a brave man, and that when he was a schoolboy he had read his life at the end of the dictionary. My friend asked me, in the next place, if there would not be some danger in coming home late, in case the Mohocks should be abroad. "I assure you (says he), I thought I had fallen into their hands last night; for I observed two or three lusty black men that followed me halfway up Fleet Street, and mended their pace behind me, in proportion as I put on to get away from them. You must know (continued the knight with a smile) I fancied they had a mind to hunt me: for I remember an honest gentleman in my neighborhood who was served such a trick in King Charles the Second's time; for which reason he has not ventured himself in town ever since. I might have shown them very good sport, had this been their design; for as I am an old fox hunter, I should have turned and dodged, and have played them a thousand tricks they had never seen in their lives before." Sir Roger added that if these gentlemen had any such intention, they did not succeed very well in it; " for I threw them out (says he) at the end of Norfolk Street, where I doubled the corner, and got shelter in my lodgings before they could imagine what was become of me. However (says the knight), if Captain Sentry will make one with us to-morrow night, and if you will both of you call on me about four o'clock, that we may be at the house before it is full, I will have my own coach in readiness to attend you, for John tells me he has got the fore wheels mended."

The captain, who did not fail to meet me there at the appointed hour, bid Sir Roger fear nothing, for that he had put on the same sword which he had made use of at the battle of Steenkirk. Sir Roger's servants, and among the rest my old friend the butler had, I found, provided themselves with good oaken plants, to attend their master upon this occasion. When he had placed him in his coach, with myself at his left hand, the captain before him, and his butler at the head of his footmen in the rear, we convoyed him in safety to the playhouse; where, after having marched up the entry in good order, the captain and I went in with him, and seated him betwixt us in the pit. As soon as the house was full, and the candles lighted, my old friend stood up and looked about him with that pleasure which a mind seasoned with humanity naturally feels in itself at the sight of a multitude of people who seem pleased with one another and partake of the same common entertainment. I could not but fancy to myself, as the old man stood up in the middle of the pit, that he made a very proper center to a tragic audience. Upon the entering of Pyrrhus, the knight told me that he did not believe the King of France himself had a better strut. I was, indeed, very attentive to my old friend's remarks, because I looked upon them as a piece of natural criticism, and was well pleased to hear him, at the conclusion of almost every scene, telling me that he could not imagine how the play would end. One while he appeared much concerned for Andromache; and a little while after as much for Hermione; and was extremely puzzled to think what would become of Pyrrhus.

When Sir Roger saw Andromache's obstinate refusal to her lover's importunities, he whispered me in the ear that he was sure she would never have him; to which he added, with a more than ordinary vehemence, you cannot imagine, sir, what it is to have to do with a widow. Upon Pyrrhus his threatening afterwards to leave her, the knight shook his head, and muttered to himself, Ay, do if you can. This part dwelt so much upon my friend's imagination, that at the close of the third act, as I was thinking of something else, he whispered in my ear, " These widows, sir, are the most perverse creatures in the world. But pray (says he), you that are a critic, is this 'play according to your dramatic rules, as you call them? Should your people in tragedy always talk to be understood? Why, there is not a single sentence in this play that I do not know the meaning of."

The fourth act very luckily begun before I had time to give the old gentleman an answer. " Well (says the knight, sitting down with great satisfaction), I suppose we are now to see Hector's ghost." He then renewed his attention, and, from time to time, fell a praising the widow. He made, indeed, a little mistake as to one of her pages, whom, at his first entering, he took for Astyanax; but he quickly set himself right in that particular, though, at the same time, he owned he should have been very glad to have seen the little boy, "who," says he, "must needs be a very fine child by the account that is given of him." Upon Hermione's going off with a menace to Pyrrhus, the audience gave a loud clap; to which Sir Roger added, "On my word, a notable young baggage!"

As there was a very remarkable silence and stillness in the audience during the whole action, it was natural for them to take the opportunity of the intervals between the acts to express their opinion of the players, and of their respective parts. Sir Roger, hearing a cluster of them praise Orestes, struck in with them, and told them that he thought his friend Pylades was a very sensible man; as they were afterwards applauding Pyrrhus, Sir Roger put in a second time, "And let me tell you (says he), though he speaks but little, I like the old fellow in whiskers as well as any of them." Captain Sentry, seeing two or three wags who sat near us lean with an attentive ear towards Sir Roger, and fearing lest they should smoke the knight, plucked him by the elbow, and whispered something in his ear, that lasted till the opening of the fifth act. The knight was wonderfully attentive to the account which Orestes gives of Pyrrhus his death, and at the conclusion of it told me it was such a bloody piece of work that he was glad it was not done upon the stage. Seeing afterwards Orestes in his raving fit, he grew more than ordinary serious, and took occasion to moralize (in his way) upon an evil conscience, adding that "Orestes, in his madness, looked as if he saw something."

As we were the first that came into the house, so we were the last that went out of it; being resolved to have a clear passage for our old friend, whom we did not care to venture among the jostling of the crowd. Sir Roger went out fully satisfied with his entertainment, and we guarded him to his lodgings in the same manner that we brought him to the playhouse; being highly pleased, for my part, not only with the performance of the excellent piece which had been presented, but with the satisfaction which it had given to the good old man.

SIR ROGER AS A HOST

(From the "Spectator")

HAVING often received an invitation from my friend Sir Roger de Coverley, to pass away a month with him in the country, I last week accompanied him thither, and am settled with him for some time at his country house, where I intend to form several of my ensuing speculations. Sir Roger, who is very well acquainted with my humor, lets me rise and go to bed when I please, dine at his own table or in my chamber, as I think fit, sit still and say nothing without bidding me be merry. When the gentlemen of the country come to see him he only shows me at a distance. As I have been walking in his fields I have observed them stealing a sight of me over a hedge, and have heard the knight desiring them not to let me see them, for that I hated to be stared at.

"I am the more at ease in Sir Roger's family, because it consists of sober, staid persons; for as the knight is the best master in the world, he seldom changes his servants; and as he is beloved by all about him, his servants never care for leaving him; by this means his domestics are all in years, and grown old with their master. You would take his *valet-de-chambre* for his brother, his butler is gray-headed, his groom is one of the gravest men that I have ever seen, and his coachman has the looks of a privy councillor. You see the goodness of the master even in his old house-dog, and in a gray pad that is kept in the stable with great care and tenderness, out of regard for his past services, though he has been useless for several years.

"I could not but observe, with a great deal of pleasure, the joy that appeared in the countenances of these ancient domestics upon my friend's arrival at his country-seat. Some of them could not refrain from tears at the sight of their old master; every one of them pressed forward to do something for him, and seemed discouraged if they were not employed. At the same time the good old knight, with a mixture of the father and the master of the family, tempered the inquiries after his own affairs with several kind questions relating to themselves. This humanity and good nature engages everybody to him, so that when he is pleasant upon any of them, all his family are in good humor, and none so much as the person whom he diverts himself with; on the contrary, if he coughs, or betrays any infirmity of old age, it is easy for a stander-by to observe a secret concern in the looks of all his servants.

"My worthy friend has put me under the particular care of his butler, who is a very prudent man, and, as well as the rest of his fellow-servants, wonderfully desirous of pleasing me, because they have often heard their master talk of me as of his particular/friend."

"My chief companion when Sir Roger is diverting himself in the woods or the fields, is a very venerable man who is ever with Sir Roger, and has lived at his house in the nature of a chaplain above thirty years. This gentleman is a person of good sense and some learning, of a very regular life and obliging conversation; he heartily loves Sir Roger, and knows that he is very much in the old knight's esteem, so that he lives in the family rather as a relation than a dependent.

"I have observed in several of my papers that my friend Sir Roger amidst all his good qualities, is something of a humorist; and that his virtues as well as imperfections are, as it were, tinged by a certain extravagance which makes them particularly his, and distinguishes them from those of other men. This cast of mind, as it is generally very innocent in itself, so it renders his conversation highly agreeable and more delightful than the same degree of sense and virtue would appear in their common and ordinary colors. As I was walking with him last night, he asked me how I liked the good man whom I have just now mentioned: and without staying for my answer, told me that he was afraid of being insulted with Latin and Greek at his own table; for which reason he desired a particular friend of his at the university to find him out a clergyman rather of plain sense than much learning, of a good aspect, a clear voice, a sociable temper, and, if possible, a man that understood a little of backgammon. 'My friend (said Sir Roger) found me out this gentleman, who, besides the endowments required of him, is, they tell me, a good scholar, though he does not show it. I have given him the parsonage of the parish; and because I know his value, have set upon him a good annuity for life. If he outlives me, he shall find that he was higher in my esteem than perhaps he thinks he is. He has now been with me thirty years; and though he does not know I have taken notice of it, has never in all that time asked anything of me for himself, though he is every day soliciting me for something in behalf of one or other of my tenants, his parishioners. There has not been a law-suit in the parish since he has lived among them; if any dispute arises, they apply themselves to him for the decision; if they do not acquiesce in his judgment, which I think never happened above once or twice at most, they appeal to me. At his first settling with me, I made him a present of all the good sermons which have been printed in English, and only begged of him that every Sunday he would pronounce one of them in the pulpit. Accordingly, he has digested them into such a series that they follow one another naturally, and make a continued system of practical divinity.' "

Sir Roger's picture gallery is an interesting portion of his ancient mansion. There is one picture in it which has reference to his own personal history:

" At the very upper end of this handsome structure I saw the portraiture of two young men standing in a river, the one naked, the other in a livery. The person supported seemed half dead, but still so much alive as to show in his face exquisite joy and love towards the other. I thought the fainting figure resembled my friend Sir Roger; and looking at the butler, who stood by me, for an account of it, he informed me that the person in the livery was a servant of Sir Roger's, who stood on the shore while his master was swimming, and observing him taken with some sudden illness, and sink under water, jumped in and saved him. He told me Sir Roger took off the dress he was in as soon as he came home, and by a great bounty at that time, followed by his favor ever since, had made him master of that pretty seat which we saw at a distance as we came to this house. I remembered, indeed, Sir Roger said, there lived a very worthy gentleman to whom he was highly obliged, without mentioning anything further. Upon my looking a little dissatisfied at some part of the picture, my attendant informed me that it was against Sir Roger's will, and at the earnest request of the gentleman himself, that he was drawn in the habit in which he had saved his master."

But the gallery is chiefly filled with the portraits of the old De Coverleys. There we have the knight in buff of the days of Elizabeth, who won "a maid of honor, the greatest beauty of her time," in a tournament in the tilt-yard. The spendthrift of the next generation—the fine gentleman who "ruined everybody that had anything to do with him, but never said a rude thing in his life," is drawn at full length, with his "little boots, laces, and slashes." But the real old English country gentleman, who kept this course of honor in evil times—in days of civil commotion, and afterwards in a period of court profligacy—is a character which we trust will never be obsolete:

"This man (pointing to him I looked at) I take to be the honor of our house, Sir Humphrey de Coverley: he was in his dealings as punctual as a tradesman, and as generous as a gentleman. He would have thought himself as much undone by breaking his word as if it were to be followed by bankruptcy. He served his country as knight of this shire to his dying day. He found it no easy matter to maintain an integrity in his words and actions, even in things that regarded the offices which were incumbent upon him in the care of his own affairs and relations of life, and therefore dreaded (though he had great talents) to go into employments of state, where he must be exposed to the snares of ambition. Innocence of life and great ability were the distinguishing parts of his character; the latter, he had often observed, had led to the destruction of the former, and he used frequently to lament that great and good had not the same signification. He was an excellent husbandman, but had resolved not to exceed such a degree of wealth; all above it he bestowed in secret bounties, many years after the sum he aimed at for his own use was attained. Yet he did not slacken his industry, but to a decent

old age spent the life and fortune which was superfluous to himself in the service of his friends and
neighbors."

The ghosts which used to haunt Sir Roger's mansion were laid, even in his time, by a good orthodox
process:

"My friend Sir Roger has often told me, with a
great deal of mirth, that at his first coming to his
estate he found three parts of his house altogether
useless; that the best room in it had the reputation
of being haunted, and by that means was locked up;
that noises had been heard in his long gallery, so
that he could not get a servant to enter it after
eight o'clock at night; that the door of one of his
chambers was nailed up, because there went a story
in the family, that a butler had formerly hanged
himself in it; and that his mother, who lived to a
great age, had shut up half the rooms in the house,
in which either her husband, a son, or daughter had
died. The knight, seeing his habitation reduced to
so small a compass, and himself in a manner shut
out of his own house, upon the death of his mother
ordered all the apartments to be flung open, and
exorcised by his chaplain, who lay in every room,
one after another, and by that means dissipated the
fears which had so long reigned in the family."

But the belief in apparitions was not passed away.
The haunted ruins are described by Addison with
his usual grace:

"At a little distance from Sir Roger's house,
among the ruins of an old abbey, there is a long
walk of aged elms, which are shot up so very high,
that when one passes under them, the rooks and
crows that rest upon the tops of them seem to be
cawing in another region. I am very much delighted
with this sort of noise, which I consider as a kind of
natural prayer to that Being who supplies the wants
of His whole creation, and who, in the beautiful

language of the Psalms, feedeth the young ravens that call upon him. I like this retirement the better, because of an ill report it lies under of being haunted; for which reason (as I have been told in the family) no living creature ever walks in it besides the chaplain. My good friend the butler desired me, with a very grave face, not to venture myself in it after sunset, for that one of the footmen had been almost frightened out of his wits by a spirit that appeared to him in the shape of a black horse without a head; to which he added, that about a month ago one of the maids, coming home late that way with a pail of milk upon her head, heard such a rustling among the bushes that she let it fall."

A COUNTRY SUNDAY

(From the " Spectator ")

I AM always very well pleased with a country Sunday, and think, if keeping holy the seventh day were only a human institution it would be the best method that could have been thought of for the polishing and civilizing of mankind. It is certain the country people would soon degenerate into a kind of savages and barbarians, were there not such frequent returns of a stated time, in which the whole village meet together with their best faces, and in their cleanest habits, to converse with one another upon indifferent subjects, hear their duties explained to them and join together in adoration of the Supreme Being. Sunday clears away the rust of the whole week, not only as it refreshes in their minds the notions of religion, but as it puts both the sexes upon appearing in their most agreeable forms, and exerting all such qualities as are apt to give them a figure in the eye of the village. A country fellow distinguishes himself as much in the churchyard as a citizen does upon the 'Change, the whole parish politics being generally discussed in that place, either after sermon or before the bell rings.

"My friend Sir Roger, being a good churchman, has beautified the inside of his church with several texts of his own choosing. He has likewise given a handsome pulpit-cloth, and railed in the communion table at his own expense. He has often told me, that at his coming to his estate, he found his parishioners very irregular: and that in order to make them kneel, and join in the responses, he gave every one of them a hassock and a Common Prayer Book; and at the same time employed an itinerant singing-master, who goes about the country for that purpose, to instruct them rightly in the tunes of the Psalms, upon which they now very much value themselves, and indeed outdo most of the country churches that I have ever heard.

"As Sir Roger is landlord to the whole congregation, he keeps them in very good order, and will suffer nobody to sleep in it besides himself; for if by chance he has been surprised into a short nap at sermon, upon recovering out of it, he stands up and looks about him, and if he sees anybody else nodding, either wakes them himself, or sends his servants to them. Several other of the old knight's particularities break out upon these occasions. Sometimes he will be lengthening out a verse in the singing Psalms, half a minute after the rest of the congregation have done with it; sometimes, when he is pleased with the matter of his devotion, he pronounces Amen three or four times in the same prayer; and sometimes stands up when everybody else is upon their knees, to count the congregation, or see if any of his tenants are missing.

"I was yesterday very much surprised to hear of my old friend, in the midst of the service, calling

out to one John Matthews to mind what he was
about and not disturb the congregation. This John
Matthews, it seems, is remarkable for being an idle
fellow, and at that time was kicking his heels for his
diversion. This authority of the knight, though ex-
erted in that odd manner which accompanies him
in all circumstances of life, has a very good effect upon the parish, who are not polite enough to
see anything ridiculous in his behavior; besides that
the general good sense and worthiness of his character make his friends observe these little singular-
ities as foils that rather set off than blemish his
good qualities.

"As soon as the sermon is finished, nobody pre-
sumes to stir till Sir Roger is gone out of the
church. The knight walks down from his seat in
the chancel between a double row of his tenants,
that stand bowing to him on each side; and every
now and then inquires how such a one's wife, or
mother, or son, or father do, whom he does not see
at church; which is understood as a secret repri-
mand to the person that is absent.

"The chaplain has often told me, that upon a
catechising day, when Sir Roger has been pleased
with a boy that answers well, he has ordered a Bible
to be given to him next day for his encouragement,
and sometimes accompanies it with a flitch of bacon
to his mother. Sir Roger has likewise added five
pounds a year to the clerk's place; and, that he may
encourage the young fellows to make themselves
perfect in the church service, has promised upon
the death of the present incumbent, who is very old,
to bestow it according to merit.

"The fair understanding between Sir Roger and
his chaplain, and their mutual concurrence in doing
good, is the more remarkable, because the very next
village is famous for the differences and contentions
that arise between the parson and the 'squire, who

live in a perpetual state of war. The parson is always preaching at the 'squire, and the 'squire, to be revenged on the parson, never comes to church. The 'squire has made all his tenants atheists and tithe-stealers, while the parson instructs them every Sunday in the dignity of his order, and insinuates to them, in almost every sermon, that he is a better man than his patron. In short, matters are come to such an extremity, that the 'squire has not said his prayers either in public or private this half-year; and the parson threatens him, if he does not mend his manners, to pray for him in the face of the whole congregation.

"Feuds of this nature, though too frequent in the country, are very fatal to the ordinary people; who are so used to be dazzled with riches that they pay as much deference to the understanding of a man of an estate as of a man of learning; and are very hardly brought to regard any truth, how important soever it may be, that is preached to them, when they know there are several men of five hundred a year who do not believe it."

ÆSCHYLUS

ÆSCHYLUS, the greatest name in Greek drama, was born at Eleusis, 525 B.C. He fought against the Persian invaders, greatly distinguishing himself at Marathon, and at Salamis ten years later. This lent coloring to one of the poet's most striking pictures in "The Persians." He first appeared in the rôle of tragedy when twenty-six. His dramas were produced in rapid succession, but only seven survive. He died 456 B.C. The Middle Ages paid the most profound reverence to his name.

THE COMPLAINT OF PROMETHEUS

(From "Prometheus Bound," Translation of Elizabeth Barrett Browning)

PROMETHEUS (ALONE)

O Holy Æther, and swift-winged Winds,
    And River-wells, and laughter innumerous
    Of yon Sea-waves! Earth, mother of us all,
And all-viewing cyclic Sun, I cry on you,—
Behold me a god, what I endure from gods!
    Behold, with throe on throe,
    How, wasted by this woe,
I wrestle down the myriad years of Time!
    Behold, how fast around me
The new King of the happy ones sublime
Has flung the chain he forged, has shamed and
      bound me!
Woe, woe! to-day's woe and coming morrow's
    I cover with one groan. And where is found me
      A limit to these sorrows?

24

And yet what word do I say? I have foreknown
Clearly all things that should be; nothing done
Comes sudden to my soul—and I must bear
What is ordained with patience, being aware
Necessity doth front the universe
With an invincible gesture. Yet this curse
Which strikes me now, I find it hard to brave
In silence or in speech. Because I gave
Honor to mortals, I have yoked my soul
To this compelling fate. Because I stole
The secret fount of fire, whose bubbles went
Over the ferrule's brim, and manward sent
Art's mighty means and perfect rudiment,
That sin I expiate in this agony,
Hung here in fetters, 'neath the blanching sky.
    Ah, ah me! what a sound,
What a fragrance sweeps up from a pinion unseen
Of a god, or a mortal, or nature between,
Sweeping up to this rock where the earth has he,
        bound,
To have sight of my pangs, or some guerdon obtain—
Lo, a god in the anguish, a god in the chain!
      The god Zeus hateth sore,
      And his gods hate again,
As many as tread on his glorified floor,
Because I loved mortals too much evermore.
Alas me! what a murmur and motion I hear,
    As of birds flying near!
    And the air undersings
    The light stroke of their wings—
And all life that approaches I wait for in fear.

A PRAYER TO ARTEMIS

(From Miss Swanwick's Translation of "The Suppliants")

STROPHE IV.

Though Zeus plan all things right,
Yet is his heart's desire full hard to trace;

Nathless in every place
Brightly it gleameth, e'en in darkest night,
Fraught with black fate to man's speech-gifted race.

ANTISTROPHE IV.

Steadfast, ne'er thrown in fight,
The deed in brow of Zeus to ripeness brought;
For wrapt in shadowy night,
Tangled, unscanned by mortal sight,
Extend the pathways of his secret thought.

STROPHE V.

From towering hopes mortals he hurleth prone
To utter doom: but for their fall
No force arrayeth he; for all
That gods devise is without effort wrought.
A mindful Spirit aloft on holy throne
By inborn energy achieves his thought.

ANTISTROPHE V.

But let him mortal insolence behold:—
How with proud contumacy rife,
Wantons the stem in lusty life
My marriage craving;—frenzy over-bold,
Spur ever-pricking, goads them on to fate,
By ruin taught their folly all too late.

STROPHE VI.

Thus I complain, in piteous strain,
Grief-laden, tear-evoking, shrill;
Ah woe is me! woe! woe!
Dirge-like it sounds; mine own death-trill
I pour, yet breathing vital air.
Hear, hill-crowned Apia, hear my prayer!
Full well, O land,
My voice barbaric thou canst understand;
While oft with rendings I assail
My byssine vesture and Sidonian veil.

A PRAYER TO ARTEMIS

ANTISTROPHE VI.

My nuptial right in Heaven's pure sight
  Pollution were, death-laden, rude;
    Ah woe is me! woe! woe!
  Alas for sorrow's murky brood!
Where will this billow hurl me? Where?
Hear, hill-crowned Apia, hear my prayer!
  Full well, O land,
My voice barbaric thou canst understand;
  While oft with rendings I assail
My byssine vesture and Sidonian veil.

STROPHE VII.

The oar indeed and home with sails
Flax-tissued, swelled with favoring gales,
Stanch to the wave, from spear-storm free,
Have to this shore escorted me,
Not so far blame I destiny.
But may the all-seeing Father send
In fitting time propitious end;
So our dread Mother's mighty brood
The lordly couch may 'scape, ah me,
    Unwedded, unsubdued!

ANTISTROPHE VII.

Meeting my will with will divine,
Daughter of Zeus, who here dost hold
  Steadfast thy sacred shrine—
Me, Artemis unstained, behold.
Do thou, who sovereign might dost wield,
Virgin thyself, a virgin shield;
So our dread Mother's mighty brood
The lordly couch may 'scape, ah me,
    Unwedded, unsubdued!

THE VISION OF CASSANDRA

(From Edward Fitzgerald's Version of " Agamemnon")

CASSANDRA.

Phœbus Apollo!

CHORUS.

Hark!
The lips at last unlocking.

CASSANDRA.

Phœbus! Phœbus!

CHORUS.

Well, what of Phœbus, maiden? though a name
'Tis but disparagement to call upon
In misery.

CASSANDRA.

Apollo! Apollo! Again!
Oh, the burning arrow through the brain!
Phœbus Apollo! Apollo!

CHORUS.

Seemingly
Possessed indeed—whether by—

CASSANDRA.

Phœbus! Phœbus!
Through trampled ashes, blood, and fiery rain,
Over water seething, and behind the breathing
War-horse in the darkness—till you rose again,
Took the helm—took the rein—

CHORUS.

As one that half asleep at dawn recalls
A night of Horror!

CASSANDRA.

Hither, whither, Phœbus? And with whom,
Leading me, lighting me—

CHORUS.

I can answer that—

CASSANDRA.

Down to what slaughter-house!
Foh! the smell of carnage through the door
Scares me from it—drags me toward it—
    Phœbus Apollo! Apollo!

CHORUS.

One of the dismal prophet-pack, it seems,
That hunt the trail of blood. But here at fault—
This is no den of slaughter, but the house
Of Agamemnon.

CASSANDRA.

        Down upon the towers,
Phantoms of two mangled children hover—and a
        famished man,
At an empty table glaring, seizes and devours!

CHORUS.

Thyestes and his children! Strange enough
For any maiden from abroad to know,
Or, knowing—

CASSANDRA.

        And look! in the chamber below
The terrible Woman, listening, watching,
Under a mask, preparing the blow
In the fold of her robe—

29

CHORUS.

          Nay, but again at fault:
For in the tragic story of this House—
Unless, indeed the fatal Helen—
No woman—

CASSANDRA.

          No Woman—Tisiphone! Daughter
Of Tartarus—love-grinning Woman above,
Dragon-tailed under—honey-tongued, Harpy-
          clawed,
Into the glittering meshes of slaughter
She wheedles, entices him into the poisonous
Fold of the serpent—

CHORUS.

          Peace, mad woman, peace!
Whose stony lips once open vomit out
Such uncouth horrors.

CASSANDRA.

     I tell you the lioness
Slaughters the Lion asleep; and lifting
Her blood-dripping fangs buried deep in his mane,
Glaring about her insatiable, bellowing,
Bounds hither—Phœbus Apollo, Apollo, Apollo!
Whither have you led me, under night alive with fire,
Through the trampled ashes of the city of my sire,
From my slaughtered kinsmen, fallen throne, in-
          sulted shrine,
Slave-like to be butchered, the daughter of a royal
          line!

ÆSOP

Æsop, famed for his fables, flourished about 600 B.C. He was by birth a Phrygian, but for several years he lived as a slave in Greece, where his fame was made as a writer. Invited by Crœsus, the Lydian king, Æsop passed his last days at the court of that famous monarch.

THE ASS IN THE LION'S SKIN

AN Ass, finding the skin of a Lion, put it on; and, going into the woods and pastures, threw all the flocks and herds into a terrible consternation. At last, meeting his owner, he would have frightened him also; but the good man, seeing his long ears stick out, presently knew him, and with a good cudgel made him sensible that, notwithstanding his being dressed in a Lion's skin, he was really no more than an Ass.

THE WOLF IN SHEEP'S CLOTHING

A WOLF, clothing himself in the skin of a sheep, and getting in among the flock, by this means took the opportunity to devour many of them. At last the shepherd discovered him, and cunningly fastening a rope about his neck, tied him to a tree which stood hard by. Some other shepherds happening to pass that way, and observing what he was about, drew near, and expressed their admiration at it. "What!" says one of them, "brother, do you make hanging of a sheep?" "No," replied the other "but I make hanging of a Wolf whenever I catch him, though in the habit and garb of a sheep." Then he showed them their mistake, and they applauded the justice of the execution.

THE COUNTRY MOUSE AND THE CITY MOUSE

AN honest, plain, sensible Country Mouse is said to have entertained at his hole one day a fine Mouse of the Town. Having formerly been play-fellows together, they were old acquaintances, which served as an apology for the visit. However, as master of the house, he thought himself obliged to do the honors of it in all respects, and to make as great a stranger of his guest as he possibly could. In order to do this he set before him a reserve of delicate gray pease and bacon, a dish of fine oat-meal, some parings of new cheese, and, to crown all with a dessert, a remnant of a charming mellow apple. In good manners, he forebore to eat any himself, lest the stranger should not have enough; but that he might seem to bear the other company, sat and nibbled a piece of a wheaten straw very busily. At last, says the spark of the town: "Old crony, give me leave to be a little free with you: how can you bear to live in this nasty, dirty, melancholy hole here, with nothing but woods, and meadows, and mountains, and rivulets about you? Do not you prefer the conversation of the world to the chirping of birds, and the splendor of a court to the rude aspect of an uncultivated desert? Come, take my word for it, you will find it a change for the better. Never stand considering, but away this moment. Remember, we are not immortal, and therefore have no time to lose. Make sure of to-day, and spend it as agreeably as you can: you know not what may happen to-morrow." In short, these and such like arguments prevailed, and his Country Acquaintance was resolved to go to town that night. So they both set out upon their journey together, proposing to sneak in after the close of the evening. They did so; and about midnight made their entry into a certain great house, where there had been an extraordinary entertainment the day before, and several tit-bits, which some of the servants had purloined, were hid under the seat of a window. The Country Guest was immediately placed in the midst of a rich Persian carpet: and now it was the Courtier's turn to entertain; who indeed acquitted himself in that capacity with the utmost readiness and address, changing the courses as elegantly, and tasting everything first as judiciously, as any clerk of the kitchen. The other sat and enjoyed himself like a delighted epicure, tickled to the last degree with this new turn of his affairs; when on a sudden, a noise of somebody opening the door made them start from their seats and scuttle in confusion about the dining-room. Our Country Friend, in particular, was ready to die with fear at the barking of a huge mastiff or two, which opened their throats just about the same time, and made the whole house echo. At last, recovering himself:—" Well," says he, " if this be your town-life, much good may you do with it: give me my poor, quiet hole again, with my homely but comfortable gray pease."

THE WOLF AND THE LAMB

AS a Wolf was lapping at the head of a running brook, he spied a stray Lamb paddling at some distance down the stream. Having made up his mind to seize her, he bethought himself how he might justify his violence. "Villain!" said he, running up to her, "how dare you muddle the water that I am drinking?" "Indeed," said the Lamb, humbly. "I do not see how I can disturb the water, since it runs from you to me, not from me to you." "Be that as it may," replied the Wolf, "it was but a year ago that you called me ill names." "Oh, Sir," said the Lamb, trembling, "a year ago I was not born." "Well," replied the Wolf, "if it was not you, it was your father, and that is all the same; but it is no use trying to argue me out of my supper." And without another word he fell upon the poor helpless Lamb, and tore her to pieces.

THE BUNDLE OF STICKS

(Translation of James)]

A HUSBANDMAN who had a quarrelsome family, after having tried in vain to reconcile them by words, thought he might more readily prevail by an example. So he called his sons and bade them lay a bundle of sticks before him. Then having tied them up into a fagot, he told the lads, one after another, to take it up and break it. They all tried, but tried in vain. Then, untying the fagot, he gave them the sticks to break one by one. This they did with the greatest ease. Then said the father: "Thus, my sons, as long as you remain united, you are a match for all your enemies; but differ and separate, and you are undone."

THOMAS BAILEY ALDRICH

THOMAS BAILEY ALDRICH, poet, journalist and novelist, was born at Portsmouth, N. H., in 1836; came to New York as a young man and engaged in business; while there began writing for periodicals. He was editor of the "Atlantic Monthly" from 1883 to 1892. His best known poems are "The Bells," "Flower and Thorn," "Mercedes," and those given below.

BABY BELL

(The poems of T. B. Aldrich are used by permission of, and by special arrangement with Houghton, Mifflin & Co., publishers.)

I

HAVE you not heard the poets tell
How came the dainty Baby Bell
Into this world of ours?
The gates of heaven were left ajar:
With folded hands and dreamy eyes,
Wandering out of Paradise,
She saw this planet, like a star,
Hung in the glistening depths of even—
Its bridges, running to and fro,
O'er which the white-winged Angels go,
Bearing the holy Dead to heaven.
She touched a bridge of flowers—those feet
So light they did not bend the bells
Of the celestial asphodels,
They fell like dew upon the flowers:

35

Then all the air grew strangely sweet.
And thus came dainty Baby Bell
Into this world of ours.

II

She came and brought delicious May;
The swallows built beneath the eaves;
Like sunlight, in and out the leaves
The robins went, the livelong day;
The lily swung its noiseless bell;
And on the porch the slender vine
Held out its cups of fairy wine.
How tenderly the twilights fell!
Oh, earth was full of singing birds
And opening springtide flowers,
When the dainty Baby Bell
Came to this world of ours.

III

O Baby, dainty Baby Bell,
How fair she grew from day to day!
What woman nature filled her eyes,
What poetry within them lay—
Those deep and tender twilight eyes,
So full of meaning, pure and bright
As if she yet stood in the light
Of those oped gates of Paradise.
And so we loved her more and more:
Ah, never in our hearts before
Was love so lovely born.
We felt we had a link between
This real world and that unseen—
The land beyond the morn;
And for the love of those dear eyes,
For love of her whom God led forth,
(The mother's being ceased on earth
When Baby came from Paradise,)—

For love of Him who smote our lives,
And woke the chords of joy and pain,
We said, *Dear Christ !*—our hearts bowed down
Like violets after rain.

IV

And now the orchards, which were white
And pink with blossoms when she came,
Were rich in autumn's mellow prime;
The clustered apples burnt like flame,
The folded chestnut burst its shell,
The grapes hung purpling, range on range:
And time wrought just as rich a change
In little Baby Bell.
Her lissome form more perfect grew,
And in her features we could trace,
In softened curves, her mother's face.
Her angel nature ripened too:
We thought her lovely when she came,
But she was holy, saintly now. . . .
Around her pale, angelic brow
We saw a slender ring of flame.

V

God's hand had taken away the seal
That held the portals of her speech;
And oft she said a few strange words
Whose meaning lay beyond our reach.
She never was a child to us,
We never held her being's key;
We could not teach her holy things
Who was Christ's self in purity.

VI

It came upon us by degrees,
We saw its shadow ere it fell—
The knowledge that our God had sent
His messenger for Baby Bell.

We shuddered with unlanguaged pain,
And all our hopes were changed to fears,
And all our thoughts ran into tears
Like sunshine into rain.
We cried aloud in our belief,
"Oh, smite us gently, gently, God!
Teach us to bend and kiss the rod,
And perfect grow through grief."
Ah! how we loved her, God can tell;
Her heart was folded deep in ours.
Our hearts are broken, Baby Bell!

VII

At last he came, the messenger,
The messenger from unseen lands:
And what did dainty Baby Bell?
She only crossed her little hands,
She only looked more meek and fair!
We parted back her silken hair,
We wove the roses round her brow—
White buds, the summer's drifted snow—
Wrapt her from head to foot in flowers . . .
And thus went dainty Baby Bell
Out of this world of ours.

PRESCIENCE

THE new moon hung in the sky, the sun was low
in the west,
And my betrothed and I in the churchyard paused
to rest:
Happy maid and lover, dreaming the old dream
over:
The light winds wandered by, and robins chirped
from the nest.

And lo! in the meadow sweet was the grave of a little
child,
With a crumbling stone at the feet, and the ivy running wild:
Tangled ivy and clover folding it over and over:
Close to my sweetheart's feet was the little mound
up-piled.

Stricken with nameless fears, she shrank and clung
to me,
And her eyes were filled with tears for a sorrow I
did not see:
Lightly the winds were blowing, softly her tears
were flowing—
Tears for the unknown years and a sorrow that was
to be!

SWEETHEART, SIGH NO MORE

IT was with doubt and trembling
I whispered in her ear.
Go, take her answer, bird-on-bough,
That all the world may hear—
Sweetheart, sigh no more!

Sing it, sing it, tawny throat,
Upon the wayside tree,
How fair she is, how true she is,
How dear she is to me—
Sweetheart, sigh no more!

Sing it, sing it, and through the summer long
The winds among the clover-tops,
And brooks, for all their silvery stops,
Shall envy you the song—
Sweetheart, sigh no more!

WILLIAM ALLINGHAM

WILLIAM ALLINGHAM, born in Ireland in 1828, died 1889. He removed to England and became editor of "Fraser's Magazine." He was the author of numerous poems. "Lawrence Bloomfield in Ireland" and "Day and Night Songs" are the best known.

THE RUINED CHAPEL

(From "Day and Night Songs")

BY the shore, a plot of ground
    Clips a ruined chapel round,
Buttressed with a grassy mound;
    Where Day and Night and Day go by
And bring no touch of human sound.

Washing of the lonely seas,
Shaking of the guardian trees,
Piping of the salted breeze;
    Day and Night and Day go by
To the endless tune of these.

Or, when, as winds and waters keep
A hush more dead than any sleep,
Still morns to stiller evenings creep,
    And Day and Night and Day go by;
Here the silence is most deep.

The empty ruins, lapsed again
Into Nature's wide domain,
Sow themselves with seed and grain
    As Day and Night and Day go by;
And hoard June's sun and April's rain.

Here fresh funeral tears were shed;
Now the graves are also dead;

And suckers from the ash-tree spread,
  While Day and Night and Day go by;
And stars move calmly overhead.

SONG

(From "Day and Night Songs")

O SPIRIT of the Summer-time!
  Bring back the roses to the dells;
The swallow from her distant clime,
  The honey-bee from drowsy cells.

Bring back the friendship of the sun;
  The gilded evenings calm and late,
When weary children homeward run,
  And peeping stars bid lovers wait.

Bring back the singing; and the scent
  Of meadow-lands at dewy prime;
Oh, bring again my heart's content,
  Thou spirit of the Summer-time!

THE BUBBLE

(From "Ballads and Songs")

SEE the pretty planet!
  Floating sphere!
Faintest breeze will fan it
  Far or near;

World as light as feather;
  Moonshine rays,
Rainbow tints together,
  As it plays.

*   *   *   *   *   *

ROBIN REDBREAST

GOOD-BYE, good-bye to Summer!
  For Summer's nearly done;

The garden smiling faintly,
  Cool breezes in the sun;
Our thrushes now are silent,
  Our swallows flown away—
But Robin's here in coat of brown,
  And scarlet breast-knot gay.
Robin, Robin Redbreast,
  O Robin dear!
Robin sings so sweetly
  In the falling of the year.

Bright yellow, red, and orange,
  The leaves come down in hosts;
The trees are Indian princes,
  But soon they'll turn to ghosts;
The leathery pears and apples
  Hang russet on the bough;
It's autumn, autumn, autumn late,
  'Twill soon be winter now.
Robin, Robin Redbreast,
  O Robin dear!
And what will this poor Robin do?
  For pinching days are near.

The fireside for the cricket,
  The wheat-stack for the mouse,
When trembling night-winds whistle
  And moan all round the house.
The frosty ways like iron,
  The branches plumed with snow—
Alas! in winter dead and dark,
  Where can poor Robin go?
Robin, Robin Redbreast,
  O Robin dear!
And a crumb of bread for Robin,
  His little heart to cheer.

HANS CHRISTIAN ANDERSEN

HANS CHRISTIAN ANDERSEN, poet, dramatist and story-writer, born at Odense, Denmark, in 1805; died at Copenhagen in 1875. From his early youth he was a maker of tales, and on the banks of the silver Odense River he walked and dreamed of the days of old, and the famous days to come. Primarily a writer of tales for children, his work possesses such deep insight into human nature, such tenderness, that the person who has not read them has a gap on the shelves of his mental library. Before he laid down his pen at the close of his life's work, it took fifty volumes to contain his writings.

THE GARDENER OF THE MANOR

ABOUT one Danish mile from the capital stood an old manor-house, with thick walls, towers, and pointed gable-ends. Here lived, but only in the summer season, a rich and courtly family. This manor-house was the best and the most beautiful of all the houses they owned. It looked outside as if it had just been cast in a foundry, and within it was comfort itself. The family arms were carved in stone over the door; beautiful roses twined about the arms and the balcony; a grass-plot extended before the house with red-thorn and white-thorn, and many rare flowers grew even outside the conservatory. The manor kept also a very skilful gardener. It was a real pleasure to see the flower-garden, the orchard, and the kitchen-garden. There was still to be seen a portion of the manor's original garden, a few box-tree hedges cut in shape of crowns and pyramids, and behind these two mighty old trees almost always without leaves. One might always think that a storm or waterspout had scattered great lumps of manure on their branches, but each lump was a bird's nest. A swarm of rooks and crows from time immemorial had built their nests here. It was a townful of birds, and the birds were the manorial lords here. They did not care for the proprietors, the manor's oldest family branch, nor for the present owner of the manor— these were nothing to them; but they bore with the wandering creatures below them, notwithstanding that once in a while they shot with guns in a way that made the birds' backbones shiver, and made every bird fly up, crying, " Rak, Rak ! "

The gardener very often explained to the master the necessity of felling the old trees, as they did not look well, and by taking them away they would probably also get rid of the screaming birds, which would seek another place. But he never could be induced either to give up the trees or the swarm of birds: the manor could not spare them, as they were relics of the good old times, that ought always to be kept in remembrance.

" The trees are the birds' heritage by this time," said the master. " So let them keep them, my good Larsen." Larsen was the gardener's name, but that is of very little consequence in this story. " Haven't you room enough to work in, little Larsen? Have you not the flower-garden, the green-houses, the orchard, and the kitchen-garden? " He cared for them, he kept them in order and cultivated them with zeal and ability, and the family knew it; but they did not conceal from him that they often tasted fruits and saw flowers in other houses that surpassed what he had in his garden, and that was a sore trial to the gardener, who always wished to do the best, and really did the best he could. He was good-hearted and a faithful servant.

The owner sent one day for him, and told him kindly that the day before, at a party given by some friends of rank, they had eaten apples and pears which were so juicy and well-flavored that all the guests had loudly expressed their admiration. To be sure, they were not native fruits, but they ought by all means to be introduced here, and to be acclimatized if possible. They learned that the fruit was bought of one of the first fruit-dealers in the city, and the gardener was to ride to town, and find out about where they came from, and then order some slips for grafting. The gardener was very well acquainted with the dealer, because he was the very person to whom he sold the fruit that grew in the manor-garden, beyond what was needed by the family. So the gardener went to town and asked the fruit-dealer where he had found those apples and pears that were praised so highly.

"They are from your own garden," said the fruit-dealer, and he showed him both the apples and the pears, which he recognized. Now, how happy the gardener felt! He hastened back to his master, and told him that the apples and pears were from his own garden. But he would not believe it.

"It cannot be possible, Larsen. Can you get a written certificate of that from the fruit-dealer?" And that he could; and brought him a written certificate.

"This is certainly wonderful!" said the family.

And now every day were set on the table great dishes filled with beautiful apples and pears from their own garden; bushels and barrels of these fruits were sent to friends in the city and country —nay, were even sent abroad. It was exceedingly pleasant; but when they talked with the gardener, they said that the last two seasons had been re-

markably favorable for fruits, and that fruits had
done well all over the country.

Some time passed. The family were at dinner at
court. The next day the gardener was sent for.
They had eaten melons at the royal table which they
found very juicy and well-flavored; they came from
his majesty's green-house.

"You must go and see the court-gardener, and
let him give you some seeds of those melons."

"But the gardener at the court got his melon-
seeds from us," said the gardener, highly delighted.

"But then that man understands how to bring
the fruit to a higher perfection," was the answer.
"Each particular melon was delicious."

"Well, then, I really may feel proud," said the
gardener. "I must tell your lordship that the gardener at the court did not succeed very well with
his melons this year, and so, seeing how beautiful
ours looked, he tasted them, and ordered from me
three of them for the castle."

"Larsen, do not pretend to say that those were
melons from our garden."

"Really, I dare say as much," said the gardener,
who went to the court-gardener and got from him
a written certificate to the effect that the melons
on the royal table were from the manor. That was
certainly a great surprise to the family, and they
did not keep the story to themselves. Melon seeds
were sent far and wide, in the same way as had been
done with the slips, which they were now hearing
had begun to take, and to bear fruit of an excellent
kind. The fruit was named after the manor, and
the name was written in English, German and
French.

This was something they never had dreamed of.

"We are afraid that the gardener will come to
think too much of himself," said they; but he looked
on it in another way: what he wished was to get

the reputation of being one of the best gardeners in the country, and to produce every year something exquisite out of all sorts of garden stuff, and that he did. But he often had to hear that the fruits which he first brought, the apples and pears, were after all the best. All other kinds of fruit were inferior to these. The melons, too, were very good, but they belonged to quite another species. His strawberries were very excellent, but by no means better than many others; and when it happened one year that his radishes did not succeed, they only spoke of them, and not of other good things he had made succeed.

It really seemed as if the family felt some relief in saying: "It won't turn out well this year, little Larsen!" They seemed quite glad when they could say, "It won't turn out well!"

The gardener used always twice a week to bring them fresh flowers, tastefully arranged, and the colors by his arrangements were brought out in stronger light.

"You have a good taste, Larsen," said the owner. "But that is a gift from our Lord, not from yourself."

One day the gardener brought a great crystal vase with a floating leaf of a white water-lily, upon which was laid, with its long thick stalk descending into the water, a sparkling blue flower, as large as a sunflower.

"The sacred lotos of Hindostan!" exclaimed the family. They had never seen such a flower; it was placed every day in the sunshine, and in the evening under artificial light. Every one who saw it found it wonderfully beautiful and rare; and that said the most noble young lady in the country, the wise and kind-hearted princess. The lord of the manor deemed it an honor to present her with the flower, and the princess took it with her to the castle.

Now the master of the house went down to the garden to pluck another flower of the same sort, but he could not find any. So he sent for the gardener, and asked him where he kept the blue lotos.

"I have been looking for it in vain," said he. "I went into the conservatory, and round about the flower-garden."

"No, it is not there," said the gardener. "It is nothing else than a common flower from the kitchen-garden, but do you not find it beautiful? It looks as if it were the blue cactus, and yet it is only a kitchen-herb. It is the flower of the artichoke."

"You should have told us that at the time," said the master. "We supposed, of course, that it was a strange and rare flower. You have made us ridiculous in the eyes of the young princess! She saw the flower in our house and thought it beautiful. She did not know the flower, and she is versed in botany, too; but then that has nothing to do with kitchen-herbs. How could you take it into your head, my good Larsen, to put such a flower up in our drawing-room? It makes us ridiculous."

And the magnificent blue flower from the kitchen-garden was turned out of the drawing-room, which was not at all the place for it. The master made his apology to the princess, telling her that it was only a kitchen-herb which the gardener had taken into his head to exhibit, but that he had been well reprimanded for it.

"That was a pity," said the princess, "for he has really opened our eyes to see the beauty of a flower in a place where we should not have thought of looking for it. Our gardener shall every day, as long as the artichoke is in bloom, bring one of them up into the drawing-room."

Then the master told his gardener that he might again bring them a fresh artichoke-flower.

"It is, after all, a very nice flower," said he, "and

48

a truly remarkable one." And so the gardener was praised again. "Larsen likes that," said the master; "he is a spoiled child."

In the autumn there came up a great gale, which increased so violently in the night that several large trees in the outskirts of the wood were torn up by the roots; and to the great grief of the household, but to the gardener's delight, the two big trees blew down, with all their birds' nests on them. In the manor-house they heard during the storm the screaming of rooks and crows, beating their wings against the windows.

"Now I suppose you are happy, Larsen," said the master; "the storm has felled the trees, and the birds have gone off to the woods; there is nothing left from the good old days; it is all gone, and we are very sorry for it."

The gardener said nothing, but he thought of what he long had turned over in his mind, how he could make that pretty, sunny spot very useful, so that it could become an ornament to the garden and a pride to the family. The great trees which had been blown down had shattered the venerable hedge of box, that was cut into fanciful shapes.

Here he set out a multitude of plants that were not to be seen in other gardens. He made an earthen wall, on which he planted all sorts of native flowers from the fields and the woods. What no other gardener had ever thought of planting in the manor-garden he planted, giving each its appropriate soil, and the plants were in sunlight or shadow, according as each species required. He cared tenderly for them, and they grew up finely. The juniper-tree from the heaths of Jutland rose in shape and color like the Italian cypress; the shining, thorny Christ-thorn, as green in the winter's cold as in the summer's sun, was splendid to see. In the foreground grew ferns of various species; some of them looked as if they were children of the palm-tree; others, as if they were parents of the pretty plants called "Venus's golden locks" or "Maiden-hair." Here stood the despised burdock, which is so beautiful in its freshness that it looks well even in a bouquet. The burdock stood in a dry place, but below, in the moist soil, grew the colt's-foot, also a despised plant, but yet most picturesque, with its tall stem and large leaf. Like a candelabrum with a multitude of branches six feet high, and with flower over against flower, rose the mullein, a mere field plant. Here stood the woodroof and the lily of the valley, the wild calla and the fine three-leaved wood-sorrel. It was a wonder to see all this beauty.

In the front grew in rows very small pear-trees from French soil, trained on wires. By plenty of sun and good care they soon bore as juicy fruits as in their own country. Instead of the two old, leafless trees was placed a tall flag-staff, where the flag of Dannebrog was displayed; and near-by stood another pole, where the hop-tendril in summer or harvest-time wound its fragrant flowers; but in winter time, after ancient custom, oat-sheaves were fastened to it, that the birds of the air might find here a good meal in the happy Christmas-time.

"Our good Larsen is growing sentimental as he grows old," said the family; "but he is faithful, and quite attached to us."

In one of the illustrated papers there was a picture at New Year's of the old manor, with the flag-staff and the oat-sheaves for the birds of the air, and the paper said that the old manor had preserved that beautiful old custom, and deserved great credit for it.

"They beat the drum for all Larsen's doings," said the family. "He is a lucky fellow, and we may almost be proud of having such a man in our service."

But they were not a bit proud of it. They were very well aware that they were the lords of the manor; they could give Larsen warning, in fact, but they did not. They were good people, and fortunate it is for every Mr. Larsen that there are so many good people like them.

Yes, that is the story of the Gardener of the Manor. Now you may think a little about it.

THE LITTLE MATCH-GIRL

IT was very cold, the snow fell, and it was almost quite dark; for it was evening—yes, the last evening of the year. Amid the cold and the darkness, a poor little girl, with bare head and naked feet, was roaming through the streets. It is true, she had a pair of slippers when she left home, but they were not of much use. They were very large slippers; so large, indeed, that they had hitherto been used by her mother; besides, the little creature lost them as she hurried across the street, to avoid two carriages that were driving very quickly past. One of the slippers was not to be found, and the the other was pounced upon by a boy, who ran away with it, saying that it would serve for a cradle when he should have children of his own. So the little girl went along, with her little bare feet that were red and blue with cold. She carried a number of matches in an old apron, and she held a bundle of them in her hand. Nobody had bought anything from her the whole livelong day; nobody had even given her a penny.

Shivering with cold and hunger, she crept along, a perfect picture of misery—poor little thing! The snow-flakes covered her long, flaxen hair, which hung in pretty curls around her throat; but she heeded them not now. Lights were streaming from all the windows, and there was a savory smell of roast goose; for it was New Year's Eve. And this she *did* heed.

She now sat down, cowering in a corner formed by two houses, one of which projected beyond the other. She had drawn her little feet under her, but she felt colder than ever; yet she dared not return home, for she had not sold a match, and could not bring home a penny! She would certainly be beaten by her father; and it was cold enough at home, besides—for they had only the roof above them, and the wind came howling through it, though the largest holes had been stopped with straw and rags. Her little hands were nearly frozen with cold. Alas! a single match might do her some good, if she might only draw one out of the bundle, and rub it against the wall, and warm her fingers.

So at last she drew one out. Ah! how it sheds sparks, and how it burns! It gave out a warm, bright flame, like a little candle, as she held her hands over it—truly it was a wonderful little sight! It really seemed to the little girl as if she were sitting before a large iron stove, with polished brass feet, and brass shovel and tongs. The fire burned so brightly, and warmed so nicely, that the little creature stretched out her feet to warm them likewise, when lo! the flame expired, the stove vanished, and left nothing but the little half-burned match in her hand.

She rubbed another match against the wall. It gave a light, and where it shone upon the wall, the latter became as transparent as a veil, and she could see into the room. A snow-white table-cloth was spread upon the table, on which stood a splendid china dinner-service, while a roast goose stuffed with apples and prunes, sent forth the most savory fumes. And what was more delightful still to see, the goose jumped down from the dish, and waddled along the ground with a knife and fork in its breast, up to the poor girl. The match then went out, and nothing remained but the thick, damp wall.

She lit yet another match. She now sat under the most magnificent Christmas tree, that was larger, and more superbly decked, than even the one she had seen through the glass door at the rich merchant's. A thousand tapers burned on its green branches, and gay pictures, such as one sees on shields, seemed to be looking down upon her. She stretched out her hands, but the match then went out. The Christmas lights kept rising higher and higher. They now looked like stars in the sky. One of them fell down, and left a long streak of fire. "Somebody is now dying," thought the little girl—for her old grandmother, the only person who had ever loved her, and who was now dead, had told her that, when a star falls, it is a sign that a soul is going up to heaven.

She again rubbed a match upon the wall, and it was again light all round; and in the brightness stood her old grandmother, clear and shining like a spirit, yet looking so mild and loving. "Grandmother," cried the little one, "oh, take me with you! I know you will go away when the match goes out—you will vanish like the warm stove, and the delicious roast goose, and the fine, large Christmas-tree!" And she made haste to rub the whole bundle of matches, for she wished to hold her grandmother fast. And the matches gave a light that was brighter than noonday. Her grandmother had never appeared so beautiful nor so large. She took the little girl in her arms, and both flew upwards, all radiant and joyful, far, far above mortal ken, where there was neither cold, nor hunger, nor care to be found; where there was no rain, no snow, or stormy wind, but calm, sunny days the whole year round.

But, in the cold dawn, the poor girl might be seen

leaning against the wall, with red cheeks and smiling mouth; she had been frozen on the last night of the old year. The new year's sun shone upon the little dead girl. She sat still holding the matches, one bundle of which was burned. People said: "She tried to warm herself." Nobody dreamed of the fine things she had seen, nor in what splendor she had entered, along with her grandmother, upon the joys of the New Year.

THE SHADOW

IN the hot countries the sun burns very strongly; there the people become quite mahogany brown, and in the very hottest countries they are even burned into negroes. But this time it was only to the hot countries that a learned man out of the cold regions had come. He thought he could roam about there just as he had been accustomed to do at home; but he soon altered his opinion. He and all sensible people had to remain at home, where the window-shutters and doors were shut all day long, and it looked as if all the inmates were asleep or had gone out. The narrow street with the high houses in which he lived was, however, built in such a way that the sun shone upon it from morning till evening; it was really quite unbearable! The learned man from the cold regions was a young man and a clever man; it seemed to him as if he were sitting in a glowing oven that exhausted him greatly, and he became quite thin; even his Shadow shriveled up and became much smaller than it had been at home; the sun even took the Shadow away, and it did not return till the evening, when the sun went down. It was really a pleasure to see this. As soon as a light was brought into the room the Shadow stretched itself quite up the wall, farther even than

the ceiling, so tall did it make itself; it was obliged
to stretch to get strength again. The learned man
went out into the balcony to stretch himself, and
as soon as the stars came out in the beautiful clear
sky, he felt himself reviving. On all of the bal-
conies in the streets—and in the hot countries there
is a balcony to every window—young people now
appeared; for one must breathe fresh air, even if one
has got used to becoming mahogany brown; then it
became lively above and below; the tinkers and
tailors—by which we mean all kinds of people—sat
below in the street; then tables and chairs were
brought out, and candles burned, yes, more than a
thousand candles; one talked and then sang, and
the people walked to and fro; carriages drove past,
mules trotted "Kling-ling-ling!" for they had bells
on their harness; dead people were buried with solemn songs; the church bells rang, and it was indeed very lively in the street. Only in one house,
just opposite to that in which the learned man
dwelt, it was quite quiet, and yet somebody lived
there, for there were flowers upon the balcony,
blooming beautifully in the hot sun, and they could
not have done this if they had not been watered, so
that some one must have watered them; therefore,
there must be people in that house. Towards evening the door was half opened, but it was dark, at
least in the front room; farther back, in the interior,
music was heard. The strange learned man thought
this music very lovely, but it was quite possible that
he only imagined this, for out there in the hot countries he found everything requisite, if only there had
been no sun. The stranger's landlord said that he
did not know who had taken the opposite house—
one saw nobody there, and so far as the music was
concerned, it seemed very monotonous to him.

"It was just," he said, "as if some one sat there,
always practicing a piece that he could not manage

—always the same piece. He seemed to say, 'I shall manage it, after all;' but he did not manage it, however long he played."

Will the stranger awake at night? He slept with the balcony door open: the wind lifted up the curtain before it, and he fancied that a wonderful radiance came from the balcony of the house opposite all the flowers appeared like flames of the most gorgeous colors, and in the midst, among the flowers, stood a beautiful slender maiden; it seemed as if a radiance came from her also. His eyes were quite dazzled; but he had only opened them too wide just when he awoke out of his sleep. With one leap he was out of bed; quite quietly he crept behind the curtain; but the maiden was gone, the splendor was gone, the flowers gleamed no longer, but stood there as beautiful as ever. The door was ajar, and from within sounded music, so lovely, so charming, that one fell into sweet thought at the sound. It was just like magic work. But who lived there? Where was the real entrance? for towards the street and towards the lane at the side the whole ground floor was shop by shop, and the people could not always run through there.

One evening the stranger sat upon his balcony; in the room just behind him a light was burning, and so it was quite natural that his Shadow fell upon the wall of the opposite house; yes, it sat just among the flowers on the balcony, and when the stranger moved his Shadow moved too.

"I think my Shadow is the only living thing we see yonder," said the learned man. "Look how gracefully it sits among the flowers. The door is only ajar, but the Shadow ought to be sensible enough to walk in and look around, and then come back and tell me what it has seen.

"Yes, you would thus make yourself very useful," said he, as if in sport. "Be so good as to slip in.

Now, will you go?" And then he nodded at the Shadow, and the Shadow nodded back at him. "Now go, but don' stay away altogether."

And the stranger stood up, and the Shadow on the balcony opposite stood up too, and the stranger moved around, and if any one had noticed closely he would have remarked how the Shadow went away in the same moment, straight through the half-opened door of the opposite house, as the stranger returned into his room and let the curtain fall.

Next morning the learned man went out to drink coffee and read the papers.

"What is this?" said he, when he came out into the sunshine. "I have no Shadow! So it really went away yesterday evening, and did not come back; that's very tiresome."

And that fretted him, but not so much because the Shadow was gone as because he knew that there was a story of a man without a shadow. All the people in the house knew this story, and if the learned man came home and told his own history, they would say that it was only an imitation, and he did not choose them to say that of him. So he would not speak of it at all, and that was a very sensible idea of his.

In the evening he again went out on his balcony; he had placed the light behind him, for he knew that a shadow always wants its master for a screen, but he could not coax it forth. He made himself little, he made himself long, but there was no shadow, and no shadow came. He said, "Here, here!" but that did no good.

That was vexatious, but in the warm countries everything grows very quickly, and after the lapse of a week he remarked to his great joy that a new shadow was growing out of his legs when he went into the sunshine, so that the root must have remained behind. After three weeks he had quite a respectable shadow, which, when he started on his return to the North, grew more and more, so that at last it was so long and great that he could very well have parted with half of it.

When the learned man got home he wrote books about what is true in the world, and what is good, and what is pretty; and days went by, and years went by, many years.

He was one evening sitting in his room when there came a quiet little knock at the door. "Come in!" said he; but nobody came. Then he opened the door, and there stood before him such a remarkably thin man that he felt quite uncomfortable. This man was, however, very respectably dressed; he looked like a man of standing.

"Whom have I the honor to address?" asked the professor.

"Ah!" replied the genteel man, "I thought you would not know me; I have become so much a body that I have got real flesh and clothes. You never thought to see me in such a condition. Don't you know your old Shadow? You certainly never thought that I would come again. Things have gone remarkably well with me since I was with you last. I've become rich in every respect: if I want to buy myself free from servitude I can do it!"

And he rattled a number of valuable charms, which hung by his watch, and put his hand upon the thick gold chain he wore round his neck; and how the diamond rings glittered on his fingers! and everything was real!

"No, I cannot regain my self-possession at all!" said the learned man. "What's the meaning of all this?"

"Nothing common," said the Shadow. "But you yourself don't belong to common folks; and I have, as you very well know, trodden in your footsteps from my childhood upwards. As soon as I found that I was experienced enough to find my way through the world alone, I went away. I am in the most brilliant circumstances; but I was seized with a kind of longing to see you once more before you die, and I wanted to see these regions once more, for one always holds by one's fatherland. I know that you have got another shadow: have I anything to pay to it, or to you? You have only to tell me."

"Is it really you?" said the learned man. "Why, that is wonderful! I should never have thought that I should ever meet my old Shadow as a man!"

"Only tell me what I have to pay," said the Shadow, "for I don't like to be in any one's debt."

"How can you talk in that way?" said the learned man. "Of what debt can there be a question here? You are as free as any one! I am exceedingly pleased at your good fortune! Sit down, old friend, and tell me a little how it has happened, and what you saw in the warm countries, and in the house opposite ours."

"Yes, that I will tell you," said the Shadow; and it sat down. "But then you must promise me never to tell any one in this town, when you meet me, that I have been your Shadow! I have the intention of engaging myself to be married; I can do more than support a family."

"Be quite easy," replied the learned man; "I will tell nobody who you really are. Here's my hand. I promise it, and my word's as good as my bond."

"A Shadow's word in return!" said the Shadow, for he was obliged to talk in that way. But, by the way, it was quite wonderful how complete a man he had become. He was dressed all in black, and wore the very finest black cloth, polished boots, and a hat that could be crushed together till it was nothing but crown and rim, besides what we have already noticed of him, namely, the charms, the gold neck-chain, and the diamond rings. The Shadow was indeed wonderfully well clothed; and it was just this that made a complete man of him.

"Now I will tell you," said the Shadow; and then he put down his polished boots as firmly as he could on the arm of the learned man's new shadow that lay like a poodle dog at his feet. This was done perhaps from pride, perhaps so that the new shadow might stick to his feet; but the prostrate shadow remained quite quiet, so that it might listen well, for it wanted to know how one could get free and work up to be one's own master.

"Do you know who lived in the house opposite to us?" asked the Shadow. "That was the most glorious of all; it was Poetry! I was there for three weeks, and that was just as if one had lived there a thousand years, and could read all that has been written and composed. For this I say, and it is truth, I have seen everything, and I know everything!"

"Poetry!" cried the learned man. "Yes, she often lives as a hermit in great cities. Poetry! Yes, I myself saw her for one single brief moment, but sleep was heavy on my eyes: she stood on the balcony, gleaming as the Northern Light gleams, flowers with living flames. Tell me! tell me! You were upon the balcony. You went through the door, and then——"

"Then I was in the anteroom," said the Shadow. "You sat opposite, and were always looking across at the anteroom. There was no light; a kind of semi-obscurity reigned there; but one door after another in a whole row of halls and rooms stood open, and there it was light; and the mass of light would have killed me if I had got as far as to where the maiden sat. But I was deliberate, I took my time; and that's what one must do."

"And what didst thou see then?" asked the learned man.

"I saw everything, and I will tell you what; but—it is really not pride on my part—as a free man, and with the acquirements I possess, besides my good position and my remarkable fortune, I wish you would say *you* to me."

"I beg your pardon," said the learned man. This *thou* is an old habit, and old habits are difficult to alter. You are perfectly right, and I will remember it. But now tell me everything you saw."

"Everything," said the Shadow; "for I saw everything, and I know everything."

"How did things look in the inner room?" asked the learned man. "Was it there as in a cool grave? Was it there like in a holy temple? Were the chambers like the starry sky, when one stands on the high mountains?"

"Everything was there," said the Shadow. "I was certainly not quite inside; I remained in the front room, in the half-darkness; but I stood there remarkably well. I saw everything and know everything. I have been in the anteroom at the Court of Poetry."

"But what did you see? Did all the gods of antiquity march through the halls? Did the old heroes fight there? Did lovely children play there, and relate their dreams?"

"I tell you that I have been there, and so you will easily understand that I saw everything that was to be seen. If *you* had got there you would not have remained a man; but I became one, and at the same time I learned to understand my inner being and the relation in which I stood to Poetry. Yes, when I was with you, I did not think of these things; but you know that whenever the sun rises or sets I am wonderfully great. In the moonshine I was almost more noticeable than you yourself. I did not then understand my inward being; in the anteroom it was revealed to me. I became a man! I came out ripe. But you were no longer in the warm countries. I was ashamed to go about as a man in the state I was then in: I required boots, clothes, and all this human varnish by which a man is known. I hid myself; yes, I can confide a secret to you—you will not put it into a book. I hid myself under the cake-woman's gown; the woman had no idea how much she concealed. Only in the evening did I go out: I ran about the streets by moonlight; I stretched myself quite long up the wall: that tickled my back quite agreeably. I ran up and down, looked through the highest windows into the halls and through the roof, where nobody could see, and I saw what nobody saw and what nobody ought to see. On the whole it is a bad world: I should not like to be a man if I were not allowed to be of some consequence. I saw the most incomprehensible things going on among men, and women, and parents, and 'dear incomparable children.' I saw what no one else knows, but what they all would be very glad to know, namely, bad goings on at their neighbors. If I had written a newspaper, how it would have been read! But I wrote directly to the persons interested, and there was terror in every town to which I came. They were so afraid of me that they were remarkably fond of me. The professor made me a professor; the tailor gave me new clothes (I am well provided); the coining superintendent coined money for me; the women declared I was handsome: and thus I became the man I am. And now, farewell! Here is my card; I live on the sunny side, and am always at home in rainy weather."

And the Shadow went away.

*　　*　　*　　*　　*　　*　　*　　*　　*

MICHEL ANGELO

MICHEL ANGELO, painter, architect, sculptor, and poet, born at Caprese, Italy, 1475; died, 1564, at Rome. He was undoubtedly the greatest figure produced by the Italian Renaissance in the world of art. He wrote a number of poems and a series of letters that have given him a niche in the Temple of Literary Fame.

SONNETS TO VITTORIA

(Translated by J. A. Symonds)

NOW on the one foot, on the other now,
  'Twixt vice and virtue balancing below,
Wearied and anxious in my troubled mind,
Seeking where'er I may salvation find.
Like one to whom the stars by clouds are crossed;
Who, turn which way he will, errs, and is lost.
Therefore take thou my heart's unwritten page,
And write thou on it what is wanted there;
And hold before it, in life's daily stage,
The line of action which it craves in prayer.
So that, amid the errors of my youth,
My own shortcomings may not hide the truth:
If humble sinners lower in heaven stood,
Than the proud doers of superfluous good.

Not all unworthy of the boundless grace
Which thou, most noble lady, hast bestowed,
I fain at first would pay the debt I owed,
And some small gift for thy acceptance place.
But soon I felt, 't is not alone desire
That opes the way to reach an aim so high;

My rash pretensions their success deny,
And I grow wise while failing to aspire.
And well I see how false it were to think
That any work, faded and frail, of mine,
Could emulate the perfect grace of thine,
Genius and art and daring backward shrink;
A thousand works from mortals like to me
Can ne'er repay what Heaven has given thee!

When godlike art has, with superior thought,
The limbs and motions in idea conceived,
A simple form, in humble clay achieved,
Is the first offering into being brought:
Then stroke on stroke from out the living rock
Its promised work the practised chisel brings,
And into life a form so graceful springs,
That none can fear for it time's rudest shock.
Such was my birth: in humble mould I lay
At first; to be by thee, oh, lady high!
Renewed, and to a work more perfect brought;
Thou giv'st what lacking is, and filest away
All roughness: yet what tortures lie,
Ere my wild heart can be restrained and taught!

SONNET ON THE DEATH OF VIC-
TORIA

WHEN she, the aim of every hope and prayer,
    Was called by death to yon celestial spheres,
Nature, who ne'er had fashioned aught so fair,
Stood there ashamed, and all who saw shed tears.
O cruel fate, quenching the dreams of love!
O empty hopes! O spirit rare and blest!
Where art thou now? On earth thy fair limbs rest:
Thy holy thoughts have found their home above.
Yet let us think not cruel death could e'er

Have stilled the sound of all thy virtuous ways:
Lethe's oblivion could extinguish nought;
For, robbed of thee, a thousand records fair
Speak of thee yet; and death from heaven conveys
Thy powers divine, and thy immortal thought.

ON DANTE

THERE is no tongue to speak his eulogy;
    Too brightly burned his splendor for our eyes;
Far easier to condemn his injurers,
Than for the tongue to reach his smallest worth.
He to the realms of sinfulness came down,
To teach mankind; ascending then to God,
Heaven unbarred to him her lofty gates,
To whom his country hers refused to ope.
Ungrateful land! to its own injury,
Nurse of his fate! Well, too, does this instruct
That greatest ills fall to the perfectest.
And, midst a thousand proofs, let this suffice,—
That, as his exile had no parallel,
So never was there man more great than he.

THE ARABIAN NIGHTS

The Thousand and One Nights, commonly called "The Arabian Nights," have now delighted the Western World for two hundred years, as they have the East for centuries. The various stories were undoubtedly the work of many authors, combined much in the same way as the Canterbury Tales of Chaucer. All the color, the fascination of Oriental life, is in them, and the reader loses himself in the oases of Arabian deserts or walks the streets of Bagdad in the reign of Caliph Harun-al-Rashid.

THE FORTY THIEVES

THERE once lived in a town of Persia two brothers, one named Cassim and the other Ali Baba. Their father divided a small inheritance equally between them. Cassim married a very rich wife, and became a wealthy merchant. Ali Baba married a woman as poor as himself, and lived by cutting wood, and bringing it upon three asses into the town to sell.

One day, when Ali Baba was in the forest, and had just cut wood enough to load his asses, he saw at a distance a great cloud of dust, which seemed to approach him. He observed it with attention, and distinguished soon after a body of horsemen, whom he suspected might be robbers. He determined to leave his asses to save himself. He climbed up a large tree, planted on a high rock, whose branches were thick enough to conceal him, and yet enabled him to see all that passed without being discovered.

The troop, who were to the number of forty, all well mounted and armed, came to the foot of the rock on which the tree stood, and there dismounted. Every man unbridled his horse, tied him to some shrub, and hung about his neck a bag of corn which they brought behind them. Then each of them took off his saddle-bag, which seemed to Ali Baba to be full of gold and silver from its weight. One, whom he took to be their captain, came under the tree in which Ali Baba was concealed, and making his way through some shrubs, pronounced these words: "Open, Sesame!"* As soon as the captain of the robbers had thus spoken, a door opened in the rock; and after he had made all his troop enter before him, he followed them, when the door shut again of itself.

The robbers stayed some time within the rock, during which Ali Baba, fearful of being caught, remained in the tree.

At last the door opened again, and as the captain went in last, so he came out first, and stood to see them all pass by him; when Ali Baba heard him make the door close by pronouncing these words, "Shut, Sesame!" Every man at once went and bridled his horse, fastened his wallet, and mounted again. When the captain saw them all ready, he put himself at their head, and they returned the way they had come.

Ali Baba followed them with his eyes as far as he could see them; and afterward stayed a considerable time before he descended. Remembering the words the captain of the robbers used to cause the door to open and shut, he had the curiosity to try if his pronouncing them would have the same effect. Accordingly, he went among the shrubs,

* " Sesame " is a small grain.

and perceiving the door concealed behind them, stood before it, and said, "Open, Sesame!" The door instantly flew wide open.

Ali Baba, who expected a dark, dismal cavern, was surprised to see a well-lighted and spacious chamber, which received the light from an opening at the top of the rock, and in which were all sorts of provisions, rich bales of silk, stuff, brocade, and valuable carpeting, piled upon one another; gold and silver ingots in great heaps, and money in bags. The sight of all these riches made him suppose that this cave must have been occupied for ages by robbers, who had succeeded one another.

Ali Baba went boldly into the cave, and collected as much of the gold coin, which was in bags, as he thought his three asses could carry. When he had loaded them with the bags, he laid wood over them in such a manner that they could not be seen. When he had passed in and out as often as he wished, he stood before the door, and pronouncing the words, "Shut, Sesame!" the door closed of itself. He then made the best of his way to town.

When Ali Baba got home, he drove his asses into a little yard, shut the gates very carefully, threw off the wood that covered the panniers, carried the bags into his house, and ranged them in order before his wife. He then emptied the bags, which raised such a great heap of gold as dazzled his wife's eyes, and then he told her the whole adventure from beginning to end, and, above all, recommended her to keep it secret.

The wife rejoiced greatly at their good fortune, and would count all the gold piece by piece. "Wife," replied Ali Baba, "you do not know what you undertake, when you pretend to count the money; you will never have done. I will dig a hole, and bury it. There is no time to be lost." "You are in the right, husband," replied she, "but let us know, as nigh as possible, how much we have. I will borrow a small measure, and measure it, while you dig the hole."

Away the wife ran to her brother-in-law Cassim, who lived just by, and addressing herself to his wife, desired her to lend her a measure for a little while. Her sister-in-law asked her whether she would have a great or a small one. The other asked for a small one. She bade her stay a little, and she would readily fetch one.

The sister-in-law did so, but as she knew Ali Baba's poverty, she was curious to know what sort of grain his wife wanted to measure, and artfully putting some suet at the bottom of the measure, brought it to her, with an excuse that she was sorry that she had made her stay so long, but that she could not find it sooner.

Ali Baba's wife went home, set the measure upon the heap of gold, filled it, and emptied it often upon the sofa, till she had done, when she was very well satisfied to find the number of measures amounted to so many as they did, and went to tell her husband, who had almost finished digging the hole. While Ali Baba was burying the gold, his wife, to show her exactness and diligence to her sister-in-law, carried the measure back again, but without taking notice that a piece of gold had stuck to the bottom. "Sister," said she, giving it to her again, "you see that I have not kept your measure long. I am obliged to you for it, and return it with thanks."

As soon as Ali Baba's wife was gone, Cassim's looked at the bottom of the measure, and was in inexpressible surprise to find a piece of gold sticking to it. Envy immediately possessed her breast. "What!" said she, "has Ali Baba gold so plentiful as to measure it? Whence has he all this wealth?"

Cassim, her husband, was at his counting-house. When he came home, his wife said to him, "Cassim, I know you think yourself rich, but Ali Baba is infinitely richer than you. He does not count his money, but measures it." Cassim desired her to explain the riddle, which she did, by telling him the stratagem she had used to make the discovery, and showed him the piece of money, which was so old that they could not tell in what prince's reign it was coined.

Cassim, after he had married the rich widow, had never treated Ali Baba as a brother, but neglected him; and now, instead of being pleased, he conceived a base envy at his brother's prosperity. He could not sleep all that night, and went to him in the morning before sunrise. "Ali Baba," said he, "I am surprised at you; you pretend to be miserably poor, and yet you measure gold. My wife found this at the bottom of the measure you borrowed yesterday."

By this discourse, Ali Baba perceived that Cassim and his wife, through his own wife's folly, knew what they had so much reason to conceal; but what was done, could not be undone. Therefore, without showing the least surprise or trouble, he confessed all, and offered his brother part of his treasure to keep the secret.

"I expect as much," replied Cassim, haughtily, "but I must know exactly where this treasure is, and how I may visit it myself when I choose; otherwise, I will go and inform against you, and then you will not only get no more, but will lose all you have, and I shall have a share for my information."

Ali Baba told him all he desired, even to the very words he was to use to gain admission into the cave.

Cassim rose the next morning long before the sun, and set out for the forest with ten mules bearing great chests, which he designed to fill, and followed the road which Ali Baba had pointed out to him. He was not long before he reached the rock, and found out the place, by the tree and other marks which his brother had given him. When he reached the entrance of the cavern, he pronounced the words, "Open, Sesame!" The door immediately opened, and, when he was in, closed upon him. In examining the cave, he was in great admiration to find much more riches than he had expected from Ali Baba's relation. He quickly laid as many bags of gold as he could carry at the door of the cavern; but his thoughts were so full of the great riches he should possess, that he could not think of the necessary word to make it open, but instead of "Sesame," said, "Open, Barley!" and was much amazed to find that the door remained fast shut. He named several sorts of grain, but still the door would not open.

Cassim had never expected such an incident, and was so alarmed at the danger he was in, that the more he endeavored to remember the word "Sesame," the more his memory was confounded, and he had as much forgotten it as if he had never heard it mentioned. He threw down the bags he had loaded himself with, and walked distractedly up and down the cave, without having the least regard to the riches that were round him.

About noon the robbers visited their cave. At some distance they saw Cassim's mules straggling about the rock, with great chests on their backs. Alarmed at this, they galloped full speed to the cave. They drove away the mules, who strayed through the forest so far, that they were soon out of sight, and went directly, with their naked sabers in their hands, to the door, which, on their captain pronouncing the proper words, immediately opened.

Cassim, who heard the noise of the horses' feet, at once guessed the arrival of the robbers, and resolved to make one effort for his life. He rushed to the door, and no sooner saw the door open, than he ran out and threw the leader down, but could not escape the other robbers, who with their scimitars soon deprived him of life.

The first care of the robbers after this was to examine the cave. They found all the bags which Cassim had brought to the door, to be ready to load his mules, and carried them again to their places, but they did not miss what Ali Baba had taken away before. Then holding a council, and deliberating upon this occurrence, they guessed that Cassim, when he was in, could not get out again, but could not imagine how he had learned the secret words by which alone he could enter. They could not deny the fact of his being there; and to terrify any person or accomplice who should attempt the same thing, they agreed to cut Cassim's body into four quarters—to hang two on one side, and two on the other, within the door of the cave. They had no sooner taken this resolution than they put it in execution; and when they had nothing more to detain them, left the place of their hoards well closed. They mounted their horses, went to beat the roads again, and to attack the caravans they might meet.

In the mean time, Cassim's wife was very uneasy when night came, and her husband was not returned. She ran to Ali Baba in great alarm, and said, "I believe, brother-in-law, that you know Cassim is gone to the forest, and upon what account; it is now night, and he has not returned; I am afraid some misfortune has happened to him." Ali Baba told her that she need not frighten herself, for that certainly Cassim would not think it proper to come into the town till the night should be pretty far advanced.

Cassim's wife, considering how much it concerned her husband to keep the business secret, was the more easily persuaded to believe her brother-in-law. She went home again, and waited patiently till midnight. Then her fear redoubled, and her grief was the more sensible because she was forced to keep it to herself. She repented of her foolish curiosity, and cursed her desire of prying into the affairs of her brother and sister-in-law. She spent all the night in weeping; and as soon as it was day went to them, telling them, by her tears, the cause of her coming.

Ali Baba did not wait for his sister-in-law to desire him to go to see what was become of Cassim, but departed immediately with his three asses, begging of her first to moderate her affliction. He went to the forest, and when he came near the rock, having seen neither his brother nor the mules in his way, was seriously alarmed at finding some blood spilt near the door, which he took for an ill omen; but when he had pronounced the word, and the door had opened, he was struck with horror at the dismal sight of his brother's body. He was not long in determining how he should pay the last dues to his brother; but without adverting to the little fraternal affection he had shown for him, went into the cave to find something to enshroud his remains; and having loaded one of his asses with them, covered them over with wood. The other two asses he loaded with bags of gold, covering them with wood also as before; and then bidding the door shut, came away; but was so cautious as to stop some time at the end of the forest, that he might not go into the town before night. When he came home, he drove the two asses loaded with gold into his little yard, and left the care of unloading them to his wife, while he led the other to his sister-in-law's house.

Ali Baba knocked at the door, which was opened by Morgiana, a clever, intelligent slave, who was fruitful in inventions to meet the most difficult circumstances. When he came into the court, he unloaded the ass, and taking Morgiana aside, said to her, "You must observe an inviolable secrecy. Your master's body is contained in these two panniers. We must bury him as if he had died a natural death. Go now and tell your mistress. I leave the matter to your wit and skilful devices."

Ali Baba helped to place the body in Cassim's house, again recommended to Morgiana to act her part well, and then returned with his ass.

Morgiana went out early the next morning to a druggist, and asked for a sort of lozenge, which was considered efficacious in the most dangerous disorders. The apothecary inquired who was ill? She replied, with a sigh, "Her good master Cassim himself: and that he could neither eat nor speak." In the evening Morgiana went to the same druggist's again, and with tears in her eyes, asked for an essence which they used to give to sick people only when at the last extremity. "Alas!" said she taking it from the apothecary, "I am afraid that this remedy will have no better effect than the lozenges; and that I shall lose my good master."

On the other hand, as Ali Baba and his wife were often seen to go between Cassim's and their own house all that day, and to seem melancholy, nobody was surprised in the evening to hear the lamentable shrieks and cries of Cassim's wife and Morgiana, who gave out everywhere that her master was dead. The next morning at daybreak, Morgiana went to an old cobbler whom she knew to be always early at his stall, and bidding him good-morrow, put a piece of gold into his hand, saying, "Baba Mustapha, you must bring with you your sewing tackle, and come with me; but I must tell you, I shall blindfold you when you come to such a place."

Baba Mustapha seemed to hesitate a little at

these words. "Oh! oh!" replied he, "you would
have me do something against my conscience or
against my honor?" "God forbid," said Morgiana,
putting another piece of gold into his hand, "that
I should ask anything that is contrary to your
honor! only come along with me and fear nothing."

Baba Mustapha went with Morgiana, who, after
she had bound his eyes with a handkerchief at the
place she had mentioned, conveyed him to her deceased master's house, and never unloosed his eyes
till he had entered the room where she had put the
corpse together. "Baba Mustapha," said she, "you
must make haste and sew the parts of this body
together; and when you have done, I will give you
another piece of gold."

After Baba Mustapha had finished his task, she
blindfolded him again, gave him the third piece of
gold as she had promised, and recommending secrecy to him, carried him back to the place where
she first bound his eyes, pulled off the bandage,
and let him go home, but watched him that he returned toward his stall, till he was quite out of
sight, for fear he should have the curiosity to return and dodge her; she then went home. Morgiana, on her return, warmed some water to wash the
body, and at the same time Ali Baba perfumed it
with incense, and wrapped it in the burying clothes
with the accustomed ceremonies. Not long after
the proper officer brought the bier, and when the
attendants of the mosque, whose business it was to
wash the dead, offered to perform their duty, she
told them that it was done already. Shortly after
this the imaun and the other ministers of the mosque
arrived. Four neighbors carried the corpse to the
burying-ground, following the imaun, who recited
some prayers. Ali Baba came after with some
neighbors, who often relieved the others in carrying

the bier to the burying-ground. Morgiana, a slave to the deceased, followed in the procession, weeping, beating her breast, and tearing her hair. Cassim's wife stayed at home mourning, uttering lamentable cries with the women of the neighborhood, who came, according to custom, during the funeral, and joining their lamentations with hers filled the quarter far and near with sounds of sorrow.

In this manner Cassim's melancholy death was concealed and hushed up between Ali Baba, his widow, and Morgiana, his slave, with so much contrivance that nobody in the city had the least knowledge or suspicion of the cause of it. Three or four days after the funeral, Ali Baba removed his few goods openly to his sister-in-law's house, in which it was agreed that he should in future live; but the money he had taken from the robbers he conveyed thither by night. As for Cassim's warehouse, he intrusted it to the management of his eldest son.

While these things were being done, the forty robbers again visited their retreat in the forest. Great, then, was their surprise to find Cassim's body taken away, with some of their bags of gold. "We are certainly discovered," said the captain. "The removal of the body, and the loss of some of our money, plainly shows that the man whom we killed had an accomplice: and for our own lives' sake we must try and find him. What say you, my lads?"

All the robbers unanimously approved of the captain's proposal.

"Well," said the captain, "one of you, the boldest and most skilful among you, must go into the town, disguised as a traveler and a stranger, to try if he can hear any talk of the man whom we have killed, and endeavor to find out who he was, and where he lived. This is a matter of the first importance, and for fear of any treachery, I propose that whoever undertakes this business without success, even though the failure arises only from an error of judgment, shall suffer death."

Without waiting for the sentiments of his companions, one of the robbers started up, and said, "I submit to this condition, and think it an honor to expose my life to serve the troop."

After this robber had received great commendations from the captain and his comrades, he disguised himself so that nobody would take him for what he was; and taking his leave of the troop that night, went into the town just at daybreak; and walked up and down, till accidentally he came to Baba Mustapha's stall, which was always open before any of the shops.

Baba Mustapha was seated with an awl in his hand, just going to work. The robber saluted him, bidding him good-morrow; and perceiving that he was old, said, "Honest man, you begin to work very early: is it possible that one of your age can see so well? I question, even if it were somewhat lighter, whether you could see to stitch."

"You do not know me," replied Baba Mustapha; "for old as I am, I have extraordinary good eyes; and you will not doubt it when I tell you that I sewed the body of a dead man together in a place where I had not so much light as I have now."

"A dead body!" exclaimed the robber, with affected amazement. "Yes, yes," answered Baba Mustapha, "I see you want to have me speak out, but you shall know no more."

The robber felt sure that he had discovered what he sought. He pulled out a piece of gold, and putting it into Baba Mustapha's hand, said to him, "I do not want to learn your secret, though I can assure you you might safely trust me with it. The only thing I desire of you is to show me the house where you stitched up the dead body."

"If I were disposed to do you that favor," replied Baba Mustapha, "I assure you I cannot. I was taken to a certain place, whence I was led blindfold to the house, and afterward brought back again in the same manner; you see, therefore, the impossiblity of my doing what you desire."

"Well," replied the robber, "you may, however, remember a little of the way that you were led blindfolded. Come, let me blind your eyes at the same place. We will walk together; perhaps you may recognize some part; and as everybody ought to be paid for their trouble, there is another piece of gold for you; gratify me in what I ask you." So saying, he put another piece of gold into his hand.

The two pieces of gold were great temptations to Baba Mustapha. He looked at them a long time in his hand, without saying a word, but at last he pulled out his purse and put them in. "I cannot promise," said he to the robber, "that I can remember the way exactly; but since you desire, I will try what I can do." At these words Baba Mustapha rose up, to the great joy of the robber, and led him to the place where Morgiana had bound his eyes. "It was here," said Baba Mustapha, "I was blindfolded; and I turned this way." The robber tied his handkerchief over his eyes, and walked by him till he stopped directly at Cassim's house, where Ali Baba then lived. The thief, before he pulled off the band, marked the door with a piece of chalk, which he had ready in his hand, and then asked him if he knew whose house that was; to which Baba Mustapha replied, that as he did not live in that neighborhood, he could not tell.

The robber, finding he could discover no more from Baba Mustapha, thanked him for the trouble he had taken, and left him to go back to his stall, while he returned to the forest, persuaded that he should be very well received.

A little after the robber and Baba Mustapha had

parted, Morgiana went out of Ali Baba's house upon some errand, and upon her return, seeing the mark the robber had made, stopped to observe it. "What can be the meaning of this mark?" said she to herself; "somebody intends my master no good; however, with whatever intention it was done, it is advisable to guard against the worst." According, she fetched a piece of chalk, and marked two or three doors on each side, in the same manner, without saying a word to her master or mistress.

In the mean time, the robber rejoined his troop in the forest, and recounted to them his success; expatiating upon his good fortune, in meeting so soon with the only person who could inform him of what he wanted to know. All the robbers listened to him with the utmost satisfaction; when the captain, after commending his diligence, addressing himself to them all, said, "Comrades, we have no time to lose: let us set off well armed, without its appearing who we are; but that we may not excite any suspicion, let only one or two go into the town together, and join at our rendezvous, which shall be the great square. In the mean time, our comrade who brought us the good news and I will go and find out the house, that we may consult what had best be done."

This speech and plan was approved of by all, and they were soon ready. They filed off in parties of two each, after some interval of time, and got into the town without being in the least suspected. The captain, and he who had visited the town in the morning as spy, came in the last. He led the captain into the street where he had marked Ali Baba's residence; and when they came to the first of the houses which Morgiana had marked, he pointed it out. But the captain observed that the next door was chalked in the same manner, and in the same place; and showing it to his guide, who him which house it was, that, or the first. The guide was so confounded, that he knew not what answer to make; but still more puzzled, when he and the captain saw five or six houses similarly marked. He assured the captain, with an oath, that he had marked but one, and could not tell who had chalked the rest, so that he could not distinguish the house which the cobbler had stopped at.

The captain, finding that their design had proved abortive, went directly to the place of rendezvous, and told his troop that they had lost their labor, and must return to their cave. He himself set them the example, and they all returned as they had come.

When the troop was all got together, the captain told them the reason of their returning; and presently the conductor was declared by all worthy of death. He condemned himself, acknowledging that he ought to have taken better precaution, and prepared to receive the stroke from him who was appointed to cut off his head.

But as the safety of the troop required the discovery of the second intruder into the cave, another of the gang, who promised himself that he should succeed better, presented himself, and his offer being accepted, he went and corrupted Baba Mustapha, as the other had done; and being shown the house, marked it in a place more remote from sight, with red chalk.

Not long after, Morgiana, whose eyes nothing could escape, went out, and seeing the red chalk, and arguing with herself as she had done before, marked the other neighbors' houses in the same place and manner.

The robber, at his return to his company, valued himself much on the precaution he had taken, which he looked upon as an infallible way of distinguishing Ali Baba's house from the others; and the captain and all of them thought it must succeed. They conveyed themselves into the town with the same precaution as before; but when the robber and his captain came to the street, they found the same difficulty; at which the captain was enraged, and the robber in as great confusion as his predecessor.

Thus the captain and his troop were forced to retire a second time, and much more dissatisfied; while the robber who had been the author of the mistake underwent the same punishment, which he willingly submitted to.

The captain, having lost two brave fellows of his troop, was afraid of diminishing it too much by pursuing this plan to get information of the residence of their plunderer. He found by their example that their heads were not so good as their hands on such occasions; and therefore resolved to take upon himself the important commission.

Accordingly, he went and addressed himself to Baba Mustapha, who did him the same service he had done to the other robbers. He did not set any particular mark on the house, but examined and observed it so carefully, by passing often by it, that it was impossible for him to mistake it.

The captain, well satisfied with his attempt, and informed of what he wanted to know, returned to the forest; and when he came into the cave, where the troop waited for him, said, "Now, comrades, nothing can prevent our full revenge, as I am certain of the house; and in my way hither I have thought how to put it into execution, but if any one can form a better expedient, let him communicate it." He then told them his contrivance; and as they approved of it, ordered them to go into the villages about, and buy nineteen mules, with thirty-eight large leather jars, one full of oil, and the others empty.

In two or three days' time the robbers had purchased the mules and jars, and as the mouths of the jars were rather too narrow for his purpose, the captain caused them to be widened, and after having put one of his men into each, with the weapons which he thought fit, leaving open the seam which had been undone to leave them room to breathe, he rubbed the jars on the outside with oil from the full vessel.

Things being thus prepared, when the nineteen mules were loaded with thirty-seven robbers in jars, and the jar of oil, the captain, as their driver, set out with them, and reached the town by the dusk of the evening, as he had intended. He led them through the streets, till he came to Ali Baba's, at whose door he designed to have knocked; but was prevented by his sitting there after supper to take a little fresh air. He stopped his mules, addressed himself to him, and said, " I have brought some oil a great way, to sell at to-morrow's market; and it is now so late that I do not know where to lodge. If I should not be troublesome to you, do me the favor to let me pass the night with you, and I shall be very much obliged by your hospitality."

Though Ali Baba had seen the captain of the robbers in the forest, and had heard him speak, it was impossible to know him in the disguise of an oil merchant. He told him he should be welcome, and immediately opened his gates for the mules to go into the yard. At the same time he called to a slave, and ordered him, when the mules were unloaded, to put them into the stable, and to feed them; and then went to Morgiana, to bid her get a good supper for his guest. After they had finished supper, Ali Baba, charging Morgiana afresh to take care of his guest, said to her, " To-morrow morning I design to go to the bath before day; take care my bathing linen be ready, give them to

Abdalla (which was the slave's name), and make me some good broth against I return." After this he went to bed.

In the mean time the captain of the robbers went into the yard, and took off the lid of each jar, and gave his people orders what to do. Beginning at the first jar, and so on to the last, he said to each man: "As soon as I throw some stones out of the chamber window where I lie, do not fail to come out, and I will immediately join you." After this he returned into the house, when Morgiana, taking up a light, conducted him to his chamber, where she left him; and he, to avoid any suspicion, put the light out soon after, and laid himself down in his clothes, that he might be the more ready to rise.

Morgiana, remembering Ali Baba's orders, got his bathing linen ready, and ordered Abdalla to set on the pot for the broth; but while she was preparing it the lamp went out, and there was no more oil in the house, nor any candles. What to do she did not know, for the broth must be made. Abdalla, seeing her very uneasy, said, "Do not fret and tease yourself, but go into the yard, and take some oil out of one of the jars."

Morgiana thanked Abdalla for his advice, took the oil-pot, and went into the yard; when, as she came nigh the first jar, the robber within said softly, "Is it time?"

Though naturally much surprised at finding a man in the jar instead of the oil she wanted, she immediately felt the importance of keeping silence, as Ali Baba, his family, and herself were in great danger; and collecting herself, without showing the least emotion,. she answered, "Not yet, but presently." She went quietly in this manner to all the jars, giving the same answer, till she came to the jar of oil.

By this means Morgiana found that her master

Ali Baba had admitted thirty-eight robbers into his house, and that this pretended oil merchant was their captain. She made what haste she could to fill her oil-pot, and returned into her kitchen, where, as soon as she had lighted her lamp, she took a great kettle, went again to the oil-jar, filled the kettle, set it on a large wood fire, and as soon as it boiled, went and poured enough into every jar to stifle and destroy the robber within.

When this action, worthy of the courage of Morgiana, was executed without any noise, as she had projected, she returned into the kitchen with the empty kettle; and having put out the great fire she had made to boil the oil, and leaving just enough to make the broth, put out the lamp also, and remained silent, resolving not to go to rest till she had observed what might follow through a window of the kitchen, which opened into the yard.

She had not waited long before the captain of the robbers got up, opened the window, and finding no light, and hearing no noise, or any one stirring in the house, gave the appointed signal, by throwing little stones, several of which hit the jars, as he doubted not by the sound they gave. He then listened, but not hearing or perceiving anything whereby he could judge that his companions stirred, he began to grow very uneasy, threw stones again a second and also a third time, and could not comprehend the reason that none of them should answer his signal. Much alarmed, he went softly down into the yard, and going to the first jar, while asking the robber, whom he thought alive, if he was in readiness, smelled the hot boiled oil, which sent forth a steam out of the jar. Hence he suspected that his plot to murder Ali Baba, and plunder his house, was discovered. Examining all the jars, one after another, he found that all his gang were dead; and, enraged to despair at having failed in his design, he forced the lock of a door that led from the yard to the garden, and climbing over the walls, made his escape.

When Morgiana saw him depart, she went to bed, satisfied and pleased to have succeeded so well in saving her master and family.

Ali Baba rose before day, and, followed by his slave, went to the baths, entirely ignorant of the important event which had happened at home.

When he returned from the baths, he was very much surprised to see the oil-jars, and that the merchant was not gone with the mules. He asked Morgiana, who opened the door, the reason of it. "My good master," answered she, "God preserve you and all of your family. You will be better informed of what you wish to know when you have seen what I have to show you, if you will follow me."

As soon as Morgiana had shut the door, Ali Baba followed her, when she requested him to look into the first jar, and see if there was any oil. Ali Baba did so, and seeing a man, started back in alarm, and cried out. "Do not be afraid," said Morgiana, "the man you see there can neither do you nor anybody else any harm. He is dead." "Ah, Morgiana," said Ali Baba, "what is it you show me? Explain yourself." "I will," replied Morgiana. "Moderate your astonishment, and do not excite the curiosity of your neighbors; for it is of great importance to keep this affair secret. Look into all the other jars."

Ali Baba examined all the other jars, one after another; and when he came to that which had the oil in, found it prodigiously sunk, and stood for some time motionless, sometimes looking at the jars, and sometimes at Morgiana, without saying a word, so great was his surprise. At last, when he had recovered himself, he said, "And what is become of the merchant?"

"Merchant!" answered she; "he is as much one as I am. I will tell you who he is, and what is become of him; but you had better hear the story in your own chamber; for it is time for your health that you had your broth after your bathing."

Morgiana then told him all she had done, from the first observing the mark upon the house, to the destruction of the robbers, and the flight of the captain.

On hearing of these brave deeds from the lips of Morgiana, Ali Baba said to her—"God, by your means, has delivered me from the snares these robbers laid for my destruction. I owe, therefore, my life to you; and, for the first token of my acknowledgment, give you your liberty from this moment, till I can complete your recompense as I intend."

Ali Baba's garden was very long, and shaded at the further end by a great number of large trees. Near these he and the slave Abdalla dug a trench, long and wide enough to hold the bodies of the robbers; and as the earth was light, they were not long in doing it. When this was done, Ali Baba hid the jars and weapons; and as he had no occasion for the mules, he sent them at different times to be sold in the market by his slave.

While Ali Baba took these measures, the captain of the forty robbers returned to the forest with inconceivable mortification. He did not stay long; the loneliness of the gloomy cavern became frightful to him. He determined, however, to avenge the fate of his companions, and to accomplish the death of Ali Baba. For this purpose he returned to the town, and took a lodging in a khan, and disguised himself as a merchant in silks. Under this assumed character, he gradually conveyed a great many sorts of rich stuffs and fine linen to his lodging from the cavern, but with all the necessary precautions to conceal the place whence he brought them. In order to dispose of the merchandise, when he had thus amassed them together, he took a warehouse, which happened to be opposite to Cassim's, which Ali Baba's son had occupied since the death of his uncle.

He took the name of Cogia Houssain, and, as a new-comer, was, according to custom, extremely civil and complaisant to all the merchants his neighbors. Ali Baba's son was, from his vicinity, one of the first to converse with Cogia Houssain, who strove to cultivate his friendship more particularly. Two or three days after he was settled, Ali Baba came to see his son, and the captain of the robbers recognized him at once, and soon learned from his son who he was. After this he increased his assiduities, caressed him in the most engaging manner, made him some small presents, and often asked him to dine and sup with him, when he treated him very handsomely.

Ali Baba's son did not choose to lie under such obligation to Cogia Houssain; but was so much straitened for want of room in his house, that he could not entertain him. He therefore acquainted his father, Ali Baba, with his wish to invite him in return.

Ali Baba with great pleasure took the treat upon himself. "Son," said he, "to-morrow being Friday, which is a day that the shops of such great merchants as Cogia Houssain and yourself are shut, get him to accompany you, and as you pass by my door, call in. I will go and order Morgiana to provide a supper."

The next day Ali Baba's son and Cogia Houssain met by appointment, took their walk, and as they returned, Ali Baba's son led Cogia Houssain through the street where his father lived, and when they came to the house, stopped and knocked at the door. "This, sir," said he, "is my father's house, who, from the account I have given him of your friendship, charged me to procure him the honor of your acquaintance; and I desire you to add this pleasure to those for which I am already indebted to you."

Though it was the sole aim of Cogia Houssain to introduce himself into Ali Baba's house, that he might kill him, without hazarding his own life or making any noise, yet he excused himself, and offered to take his leave; but a slave having opened the door, Ali Baba's son took him obligingly by the hand, and, in a manner, forced him in.

Ali Baba received Cogia Houssain with a smiling countenance, and in the most obliging manner he could wish. He thanked him for all the favors he had done his son; adding, withal, the obligation was the greater as he was a young man, not much acquainted with the world, and that he might contribute to his information.

Cogia Houssain returned the compliment by assuring Ali Baba, that though his son might not have acquired the experience of older men, he had good sense equal to the experience of many others. After a little more conversation on different subjects, he offered again to take his leave, when Ali Baba, stopping him, said, "Where are you going, sir, in so much haste? I beg you would do me the honor to sup with me, though my entertainment may not be worthy your acceptance; such as it is, I heartily offer it." "Sir," replied Cogia Houssain, "I am thoroughly persuaded of your good-will; but the truth is, I can eat no victuals that have any salt in them; therefore judge how I should feel at your table. "If that is the only reason," said Ali Baba, "it ought not to deprive me of the honor of your company; for, in the first place, there is no salt ever put into my bread, and as to the meat we shall have to-night, I promise you there shall be none in that. Therefore you must do me the favor to stay. I will return immediately."

Ali Baba went into the kitchen, and ordered Morgiana to put no salt to the meat that was to be dressed that night; and to make quickly two or three ragouts besides what he had ordered, but be sure to put no salt in them.

Morgiana, who was always ready to obey her master, could not help being surprised at his strange order. "Who is this strange man," said she, "who eats no salt with his meat? Your supper will be spoiled, if I keep it back so long." "Do not be angry, Morgiana," replied Ali Baba; "he is an honest man, therefore do as I bid you."

Morgiana obeyed, though with no little reluctance, and had a curiosity to see this man who ate no salt. To this end, when she had finished what she had to do in the kitchen, she helped Abdalla to carry up the dishes; and looking at Cogia Houssain, knew him at first sight, notwithstanding his disguise, to be the captain of the robbers, and examining him very carefully, perceived that he had a dagger under his garment. "I am not in the least amazed," said she to herself, "that this wicked man, who is my masters' greatest enemy, would eat no salt with him, since he intends to assassinate him; but I will prevent him."

Morgiana, while they were at supper, determined in her own mind to execute one of the boldest acts ever meditated. When Abdalla came for the dessert of fruit, and had put it with the wine and glasses before Ali Baba, Morgiana retired, dressed herself neatly, with a suitable head-dress like a dancer, girded her waist with a silver-gilt girdle, to which there hung a poniard with a hilt and guard of the same metal, and put a handsome mask on her face. When she had thus disguised herself, she said to Abdalla, "Take your tabor, and let us go and divert our master and his son's friend, as we do sometimes when he is alone."

Abdalla took his tabor and played all the way into the hall before Morgiana, who, when she came to the door, made a low obeisance by way of asking leave to exhibit her skill, while Abdalla left off playing. "Come in, Morgiana," said Ali Baba, "and let Cogia Houssain see what you can do, that he may tell us what he thinks of your performance."

Cogia Houssain, who did not expect this diversion after supper, began to fear he should not be able to take advantage of the opportunity he thought he had found; but hoped, if he now missed his aim, to secure it another time, by keeping up a friendly correspondence with the father and son; therefore, though he could have wished Ali Baba would have declined the dance, he pretended to be obliged to him for it, and had the complaisance to express his satisfaction at what he saw, which pleased his host.

As soon as Abdalla saw that Ali Baba and Cogia Houssain had done talking, he began to play on the tabor, and accompanied it with an air, to which Morgiana, who was an excellent performer, danced in such a manner as would have created admiration in any company.

After she had danced several dances with much grace, she drew the poniard, and holding it in her hand, began a dance, in which she outdid herself by the many different figures, light movements, and the surprising leaps and wonderful exertions with which she accompanied it. Sometimes she presented the poniard to one breast, sometimes to another, and sometimes seemed to strike her own. At last, she snatched the tabor from Abdalla with her left hand, and holding the dagger in her right presented the other side of the tabor, after the manner of those who get a livelihood by dancing, and solicit the liberality of the spectators.

Ali Baba put a piece of gold into the tabor, as did also his son; and Cogia Houssain seeing that she was coming to him, had pulled his purse out of his bosom to make her a present; but while he was putting his hand into it, Morgiana, with a courage and resolution worthy of herself, plunged the poniard into his heart.

Ali Baba and his son, shocked at this action, cried out aloud. "Unhappy woman!" exclaimed Ali Baba, "what have you done to ruin me and my family?" "It was to preserve, not to ruin you," answered Morgiana; "for see here," continued she, opening the pretended Cogia Houssain's garment, and showing the dagger, "what an enemy you had entertained? Look well at him, and you will find him to be both the fictitious oil merchant, and the captain of the gang of forty robbers. Remember, too, that he would eat no salt with you; and what would you have more to persuade you of his wicked design? Before I saw him, I suspected him as soon as you told me you had such a guest. I knew him, and you now find that my suspicion was not groundless.

Ali Baba, who immediately felt the new obligation he had to Morgiana for saving his life a second time, embraced her: "Morgiana," said he, "I gave you your liberty, and then promised you that my gratitude should not stop there, but that I would soon give you higher proofs of its sincerity, which I now do by making you my daughter-in-law." Then addressing himself to his son, he said, "I believe you, son, to be so dutiful a child, that you will not refuse Morgiana for your wife. You see that Cogia Houssain sought your friendship with a treacherous design to take away my life; and if he had succeeded, there is no doubt but he would have sacrificed you also to his revenge. Consider, that by marrying Morgiana you marry the preserver of my family and your own."

The son, far from showing any dislike, readily

consented to the marriage; not only because he would not disobey his father, but also because it was agreeable to his inclination. After this they thought of burying the captain of the robbers with his comrades, and did it so privately that nobody discovered their bones till many years after, when no one had any concern in the publication of this remarkable history. A few days afterward, Ali Baba celebrated the nuptials of his son and Morgiana with great solemnity, a sumptuous feast, and the usual dancing and spectacles; and had the satisfaction to see that his friends and neighbors, whom he invited, had no knowledge of the true motives of the marriage; but that those who were not unacquainted with Morgiana's good qualities commended his generosity and goodness of heart. Ali Baba did not visit the robber's cave for a whole year, as he supposed the other two. whom he could get no account of, might be alive.

At the year's end, when he found they had not made any attempt to disturb him, he had the curiosity to make another journey. He mounted his horse, and when he came to the cave he alighted, tied his horse to a tree, then approaching the entrance, and pronouncing the words, " Open, Sesame!" the door opened. He entered the cavern, and by the condition he found things in, judged that nobody had been there since the captain had fetched the goods for his shop. From this time he believed he was the only person in the world who had the secret of opening the cave, and that all the treasure was at his sole disposal. He put as much gold into his saddle-bag as his horse would carry, and returned to town. Some years later he carried his son to the cave and taught him the secret, which he handed down to his posterity, who, using their good fortune with moderation, lived in great honor and splendor.

THE FIRST VOYAGE OF SINDBAD THE SAILOR

MY father was a wealthy merchant of much repute. He bequeathed me a large estate, which I wasted in riotous living. I quickly perceived my error, and that I was misspending my time, which is of all things most valuable. I remembered the saying of the great Solomon, which I had frequently heard from my father, "A good name is better than precious ointment," and again, "Wisdom is good with an inheritance." Struck with these reflections, I resolved to walk in my father's ways, and I entered into a contract with some merchants, and embarked with them on board a ship we had jointly fitted out.

We set sail, and steered our course toward the Indies, through the Persia Gulf, which is formed by the coasts of Arabia Felix on the right, and by those of Persia on the left. At first I was troubled with sea-sickness, but speedily recovered my health, and was not afterward subject to that complaint.

In our voyage we touched at several islands, where we sold or exchanged our goods. One day, while under sail, we were becalmed near a small island, but little elevated above the level of the water, and resembling a green meadow. The captain ordered his sails to be furled, and permitted such persons as were so inclined to land; of this number I was one.

But while we were enjoying ourselves in eating and drinking, and recovering ourselves from the fatigue of the sea, the island on a sudden trembled and shook us terribly.

The trembling of the island was perceived on board the ship, and we were called upon to re-embark speedily, or we should all be lost; for what we took for an island proved to be the back of a sea monster. The nimblest got into the sloop, others betook themselves to swimming; but as for myself, I was still upon the island when it disappeared into the sea, and I had only time to catch hold of a piece of wood that we had brought out of the ship to make a fire. Meanwhile the captain, having received those on board who were in the sloop, and taken up some of those that swam, resolved to improve the favorable gale that had just risen, and hoisting his sails pursued his voyage, so that it was impossible for me to recover the ship.

Thus was I exposed to the mercy of the waves all the rest of the day and the following night. By this time I found my strength gone, and despaired of saving my life, when happily a wave threw me against an island. The bank was high and rugged; so that I could scarcely have got up had it not been for some roots of trees which I found within reach. When the sun arose, though I was very feeble, both from hard labor and want of food, I crept along to find some herbs fit to eat, and had the good luck not only to procure some, but likewise to discover a stream of excellent water, which contributed much to recover me. After this I advanced farther into the island, and at least reached a fine plain, where I perceived some horses feeding. I went toward them, when I heard the voice of a man, who immediately appeared and asked me who I was. I related to him my adventure, after which, taking me by the hand, he led me into a cave, where there were several other people, no less amazed to see me than I was to see them.

I partook of some provisions which they offered me. I then asked them what they did in such a desert place; to which they answered, that they were grooms belonging to the maharaja, sovereign of the island, and that every year they brought thither the king's horses for pasturage. They added, that they were to return home on the morrow, and had I been one day later, I must have perished, because the inhabited part of the island was a great distance off, and it would have been impossible for me to have got thither without a guide.

Next morning they returned to the capital of the island, took me with them, and presented me to the maharaja. He asked me who I was, and by what adventure I had come into his dominions. After I had satisfied him, he told me he was much concerned for my misfortune, and at the same time ordered that I should want for nothing; which commands his officers were so generous and careful as to see exactly fulfilled.

Being a merchant, I frequented men of my own profession, and particularly inquired for those who were strangers, that perchance I might hear news from Bagdad, or find an opportunity to return. For the maharaja's capital is situated on the seacoast, and has a fine harbor, where ships arrive daily from the different quarters of the world. I frequented also the society of the learned Indians, and took delight to hear them converse; but withal, I took care to make my court regularly to the maharaja, and conversed with the governors and petty kings, his tributaries, that were about him. They put a thousand questions respecting my country; and I, being willing to inform myself as to their laws and customs, asked them concerning everything which I thought worth knowing.

There belongs to this king an island named Cassel. They assured me that every night a noise of drums was heard there, whence the mariners fancied that it was the residence of Degial. I determined to visit this wonderful place, and in my way thither saw fishes of 100 and 200 cubits long, that occasion more fear than hurt; for they are so timorous, that they will fly upon the rattling of two sticks or boards. I saw likewise other fish, about a cubit in length, that had heads like owls.

As I was one day at the port after my return, the ship arrived in which I had embarked at Bussorah. I at once knew the captain, and I went and asked him for my bales. "I am Sindbad," said I, "and those bales marked with his name are mine."

When the captain heard me speak thus, "Heavens!" he exclaimed, "whom can we trust in these times! I saw Sindbad perish with my own eyes, as did also the passengers on board, and yet you tell me you are that Sindbad. What impudence is this! and what a false tale to tell, in order to possess yourself of what does not belong to you!" "Have patience," replied I; "do me the favor to hear what I have to say." The captain was at length persuaded that I was no cheat; for there came people from his ship who knew me, paid me great compliments, and expressed much joy at seeing me alive. At last he recollected me himself, and embracing me, "Heaven be praised," said he, "for your happy escape! I cannot express the joy it affords me. There are your goods: take and do with them as you please."

I took out what was most valuable in my bales, and presented them to the maharaja, who, knowing my misfortune, asked me how I came by such rarities. I acquainted him with the circumstance of their recovery. He was pleased at my good luck, accepted my present, and in return gave me one much more considerable. Upon this I took leave of him, and went aboard the same ship after I had exchanged my goods for the commodities of that country. I carried with me wood of aloes, sandals, camphor, nutmegs, cloves, pepper, and ginger. We passed by several islands, and at last arrived at Bussorah, from whence I came to this city, with the value of 100,000 sequins.

Sindbad stopped here, and ordered the musicians to proceed with their concert, which the story had interrupted. When it was evening, Sindbad sent for a purse of 100 sequins, and giving it to the porter, said, "Take this, Sindbad, return to your home, and come back to-morrow to hear more of my adventures." The porter went away, astonished at the honor done him, and the present made him. The account of his adventure proved very agreeable to his wife and children, who did not fail to return thanks for what Providence had sent them by the hand of Sindbad.

ARISTOPHANES

ARISTOPHANES, the greatest comic poet of Greece, was born in 448 B.C. His death occurred about 380 B.C. Of his fifty-four plays only eleven are extant. "The Knights," "The Birds," "The Clouds" and "The Frogs" are best known to the moderns. All were attacks upon persons or public measures objectionable to the poet.

GRAND CHORUS OF BIRDS

(From "The Birds" : Swinburne's Translation)

COME on then, ye dwellers by nature in darkness, and like to the leaves' generations,
That are little of might, that are molded of mire, unenduring and shadowlike nations,
Poor plumeless ephemerals, comfortless mortals, as visions of shadows fast fleeing,
Lift up your mind unto us that are deathless, and dateless the date of our being;
Us, children of heaven, us, ageless for aye, us, all of whose thoughts are eternal:
That ye may from henceforth, having heard of us all things aright as to matters supernal,
Of the being of birds, and beginning of gods, and of streams, and the dark beyond reaching,
Trustfully knowing aright, in my name bid Prodicus pack with his preaching!
It was Chaos and Night at the first, and the blackness of darkness, and Hell's broad border,
Earth was not, nor air, neither heaven: when in depths of the womb of the dark without order

First thing, first-born of the black-plumed Night, was
      a wind-egg hatched in her bosom,
Whence timely with seasons revolving again sweet
      Love burst out as a blossom,
Gold wings glittering forth of his back, like whirl-
      winds gustily turning.
He, after his wedlock with Chaos, whose wings are
      of darkness, in Hell broad-burning,
For his nestlings begat him the race of us first, and
      upraised us to light new-lighted.
And before this was not the race of the gods, until
      all things by Love were united:
And of kind united in kind with communion of na-
      ture the sky and the sea are
Brought forth, and the earth, and the race of the
      gods everlasting and blest. So that we are
Far away the most ancient of all things blest. And
      that we are of Love's generation
There are manifest manifold signs. We have wings,
      and with us have the Love's habitation;
And manifold fair young folk that forswore love
      once, ere the bloom of them ended,
Have the men that pursued and desired them sub-
      dued by the help of us only befriended,
With such baits as a quail, a flamingo, a goose, or a
      cock's comb staring and splendid.
All best good things that befall men come from us
      birds, as is plain to all reason:
For first we proclaim and make known to them
      spring, and the winter and autumn in season;
Bid sow, when the crane starts clanging for Afric in
      shrill-voiced emigrant number,
And calls to the pilot to hang up his rudder again
      for the season and slumber;
And then weave a cloak for Orestes the thief, lest he
      strip men of theirs if it freezes.
And again thereafter the kite reappearing announces
      a change in the breezes,

And that here is the season for shearing your sheep
 of their spring wool. Then does the swallow
Give you notice to sell your great-coat, and provide
 something light for the heat that's to follow.
Thus are we as Ammon or Delphi unto you, Dodona,
 nay, Phœbus Apollo.
For, as first ye come all to get auguries of birds, even
 such is in all things your carriage,
Be the matter a matter of trade, or of earning your
 bread, or of any one's marriage.
And all things ye lay to the charge of a bird that belong to discerning prediction:
Winged fame is a bird, as you reckon; you sneeze,
 and the sign's as a bird for conviction;
All tokens are "birds" with you—sounds, too, and
 lackeys and donkeys. Then must it not follow
That we are to you all as the manifest godhead that
 speaks in prophetic Apollo?

THE CALL TO THE NIGHTINGALE

(From "The Birds": Frere's Translation)

AWAKE! awake!
  Sleep no more, my gentle mate!
With your tiny tawny bill,
Wake the tuneful echo shrill,
 On vale or hill;
Or in her rocky seat,
Let her listen and repeat
The tender ditty that you tell,
 The sad lament,
 The dire event,
To luckless Itys that befel
 Thence the strain
 Shall rise again,
 And soar amain,

Up to the lofty palace gate
Where mighty Apollo sits in state
In Jove's abode, with his ivory lyre,
Hymning aloud to the heavenly choir,
While all the gods shall join with thee
In a celestial symphony.

FROM "THE WOMEN'S FESTIVAL"

(Translated by W. Lucas Collins)

THEY'RE always abusing the women,
  As a terrible plague to men;
They say we're the root of all evil,
  And repeat it again and again;
Of war, and quarrels, and bloodshed,
  All mischief, be what it may;
And pray, then, why do you marry us,
  If we're all the plagues you say?
And why do you take such care of us,
  And keep us so safe at home,
And are never easy a moment,
  If ever we chance to roam?
When you ought to be thanking heaven
  That your plague is out of the way—
You all keep fussing and fretting:
  "Where *is* my Plague to-day?"
If a Plague peeps out at a window,
  Up go the eyes of the men;
If she hides, then they all keep staring
  Until she looks out again.

ARISTOTLE

ARISTOTLE was born in Macedonia in 384 B.C.; died at Chalcis in 322. He was a student in Plato's school, in Athens, and for a time acted as instructor of Alexander the Great. Aristotle wrote on a large variety of subjects. He gave direction and system to Greek thought, and for two thousand years he was the greatest force in the world of philosophy.

PROSECUTION AND DEFENSE

(From Buckley's translation in the Bohn Library)

IT will be for me next to speak of the number and nature of the sources out of which the orator must construct his reasonings, touching accusation and defense. Now we must ascertain three points: one, what and how many are the objects for the sake of which men act unjustly; the second, how themselves are disposed; and the third, towards persons of what character and of what disposition they do so act.

Let us then, after defining the acting unjustly, speak in order of the rest. Let the acting unjustly be defined to be the voluntary commission of hurt in contravention of law. Now law is either general or peculiar. The peculiar law I call that, by whose written enactments men direct their polity; the general, whatever unwritten rules appear to be recognized among all men. Men are voluntary agents in whatever they do wittingly, and without compulsion. Men, therefore, do not everything on fixed principle, which they do wittingly; but whatever they do on fixed principle, that they do wittingly; because no one is ignorant of that which he chooses on principle. Now, the principles by whose motion men deliberately choose to hurt and do evil in contravention of law are depravity and moral weakness; for if any are depraved either in one or more respects, it is in reference to that point, on which they are so depraved, that they are guilty of injustice. The illiberal man, for instance, on the subject of money; the intemperate, touching the pleasure of the body; and the effeminate, respecting objects of ease; and the coward, respecting danger (for it is by reason of fear that men abandon their comrades in danger); the ambitious man, on the score of honor; the hasty man, by reason of anger; the man eager to excel, on account of victory; the vindictive, for the sake of revenge; a silly man, owing to his being mistaken on points of right and wrong; a man of effrontery, from his contempt of character. And in other characters in the same way each [goes wrong] respecting his own particular weakness. But my meaning on these matters will be evident from what has been already said on the subject of the virtues, and from what hereafter will be stated on the subject of the passions. It merely remains for me to state on what account, how effected, and toward whom, men do commit injustice.

First, then, let us distinctly enumerate the objects, which desiring, or which avoiding, we set about injustice: because it evidently should be considered by the plaintiff how many, and what sort of those things, from a desire of which men wrong their neighbors, have an existence on the side of his adversary; and by the defendant again, what, and what number of these things do not so exist. Now all men do all things either of themselves, or not of themselves. The things which they do not of themselves, they do either by chance or from necessity; and the things done by necessity, they do either by compulsion or by nature. So that all things whatsoever which men do not of themselves, they do either by chance, or from compulsion, or by nature. Again, the things which they do of themselves, and of which they are themselves the causes, some they do through custom, and others through natural desire; and this partly through this desire influenced by reason, and in part through it devoid of reason. Now, the act of wishing is desire accompanied by reason, fixing on some good as its object; because no one wishes for anything other than what he conceives to be a good. The desires devoid of reason are anger and appetite. So that all things whatever which men do, they necessarily do from seven causes; by chance, compulsion, nature, custom, will, anger, or appetite. But to carry on distinctions in reference to age, or habits, or whatever else enacts itself in conduct, were superfluous. For, granting that it happens to young men to be passionate, it is not by motion of their youth that they act thus, but by motion of anger and appetite; neither is it by motion either of wealth or poverty simply, but (in the case of the poor) it is on account of their neediness that it happens that they cherish an appetite for wealth; and (in the case of the rich) on account of their having the means, that they risk an appetite for unnecessary pleasure; and these persons will act neither by motion of their wealth nor of their poverty, but by motion of appetite. And in exactly the same way, the just and unjust, and all such as are said to act conformably to habits, will in reality act, under all circumstances, by motion of these principles; for they act on the impulse either of reason or of passion; but some from good manners and passions, others from the contrary. Still, however, it happens that on habits of this particular character, principles of action the same in character are consequent; and on those of that kind, principles also of that kind. For on the temperate man perhaps forthwith, by motion of his temperance, are attendant good opinions and appetites respecting pleasures; but on the intemperate, the contrary on these same subjects. For which reason we must waive distinctions of such a kind; but we must consider on what conditions, what principles of conduct are wont to follow: for it is not ordained (in the nature of things) that, if a man be white or black, or tall or short, principles of this or that kind should be attendant on him; but if he be young or old, just or unjust, here some difference begins; and so, in a word, in the case of all contingent circumstances whatever, which produce a difference in the tempers of men, for instance, a man's seeming to himself to be rich or poor, fortunate or unfortunate; in all these cases there will be some essential difference. Of this, however, we will speak hereafter; let us now treat first of the remaining points. Things proceed from chance which are of such kind that their cause is not definite, and are produced in the absence of any final motive, and that neither invariably, nor usually, nor in any prescribed order. My meaning on these subjects will be plain from the definition of chance. All those things exist naturally whose cause is internal and ordinate; for they turn out, either invariably or generally, in the same way; since there is no need of an accurate inquiry on results contrary to nature, whether they be produced conformably to a certain nature, or any other cause. It would appear, too, that chance is the cause of such results. All things originate in compulsion, which are produced through the instrumentality of the agents themselves, contrary to their inclination and reason. In habit originates everything which men do because they have often done it before. From will proceed whatever of the forementioned goods appear to be useful, either as an end or as conducing to the end, when it is by reason of such their usefulness that they are realized in action: for even the intemperate do some things which are useful; but not on account of their usefulness, but on account of pleasure. Through the medium of anger and excited feeling arise acts of vengeance. Now, between revenge and punishment there is a difference; for punishment is for the sake of the sufferer, but revenge for that of the person inflicting it, in order that he may be satiated. On what subjects this excitement of feeling exists will therefore be plain in my treatise of the passions. But all such things as appear pleasant are produced in action on the impulse of appetite. But that which is familiar and has become habitual is of the number of things pleasant; for many things there are, even among such as are not pleasant naturally, which, when men have been habituated to, they do with pleasure. So that, to speak in one word comprehending the whole, everything whatsoever which men do of their own proper motion, either is good, or apparently good; pleasant, or apparently pleasant. But as they act voluntarily in whatever they do of their own motion, and involuntarily in whatever they do not of their own motion; all things whatsoever in respect to which they act voluntarily will be either good or apparently good; pleasant or apparently pleasant. For I also set down the getting quit either of evils or apparent evils, and the getting a less evil in exchange for a greater, in the class of goods; because they are in a certain way desirable things. And, among things pleasant, I likewise set down the getting quit of things bringing pain, or appearing to do so; or the getting things less so, in exchange for such as are so in greater degree.

We have, therefore, to ascertain the number of things pleasant and of what kinds they are. Now on the subject of what is useful, something has been already said in my treating of deliberative rhetoric; but on the subject of what is pleasant let us treat, beginning at this point. As to the definitions, you must deem them to be adequate [to my purpose] if they be found, on each subject, exempt from obscurity, though not accurately precise.

ON PLEASING THE JUDGES

THE materials, then, from which we must exhort and dissuade, praise and blame, accuse and defend, the notions also and propositions, useful in order to render these points credible, are those which we have discussed: for respecting these questions, and out of these sources, are enthymemes deduced, so that an orator, thus provided, may speak on each separate department of questions. But as rhetoric has in view the coming to a decision (for in deliberative oratory the assembly arrive at decisions; and the sentence of a court of justice is *ipso facto* a decision); it is necessary to look not only to your speech, in what way that will be of a character to convince and persuade, but also to invest yourself with a certain kind of character, and the judge with a certain kind of feeling. For it is a point of great consequence, particularly in deliberative cases; and, next to these, in judicial; as well that the speaker seem to be a man of a certain character as that his audience conceive him to be of a certain disposition toward themselves; moreover, it is of consequence if your audience chance to be themselves also disposed in a certain way. Now, as to a speaker's appearing to be himself of a certain character, this point is more available in deliberations: but the disposing the auditor in a certain way, in judicial cases; for things do not show themselves in the same light to persons affected by love and by hatred, nor to those under emotions of anger, as to those who are disposed to placability; but they appear either utterly different in character, or at least different in degree. For to a judge who is affected by love toward the party respecting whom he pronounces his decision, that party appears either not at all to be unjust, or to be so in a very trivial degree. To a judge, however, who is affected by hatred, the case has a contrary appearance. So also to a person who is eager and sanguine, the proposed object, if pleasant, takes the appearance, as well of being likely to accrue, as of being likely to prove really a good; while by one who is indifferent and reluctant, the opposite view is taken.

Now, there are three causes of a speaker's deserving belief; for so many in number are the qualities on account of which we lend our credit, independently of proof adduced; and these are prudence, moral excellence, and the having our interests at heart (for men are fallacious in what they allege or advise by reason, either of all, or some, of these causes; for either, from want of ability, they do not rightly apprehend the question; or, rightly apprehending it, from their depravity, they do not tell you what they think; or, being men both of ability and moral excellence, they have not your interests at heart, on which account it is possible they should not give you the best advice, though fully known what is best); and besides these there is no other: it follows, therefore, of course, that the speaker who appears to possess all these qualities is considered by his audience as deserving credit. Now, the means by which men may appear virtuous and prudent are to be derived from what has been laid down on the subject of the virtues; for it is by help of the very same things that an orator may invest himself, and any one else, in a certain character. The subject of feeling an interest, and of friendliness, must be discussed in my treatise of the passions, commencing henceforth. Passions, however, are all emotions whatsoever, on which pain and pleasure are consequent, by whose operation, undergoing a change, men differ in respect to their decisions: for instance, anger, pity, fear, and whatever other emotions are of such a nature, and those opposed to them. But it will be fitting to divide what I have to say respecting each into three considerations: to consider, respecting anger, for example, how those who are susceptible of anger are affected; with whom they usually are angry; and on what occasions. For, granted that we be in possession of one, or even two, of these points, and not of them all, it will be impossible for us to kindle anger in the breast; and in the case of the rest of the passions in a similar way. In the same way, then, as on the subjects treated of above, I have separately drawn up the several propositions, so let me do in respect of these also, and make my distinctions according to the manner specified.

ON EXCELLENCE OF STYLE

LET excellence of style be defined to consist in its being clear (a sign of this is this, that the diction, unless it make the sentiment clear, will no affect its purpose); and neither low, nor above the dignity of the subject, but in good taste; for the style of poetry, indeed, is not low, yet it is not becoming in prose.

Of nouns and verbs those which are in general use produce the effect of clearness; to prevent its being low, and to give it ornament, there are other nouns which have been mentioned in the "Poetics," for a departure [from ordinary acceptations] causes it to appear more dignified; for men are affected in respect of style in the very same way as they are to-

wards foreigners and citizens. On which account
you should give your phrase a foreign air; for men
are admirers of things out of the way, and what is
an object of admiration is pleasant. Now in the
case of metrical compositions, there are many things
which produce this effect, and they are very becoming, because both the subject and the person stand
more apart [from ordinary life]; in prose, however, these helps are much fewer, for the subject is
less exalted: since even in that art were a slave, or a
mere youth, or [any one, in fact, in speaking] of
mere trifles to express himself in terms of studied
ornament, it would be rather unbecoming; but here
too [as in poetry] the rule of good taste is that your
style be lowered or raised according to the subject.
On which account we must escape observation in
doing this, and not appear to speak in a studied
manner, but naturally, for the one is of a tendency
to persuade, the other is the very reverse; because
people put themselves on their guard, as though
against one who has a design upon them, just as they
would against adulterated wine. [Let your style
then be such] as was the case with the voice of Theo-
dorus as compared with that of the other actors; for
it appeared to be that of the character which was
speaking, theirs, however, were foreign from the
character. And the deceit is neatly passed off if one
frame his nomenclature upon a selection from ordinary conversation; the thing which Euripides does,
and first gave the hint of.

As, however, nouns and verbs are [the materials]
of which the speech is made up, and as nouns admit
so many species as have been examined in the
"Poetics," out of the number of these we must employ but sparingly, and in very few places, exotic
and compound words, and those newly coined; where
they may be employed I will state hereafter: the
reason [of the restriction] has been mentioned, *viz.*,

because they remove your style [from that of common life] more than is consistent with good taste. Words, however, of ordinary use, and in their original acceptations and metaphors, are alone available in the style of prose: a proof [that this is the fact is] that these are the only words which all persons employ; for everybody carries on conversation by means of metaphors, and words in their primary sense, and those of ordinary use. Thus it is plain that if one should have constructed his style well, it will be both of a foreign character, and that [the art of the orator] may still elude observation, and [the style itself] will have the advantage of clearness; this, however, was laid down to be the perfection of rhetorical language. But of all nouns, those which are equivocal suit the purposes of the sophist, for by their help he effects his fallacies, while synonyms are of use to the poet; I mean these which are both synonyms and of common usage, as πορεύησθαι and βαδίζειν, for these two are both of common usage and synonymous to each other.

The nature then of each of these varieties, and how many species of metaphor there are, and also that this ornament is of the greatest effect, as well in poetry as prose, has been explained (as I have observed above), in the "Poetics." In prose, however, we should bestow the greater attention on them, in proportion as an oration has to be made up of fewer adjuments than a metrical composition. Moreover, the metaphor possesses in an especial manner [the beauties of] clearness and sweetness, with an air of being foreign; and it is not possible to derive it from any other person.

You must, however, apply, in the case both of epithets and metaphors, such as are appropriate; and this will depend on their being constructed on principles of analogy, otherwise they will be sure to appear in bad taste; because contraries show themselves be such, particularly when set by each other. But you must consider, as a purple garment becomes a youth, what is equally so to an old man; since the same garment does not become [both].

And if you wish to embellish your subject, see you deduce your metaphor from such things coming under the same class as are better; and if to cry it down, from such as are worse: I mean, as the cases are opposed and come under the same genus, that the saying, for example, of a beggar, that "he prays," and of one who is praying, that "he begs" (both being species of asking), is to do the thing which has been mentioned; just as Iphicrates called Callias "a mere collector to the goddess, and not a bearer of the torch." He, howev r, replied, "that he must needs be uninitiated himself, or he would not call him a collector, but a bearer of the torch." For these are both services connected with the goddess; the one, however, is respectable, while the other is held in no repute. And some one [speaks of the courtiers of Dionysius as] Dionysian parasites; they, however, call themselves artificers. And these expressions are both metaphors; the one of persons who would depreciate, the other the contrary. Even robbers, nowadays, call themselves purveyors. On which principle we may say of a man who "has acted unjustly," that he "is in error"; and of one who "is in error," that he "has acted unjustly." Again, of one who has stolen, both that has taken, [in way of diminution,] and that has ravaged [in exaggeration]. But the saying, but the Telephus of Euripides does, "that he lords it o'er the oars, and landing in Mysia," etc., is out of taste; for the expression, "lording it o'er," is above the dignity of he subject; [the rhetorical artifice] then, is not lmed off. There will also be a fault in the sylla- s, unless they are significant of a grateful sound; instance, Dionysius, surnamed Chalcous, in his elegies, calls poetry, "the clangor of Calliope," because both are vocal sounds; the metaphor, however, is a paltry one, and couched in uncouth expressions.

Again, our metaphors should not be farfetched; but we should make the transfer, on the principle of assigning names out of the number of kindred objects, and such as are the same in species, to objects which are unnamed, of which, however, it is clear, simultaneously with their being uttered, that they are akin, as in that approved enigma,—

A man I once beheld, [and wondering view'd,]
Who, on another, brass with fire had glued.
                                        —*Twining.*

for the operation is undesignated by any name, and both are species of attaching; wherefore the writer called the application of the cupping instrument, a gluing. And, generally speaking, it is possible out of neatly constructed enigmas to extract excellent metaphors: because it is on the principles of metaphor that men construct enigmas; so that it is evident that [if the enigma be a good one] the metaphor has been properly borrowed.

The transfer also should be made from objects which are beautiful; beauty, however, of words consists, as Licymnius observes, in the sound or in the idea conveyed; as does also their inelegance. And there is, moreover, a third, which does away the sophistical doctrine; since it is not the fact, as Bryso argues, "that no one speaks inelegantly, if, indeed, the using one expression instead of another carries with it the same meaning": for this is a fallacy; because some words are nearer in their ordinary acceptations, more assimilated, and have more peculiar force of setting the object before the eyes than others. And what is more, one word represents the object under different circumstances from another; so that we may even on this principle lay it down that one word has more or less of beauty and inelegance than another; for although both words, [at the same time,] express [properties which are] beautiful, as well as such as are inelegant; yet they either express them not *qua* they are beautiful, or not *qua* they are inelegant; or granting they do, yet they express them, the one in a greater, the other in a less degree. But we are to deduce our metaphors from these sources;—from such as are beautiful either in sound, in meaning, or [in the image they present] to the sight, or any other sense. And there is a difference, in the saying, for instance, "the rosy-fingered Aurora," rather than "the purple-fingered," or, what is still worse, "the crimson-fingered."

Also, in the case of epithets, it is very possible to derive one's epithets from a degrading or disgraceful view of the case; for instance, "the murderer of his mother": and we may derive them from a view on the better side; as, "the avenger of his father." And Simonides, when the victor in a race by mules offered him a trifling present, was not disposed to write, as though feeling hurt at writing on demiasses; when, however, he offered a sufficient present, he composed the poem—

Hail! Daughters of the generous Horse,
That skim, like wind, along the course, etc.
—*Harris.*

and yet they were daughters of asses as well. Again, it is possible to express the selfsame thing diminutively. And it is the employment of diminutives which renders both good and evil less; just as Aristophanes jests in "The Babylonians"; using, instead of gold, "a tiny piece of gold"; instead of "a garment," "a little garment"; instead of "reproach," "puny reproach"; and instead of "sickness," "slight indisposition." We ought, however, to be careful, and always keep to the mean in both cases. . . .

Style will possess the quality of being in good taste if it be expressive at once of feeling and character, and in proportion to the subject-matter. This proportion, however, is preserved, provided the style be neither careless on questions of dignity, nor dignified on such as are mean: neither to a mean word let ornament be superadded; otherwise it appears mere burlesque. . . .

But [the style] expressive of feeling, supposing the case be one of assault, is the style of a man in a passion; if, however, it be one of loathsomeness and impiety, the expressing yourself with disgust and painful caution; if, however, the case demand praise, with exultation; if pity, with submission; and so on in the other cases. And a style which is appropriate, moreover, invests the subject with persuasive efficacy. For the mind is cheated into a persuasion, that the orator is speaking with sincerity, because under such circumstances men stand affected in that manner. So that people suppose things to be even as the speaker states them, what though, in reality, they are not: and the hearer has a kindred feeling with the orator, who expresses himself feelingly, even should he say nothing to the purpose; availing themselves of which, may bear down their hearers in the storm of passion.

THE HIGHEST GOOD OF MAN

EVERY art and every scientific system, and in like manner every cause of action and deliberate preference, seems to aim at some good; and consequently "the Good" has been well defined as "that which all things aim at."

But there appears to be a kind of difference in ends; for some are energies; others again beyond these, certain works; but wherever there are certain ends besides the actions, there the works are naturally better than the energies.

Now since there are many actions, arts, and sciences, it follows that there are many ends; for of medicine the end is health; of ship-building, a ship; of generalship, victory; of economy, wealth. But whatever of such arts are contained under any one faculty (as, for instance, under horsemanship is contained the art of making bridles, and all other horse furniture; and this and the whole art of war is contained under generalship; and in the same manner other arts are contained under different faculties), in all these the ends of the chief arts are more eligible than the ends of the subordinate ones; because for the sake of the former, the latter are pursued. It makes, however, no difference whether the energies themselves, or something else besides these, are the ends of actions, just as it would make no difference in the sciences above mentioned.

If, therefore, there is some end of all that we do, which we wish for on its own account, and if we wish for all other things on account of this, and do not choose everything for the sake of something else (for thus we should go on to infinity, so that desire would be empty and vain), it is evident that this must be "the good," and the greatest good. Has not, then, the knowledge of this end a great influence on the conduct of life? and, like archers, shall we not have a mark? If so, we ought to endeavor to give an outline at least of its nature, and to determine to which of the sciences or faculties it belongs.

Now it would appear to be the end of that which is especially the chief and master science, and this seems to be the political science, for it directs what sciences states ought to cultivate, what individuals should learn, and how far they should pursue them. We see, too, that the most valued faculties are comprehended under it, as for example, generalship, economy, rhetoric. Since, then, this science makes use of the practical sciences, and legislates respecting what ought to be done, and what abstained from, its end must include those of the others; so that this end must be *the good* of man. For although the good of an individual and a state be the same, still that of a state appears more important and more perfect both to obtain and to preserve. To discover the good of an individual is satisfactory, but to discover that of a state or a nation is more noble and divine. This, then, is the object of my treatise, which is of a political kind. * * * *

Since all knowledge and every act of deliberate preference aims at some good, let us show what that is, which we say that the political science aims at, and what is the highest good of all things which are done. As to its name, indeed, almost all men are agreed; for both the vulgar and the educated call it *happiness:* but they suppose that to live well and do well are synonyms with being happy. But concerning the nature of happiness they are at variance, and the vulgar do not give the same definition of it as the educated; for some imagine it to be an obvious and well-known object—such as pleasure, or wealth, or honor; but different men think differently of it; and frequently even the same person entertains different opinions respecting it at different times; for, when diseased, he believes it to be health; when poor, wealth; but, conscious of their own ignorance, they admire those who say that it is something great and beyond them. Some, again, have supposed that besides these numerous goods, there is another self-existent good, which is to all these the cause of their being goods. Now, to examine all the opinions would perhaps be rather unprofitable; but it will be sufficient to examine those which lie most upon the surface, or seem to be most reasonable.

Let it not, however, escape our notice, that arguments from principles differ from arguments to principles, for well did Plato also propose doubts on this point, and inquire whether the right way is from principle or to principles; just as in the course from the starting-post to the goal, or the contrary. For we must begin from those things that are known; and things are known in two ways; or some are known to ourselves, others are generally known; perhaps, therefore, we should begin from the things known to ourselves.

Whoever, therefore, is to study with advantage the things which are honorable and just, and in a word the subjects of political science, must have been well and morally educated; for the point from whence we must begin is *the fact,* and if this is satisfactorily proved, it will be unnecessary to add *the reason.* Such a student possesses, or would easily acquire, the principles. But let him who possesses neither of these qualifications, hear the sentiments of Hesiod:

" Far does the man all other men excel,
  Who, from his wisdom, thinks in all things well,
  Wisely considering, to himself a friend,
  All for the present best, and for the end.
  Nor is the man without his share of praise,
  Who well the dictates of the wise obeys:
  But he that is not wise himself, nor can
  Hearken to wisdom, is a useless man."

EDWIN ARNOLD

Sir Edwin Arnold, poet and journalist, was born in England in 1832. He won a scholarship at Oxford, and received the Newdigate prize for poetry. In addition to his numerous poems he wrote a number of practical books on education and administration in India. "The Light of Asia" is his most famous work.

SERENADE

(The MacMillan Co., Publishers)

LUTE! breathe thy lowest in my Lady's ear,
 Sing while she sleeps, "Ah! belle dame,
  aimexvous ? "
Till, dreaming still, she dream that I am here,
 And wake to find it, as my love is, true;
Then, while she listens in her warm white nest,
 Say in slow music,—softer, tenderer yet,
That lute-strings quiver when their tone's at rest
 And my heart trembles when my lips are set.

Stars! if my sweet love still a-dreaming lies,
 Shine through the roses for a lover's sake;
And send your silver to her lidded eyes,
 Kissing them very gently till she wake;
Then, while she wonders at the lay and light,
 Tell her, though morning endeth star and song,
That ye live still, when no star glitters bright,
 And my love lasteth, though it find no tongue.

THE LIGHT OF ASIA

Yet not to love
Alone trusted the king; love's prison-house
Stately and beautiful he bade them build,
So that in all the earth no marvel was
Like Vishramvan, the prince's pleasure-place.
Midway in those wide palace-grounds there rose
A verdant hill whose base Rohini bathed,
Murmuring adown from Himalay's broad feet.
To bear its tribute into Gunga's waves.
Southward is a growth of tamarind trees, and sâl,
Thick set with pale sky-colored ganthi-flowers,
Shut out the world, save if the city's hum
Came on the wind no harsher than when bees
Hum out of sight in thickets. Northward soared
The stainless ramps of huge Himâla's wall,
Ranged in white ranks against the blue—untrod,
Infinite, wonderful—whose uplands vast,
And lifted universe of crest and crag,
Shoulder and shelf, green slope and icy horn,
Riven ravine, and splintered precipice
Led climbing thought higher and higher, until
It seemed to stand in heaven and speak with gods.

Fronting this
The builders set the bright pavilion up,
Fair-planted on the terraced hill, with towers
On either flank and pillared cloisters round.
Its beams were carved with stories of old time—
Radha and Krishna and the sylvan girls—
Sita and Hanuman and Draupadi;
And on the middle porch god Ganesha,
With disk and hook—to bring wisdom and wealth—
Propitious safe, wreathing his sidelong trunk.
By winding ways of garden and of court
The inner gate was reached, of marble wrought,

White with pink veins; the lintel lazuli,
The threshold alabaster, and the doors
Sandal-wood, cut in pictured panelling;
Whereby to lofty halls and shadowy bowers
Passed the delighted foot, on stately stairs,
Through latticed gallerys, 'neath painted roofs
And clustering columns, where cool fountains—
    fringed
With lotus and nelumbo—danced, and fish
Gleamed through their crystal, scarlet, gold, and
    blue.
Great-eyed gazelles in sunny alcoves browsed
The blown red roses; birds of rainbow wing
Fluttered among the palms; doves, green and gray,
Built their safe nests on gilded cornices;
Over the shining pavements peacocks drew
The splendors of their trains, sedately watched
By milk-white herons and the small house-owls.
The plum-necked parrots swung from fruit to fruit
The yellow sun-birds whirred from bloom to bloom,
The timid lizards on the lattice basked
Fearless, the squirrels ran to feed from hand,
For all was peace: the shy black snake, that gives
Fortune to households, sunned his sleepy coils
Under the moon-flowers, where the musk-deer played
And brown-eyed monkeys chattered to the crows.
And all this house of love was peopled fair
With sweet attendance, so that in each part
With lovely sights were gentle faces found.
Soft speech and willing service, each one glad
To gladden, pleased at pleasure, proud to obey;
Till life glided beguiled, like a smooth stream
Banked by perpetual flow'rs, Yasôdhara
Queen of the enchanting court.

                But innermost,
Beyond the richness of those hundred halls,
A secret chamber lurked where skill had spent

All lovely fantasies to lull the mind.
The entrance of it was a cloistered square—
Roofed by the sky, and in the midst a tank—
Of milky marble built, and laid with slabs
Of milk-white marble: bordered round the tank
And on the steps, and all along the frieze
With tender inlaid work of agate-stones,
Cool as to tread in summer-time on snows
It was to loiter there; the sunbeams dropped
Their gold, and, passing into porch and niche,
Softened to shadows, silvery, pale, and dim.
As if the very day paused and grew eve
In love and silence at that bower's gate;
For there beyond the gate the chamber was,
Beautiful, sweet; a wonder of the world!
Soft light from perfumed lamps through windows fell
Of nakre and stained stars of lucent film
On golden cloths outspread, and silken beds,
And heavy splendor of the purdah's fringe,
Lifted to take only the loveliest in.
Here, whether it was night or day none knew
For always streamed that softening light, more
          bright
Than sunrise, but as tender as the eve's:
And always breathed sweet airs, more joy-giving
Than morning's, but as cool as midnight's breath;
And night and day lutes sighed, and night and day
Delicious foods were spread, and dewy fruits,
Sherbets new chilled with snows of Himalay,
And sweetmeats made of subtle daintiness,
With sweet tree-milk in its own ivory cup,
And night and day served there a chosen band
Of nautch-girls, cup-bearers, and cymballers,
Delicate, dark-browed ministers of love,
Who fanned the sleeping eyes of the happy prince,
And when he waked, led back his thoughts to bliss
With music whispering through the blooms, and
          charm

Of amorous songs and dreamy dances, linked
By chime of ankle bells and wave of arms
And silver vina-strings: while essences
Of musk and champak and the blue haze spread
From burning spices soothed his soul again
To drowse by sweet Yasôdhara; and thus
Siddârtha lived forgetting.

                    Furthermore,
The king commanded that within those walls
No mention should be made of death or age,
Sorrow, or pain, or sickness. If one dropped
In the lovely court—her dark glance dim, her feet
Faint in the dance—the guiltless criminal
Passed forth an exile from that Paradise,
Lest he should see and suffer at her woe.
Bright-eyed intendants watched to execute
Sentence on such as spake of the harsh world
Without, where aches and plagues were, tears and fears
And wail of mourners, and grim fume of pyres.
'Twas treason if a thread of silver strayed
In tress of singing-girl or nautch-dancer;
At every dawn the dying rose was plucked,
The dead leaves hid, all evil sights removed:
For said the king, " If he shall pass his youth
Far from such things as move to wistfulness,
And brooding on the empty eggs of thought,
The shadow of this fate, too vast for man,
May fade, belike, and I shall see him grow
To that great stature of fair sovereignty
When he shall rule all lands—if he will rule—
The king of kings and glory of his time."

   *   *   *   *   *   *   *

Softly the Indian night sinks on the plains
At full moon in the month of Chaitra Shud,
When mangoes redden and the asôka buds
Sweeten the breeze, and Rama's birthday comes.

And all the fields are glad and all the towns.
Softly that night fell over Vishramvan,
Fragrant with blooms and jeweled thick with stars,
And cool with mountain airs sighing adown
From snow-flats on Himâla high outspread;
For the moon swung above the eastern peaks,
Climbing the spangled vault, and lighting clear
Rohini's ripples and the hills and plains
And all the sleeping land, and near at hand
Silvering those roof-tops of the pleasure-house,
Where nothing stirred nor sign of watching was,
Save at the outer gates, whose warders cried
Mudra, the watchword, and the countersign
Angana, and the watch-drums beat a round;
Whereat the earth lay still, except for call
Of prowling jackals, and the ceaseless trill
Of crickets on the garden grounds.

                                        Within—
Where the moon glittered through the lace-worked
      stone
Lighting the walls of pearl-shell and the floors
Paved with veined marble—softly fell her beams
On such rare company of Indian girls,
It seemed some chamber sweet in Paradise
Where Devîs rested. All the chosen ones
Of Prince Siddârtha's pleasure home were there,
The brightest and most faithful of the court,
Each form so lovely in the peace of sleep,
That you had said, "This is the pearl of all!"
Save that beside her or beyond her lay
Fairer and fairer till the pleasured gaze
Roamed o'er that feast of beauty as it roams
From gem to gem in some great goldsmith-work,
Caught by each color till the next is seen.
With careless grace they lay, their soft brown limbs
Part hidden, part revealed; their glossy hair
Bound back with gold or flowers or flowing loose

In black waves down the shapely nape and neck,
Lulled into pleasant dreams by happy toils,
They slept, no wearier than jeweled birds
Which sing and love all day, then under wing
Fold head till morn bids sing and love again.
Lamps of chased silver swinging from the roof
In silver chains, and fed with perfumed oils,
Made with the moonbeams tender lights and shades,
Whereby were seen the perfect lines of grace.
The bosom's placid heave, the soft stained palms
Drooping or clasped, the faces fair and dark,
The great arched brows, the parted lips, the teeth
Like pearls a merchant picks to make a string.
The satin-lidded eyes with lashes dropped
Sweeping the delicate cheeks, the rounded wrists,
The smooth small feet with bells and bangles decked,
Tinkling low music where some sleeper moved,
Breaking her smiling dream of some new dance
Praised by the prince, some magic ring to find,
Some fairy love-gift. Here one lay full-length,
Her vina by her cheek, and in its strings
The little fingers still all interlaced
As when the last notes of her light song played
Those radiant eyes to sleep and sealed her own.
Another slumbered folding in her arms
A desert antelope, its slender head
Buried with back-sloped horns between her breasts
Soft nestling; it was eating—when both drowsed—
Red roses, and her loosening hand still held
A rose half-mumbled, while a rose-leaf curled
Between the deer's lips. Here two friends had dozed
Together, weaving môgra-buds, which bound
Their sister-sweetness in a starry chain,
Linking them limb to limb and heart to heart,
One pillowed on the blossoms, one on her.
Another, ere she slept, was stringing stones
To make a necklet—agate, onyx, sard,
Coral and moonstone—round her wrist it gleamed

A coil of splendid color, while she held,
Unthreaded yet, the bead to close it up
Green turkis, carved with golden gods and scripts.
Lulled by the cadence of the garden stream,
Thus lay they on the clustered carpets, each
A girlish rose with shut leaves, waiting dawn
To open and make daylight beautiful.
This was the antechamber of the prince;
But at the purdah's fringe the sweetest slept—
Gunga and Gotami—chief ministers
In that still house of love.

                The purdah hung,
Crimson and blue, with broidered threads of gold,
Across a portal carved in sandal wood.
Whence by three steps the way was to the bower
Of inmost splendor, and the marriage-couch
Set on dais soft with silver cloths,
Where the foot fell as though it trod on piles
Of neem-blooms. All the walls were plates of pearl,
Cut shapely from the shells of Lanka's wave;
And o'er the alabaster roof there ran
Rich inlayings of lotus and of bird,
Wrought in skilled work of lazulite and jade,
Jacynth and jasper; woven round the dome,
And down the sides, and all about the frames
Wherein were set the fretted lattices,
Through which there breathed, with moonlight and
     cool airs,
Scents from the shell flowers and the jasmine sprays
Not bringing thither grace or tenderness
Sweeter than shed from those fair presences
Within the place—the beauteous Sâkya prince,
And hers, the stately, bright Yasôdhara.
Half risen from her soft nest at his side,
The chuddah fallen to her waist, her brow
Laid in both palms, the lovely princess leaned
With heaving bosom and fast falling tears.

Thrice with her lips she touched Siddârtha's hand,
And at the third kiss moaned, "Awake, my Lord!
Give me the comfort of thy speech!" Then he—
"What is it with thee, O my life?" but still
She moaned anew before the words would come;
Then spake, "Alas, my prince! I sank to sleep
Most happy, for the babe I bear of thee
Quickened this eye, and at my heart there beat
That double pulse of life and joy and love;
Whose happy music lulled me, but—ah!—
In slumber I beheld three sights of dread,
With thought whereof my heart is throbbing yet.
I saw a white bull with wide branching horns,
A lord of pastures, pacing through the streets,
Bearing upon his front a gem which shone
As if some star had dropped to glitter there,
Or like the kantha-stone the great snake keeps
To make bright daylight underneath the earth.
Slow through the streets toward the gates he paced,
And none could stay him, though there came a voice
From Indra's temple, 'If ye stay him not,
The glory of the city goeth forth.'
Yet none could stay him. Then I wept aloud,
And locked my arms about his neck, and strove
And bade them bar the gates; but that ox-king
Bellowed, and lightly tossing free his crest,
Broke from my clasp, and bursting through the bars,
Trampled the warders down and passed away.
The next strange dream was this: Four presences
Splendid, with shining eyes, so beautiful
They seemed the regents of the earth who dwell
On mount Sumeru, lighting from the sky
With retinue of countless heavenly ones,
Swift swept unto our city, where I saw
The golden flag of Indra on the gate
Flutter and fall; and lo! there rose instead
A glorious banner, all the folds whereof
Rippled with flashing fire of rubies sewn

Thick on the silver threads, the rays wherefrom
Set forth new words and weighty sentences
Whose message made all living creatures glad;
And from the east the wind of sunrise blew
With tender waft, opening those jeweled scrolls
So that all flesh might read; and wondrous blooms—
Plucked in what clime I know not—fell in showers,
Colored as none are colored in our groves."

Then spake the prince: "All this, my lotus flower,
Was good to see." "Ah lord," the princess said,
"Save that it ended with a voice of fear
Crying, 'The time is nigh! the time is nigh!'
Thereat the third dream came; for then I sought
Thy side, sweet Lord! ah, on our bed there lay
An unpressed pillow and an empty robe—
Nothing of thee but those!—nothing of thee,
Who art my life and light, my king, my world!
And sleeping still I rose, and sleeping saw
Thy belt of pearls, tied here below my breasts,
Change to a stinging snake; my ankle-rings
Fall off, my golden bangles part and fall;
The jasmines in my hair wither to dust;
While this our bridal-couch sank to the ground,
And something rent the crimson purdah down;
Then far away I heard the white bull low,
And far away the embroidered banner flap,
And once again that cry 'The time is come!'
But with that cry—which shakes my spirit still—
I woke! O prince! what may such visions mean
Except I die, or—worse than any death—
Thou shouldst forsake me or be taken?"

                                        Sweet
As the last smile of sunset was the look
Siddârtha bent upon his weeping wife.
"Comfort thee, dear!" he said, "if comfort lives
In changeless love; for though thy dreams may be
Shadow of things to come, and though the gods

Are shaken in their seats, and though the world
Stands nigh, perchance, to know some way of help,
Yet, whatsoever fall to thee and me,
Be sure I loved and love Yasôdhara."

HE AND SHE

S HE is dead !" they said to him: " come away ;
    Kiss her and leave her,—thy love is clay !"

They smoothed her tresses of dark-brown hair;
On her forehead of marble they laid it fair ;

Over her eyes that gazed too much
They drew the lids with a gentle touch ;

With a tender touch they closed up well
The sweet thin lips that had secrets to tell ;

About her brows and beautiful face
They tied her veil and her marriage lace,

And drew on her white feet her white-silk shoes,—
Which were the whitest no eye could choose,—

And over her bosom they crossed her hands,
" Come away !" they said, " God understands."

And there was silence, and nothing there
But silence, and scents of eglantere,

And jasmine, and roses and rosemary ;
And they said, " As a lady should lie, lies she."

And they held their breath till they left the room,
With a shudder, to glance at its stillness and gloom.

But he who loved her too well to dread
The sweet, the stately, the beautiful dead,

He lit his lamp, and took the key
And turned it—alone again, he and she.

He and she; but she would not speak,
Though he kissed, in the old place, the quiet cheek.

He and she; yet she would not smile,
Though he called her the name she loved erewhile.

He and she; still she did not move
To any passionate whisper of love.

Then he said, " Cold lips and breasts without breath,
Is there no voice, no language of death,

" Dumb to the ear and still to the sense,
But to heart and to soul distinct, intense?

" See, now; I will listen with soul, not ear :
What was the secret of dying, dear ?

" Was it the infinite wonder of all
That you ever could let life's flower fall?

" Or was it a greater marvel to feel
The perfect calm o'er the agony steal ?

" Was the miracle greater to find how deep
Beyond all dreams sank downward that sleep ?

" Did life roll back its record dear,
And show, as they say it does, past things clear?

" And was it the innermost heart of the bliss
To find out so, what a wisdom love is ?

" O perfect dead ! O dead most dear !
I hold the breath of my soul to hear.

" I listen as deep as to horrible hell,
As high as to heaven, and you do not tell:

" There must be pleasure in dying, sweet,
To make you so placid from head to feet !

" I would tell you, darling, if I were dead,
And 't were your hot tears upon my brow shed,—

" I would say, though the Angel of Death had laid
His sword on my lips to keep it unsaid,—

" You should not ask vainly, with streaming eyes,
Which of all deaths was the chiefest surprise.

" The very strangest and suddenest thing
Of all the surprises that dying must bring."

Ah, foolish world ! O most kind dead !
Though he told me, who will believe it was said?

Who will believe that he heard her say,
With the sweet, soft voice, in the dear old way,

" The utmost wonder is this,—I hear
And see you, and love you, and kiss you, dear;

" I am your angel, who was your bride,
And know that though dead, I have never died."

A HOME SONG

(Swanscombe, April 1857)

THE swallow is come from his African home
        To build on the English eaves;
The sycamore wears all his glistening spears,
        And the almond rains roseate leaves;
And, dear Love ! with thee, as with bird and with
        tree
        'Tis the time of blossom and nest,
Then, what good thing of the bountiful Spring
        Shall I liken to thee—the best ?

Over the streamlet the rose-bushes bend
  Clouded with tender green,
And green the buds grow upon every bough,
  Though as yet no rose-tint is seen;
Like those, thou art come to thy promise of bloom,
  Like theirs, thine shunneth the light;
Break, rose-bud !—and let a longing heart know
  If the blossom be red or white!

Up the broad river with swelling sails
  A glorious vessel goes,
And not more clear in the soft blue air
  Than in the still water she shows!
Dost thou not go with as brave a show,
  And, sooth, with as swelling a state?
Oh, come into harbor with that thou bear'st,
  Dear ship !—for I eagerly wait.

Fair ship !—ah, Kate! none beareth a freight
  As precious and rich as thine,
And where's the rose-bush that will burgeon and
      blush
  With a blossom like thine and mine ?
Well! Well! we do as the meadow-birds too,
  Since meadows with gold were dyed,
The hen sits at rest in the hidden nest.
  And her mate sings glad at her side.

THE RAJAH'S RIDE

(A Punjab Song)

NOW is the devil-horse come to Sindh !
    Wah! wah! Gooroo!—that is true!
Now is the devil-horse come to Sindh !
  Wah! wah! Gooroo!—that is true!
His belly is stuffed with the fire and the wind,
  But a fleeter steed had Runjeet Dehu !

THE RAJAH'S RIDE

It's forty koss from Lahore to the ford
   Forty and more to far Jummoo;
Fast may go the Feringhee lord,
   But never so fast as Runjeet Dehu !

Runjeet Dehu was King of the Hill,
   Lord and eagle of every crest;
Now the swords and the spears are still,
   God will have it—and God knows best !

Rajah Runjeet sate in the sky,
   Watching the loaded Kafilas in;
Affghan, Kashmeree, passing by,
   Paid him pushm to save their skin.

Once he caracoled into the plain,
   Wah ! the sparkle of steel on steel !
And up the pass came singing again
   With a lakh of silver borne at his heel.

Once he trusted the Mussulman's word,
   Wah ! wah ! trust a liar to lie !
Down from his eyrie they tempted my Bird,
   And clipped his wings that he could not fly.

Ten months Runjeet lay in Lahore—
   Fast by the gate at the Runchenee Pul;
Sad was the soul of Chunda Kour,
   Glad the merchants of rich Kurnool.

Ten months Runjeet lay in Lahore—
   Wah ! a hero's heart is brass !
Ten months never did Chunda Kour
   Braid her hair at the tiring-glass.

There came a steed from Toorkistan,
   Wah ! God made him to match the hawk !
Fast beside him the four grooms ran,
   To keep abreast of the Toorkman's walk.

Black as the bear on Iskardoo;
    Savage at heart as a tiger chained;
Fleeter than hawk that ever flew,
    Never a Muslim could ride him reined.

" Runjeet Dehu! come forth from thy hold "—
    Wah! ten months had rusted his chain!
" Ride this Sheitan's liver cold "—
    Runjeet twisted his hand in the mane;

Runjeet sprang to the Toorkman's back,
    Wah! a king on a kingly throne!
Snort, black Sheitan! till nostrils crack,
    Rajah Runjeet sits, a stone.

Three times round the maidan he rode,
    Touched its neck at the Kashmere wall,
Struck the spurs till they spurted blood,
    Leapt the rampart before them all!

Breasted the waves of the blue Ravee,
    Forty horsemen mounting behind,
Forty bridle-chains flung free,
    Wah! wah! better chase the wind!

Chunda Kour sate sad in Jummoo:—
    Hark! what horse-hoof echoes without?
" Rise! and welcome Runjeet Dehu—
    Wash the Toorkman's nostrils out!

" Forty koss he has come, my life!
    Forty koss back he must carry me;
Rajah Runjeet visits his wife,
    He steals no steed like an Afreedee.

" They bade me teach them how to ride—
    Wah! wah! now I have taught them well ! "
Chunda Kour sank low at his side;
    Rajah Runjeet rode the hill.

When he came back to far Lahore—
　Long or ever the night began
Spake he, " Take your horse once more,
　He carries well—when he bears a man !"

Then they gave him a khillut and gold,
　All for his honor and grace and truth;
Send him back to his mountain-hold—
　Muslim manners have touch of ruth;

Send him back, with dances and drum
　Wah! my Rajah Runjeet Dehu!
To Chunda Kour and his Jummoo home—
　Wah! wah! Futtee!—wah, Gooroo!

MATTHEW ARNOLD

MATTHEW ARNOLD, English essayist and poet, son of Dr. Thomas Arnold, of Rugby, born in 1822; died at Liverpool, 1888. He graduated from Oxford with honors, receiving a prize for his poem "Cromwell." In 1857 he was elected Professor of Poetry at Oxford. His prose works cover many subjects, those dealing with theology being the best known.

THE FORSAKEN MERMAN

(The MacMillan Co., Publishers)

COME, dear children, let us away;
   Down and away below!
Now my brothers call from the bay,
Now the great winds shorewards blow,
Now the salt tides seawards flow;
Now the wild white horses play,
Champ and chafe and toss in the spray.
Children dear, let us away!
This way, this way!

Call her once before you go—
Call once yet,
In a voice that she will know:
'Margaret! Margaret!'
Children's voices should be dear
(Call once more) to a mother's ear;
Children's voices, wild with pain—
Surely she will come again!
Call her once, and come away;
This way, this way!
'Mother dear, we cannot stay!'

The wild white horses foam and fret.
Margaret! Margaret!

Come, dear children, come away down!
Call no more.
One last look at the white-walled town,
And the little gray church on the windy shore;
Then come down!
She will not come! though you call all day;
Come away, come away!

Children dear, was it yesterday
We heard the sweet bells over the bay?
In the caverns where we lay,
Through the surf and through the swell,
The far-off sound of a silver bell?
Sand-strewn caverns, cool and deep,
Where the winds are all asleep;
Where the spent lights quiver and gleam,
Where the salt weed sways in the stream,
Where the sea-beasts, ranged all round,
Feed in the ooze of their pasture-ground;
Where the sea-snakes coil and twine,
Dry their mail, and bask in the brine;
Where great whales come sailing by,
Sail and sail, with unshut eye,
Round the world for ever and aye?
When did music come this way?
Children dear, was it yesterday?

Children dear, was it yesterday
(Call yet once) that she went away?
Once she sate with you and me,
On a red gold throne in the heart of the sea,
And the youngest sate on her knee.
She combed its bright hair, and she tended it well,
When down swung the sound of the far-off bell.
She sighed, she looked up through the clear green
    sea;

She said: "I must go, for my kinsfolk pray
In the little gray church on the shore to-day.
'Twill be Easter-time in the world—ah me!
And I lose my poor soul, Merman! here with thee."
I said: "Go up, dear heart, through the waves;
Say thy prayer, and come back to the kind sea-
    caves!"
She smiled, she went up through the surf in the
    bay.
Children dear, was it yesterday?

  Children dear, were we long alone?
"The sea grows stormy, the little ones moan!
Long prayers," I said, "in the world they say;
Come!" I said; and we rose through the surf in the
    bay.
We went up the beach, by the sandy down
Where the sea-stocks bloom, to the white-walled
    town;
Through the narrow paved streets, where all was
    still,
To the little gray church on the windy hill.
From the church came a murmur of folk at their
    prayers,
But we stood without in the cold blowing airs.
We climbed on the graves, on the stones worn with
    rains,
And we gazed up the aisle through the small leaded
    panes.
She sate by the pillar; we saw her clear:
'Margaret, hist! come quick, we are here!
Dear heart," I said, "we are long alone.
The sea grows stormy, the little ones moan."
But, ah, she gave me never a look,
For her eyes were sealed to the holy book!
Loud prays the priest! shut stands the door.
Come away, children, call no more!
Come away, come down, call no more!

Down, down, down!
Down to the depths of the sea!
She sits at her wheel in the humming town,
Singing most joyfully.
Hark what she sings: "O joy, O joy,
For the humming street, and the child with its toy!
For the priest, and the bell, and the holy well;
For the wheel where I spun,
And the blessèd light of the sun!"
And so she sings her fill,
Singing most joyfully,
Till the spindle drops from her hand,
And the whizzing wheel stands still.
She steals to the window and looks at the sand,
And over the sand at the sea;
And her eyes are set in a stare;
And anon there breaks a sigh,
And anon there drops a tear,
From a sorrow-clouded eye,
And a heart sorrow-laden,
A long, long sigh;
For the cold strange eyes of a little Mermaiden
And the gleam of her golden hair.

Come away, away, children;
Come children, come down!
The hoarse wind blows coldly;
Lights shine in the town.
She will start from her slumber
When gusts shake the door;
She will hear the winds howling,
Will hear the waves roar.
We shall see, while above us
The waves roar and whirl,
A ceiling of amber,
A pavement of pearl.
Singing " Here came a mortal,
But faithless was she;

And alone dwell for ever
The kings of the sea."
But, children, at midnight,
When soft the winds blow;
When clear falls the moonlight,
When spring-tides are low;
When sweet airs come seaward
From heaths starred with broom,
And high rocks throw mildly
On the blanched sands a gloom;
Up the still, glistening beaches,
Up the creeks we will hie;
Over banks of bright seaweed
The ebb-tide leaves dry.
We will gaze, from the sand-hills,
At the white, sleeping town;
At the church on the hill-side—
And then come back down.
Singing, "There dwells a loved one,
But cruel is she!
She left lonely for ever
The kings of the sea."

MEMORIAL VERSES

(1850)

GOETHE in Weimar sleeps, and Greece,
  Long since, saw Byron's struggle cease,
But one such death remained to come;
The last poetic voice is dumb—
We stand to-day by Wordsworth's tomb.

When Byron's eyes were shut in death,
We bowed our head and held our breath.
He taught us little; but our soul
Had felt him like the thunder's roll.
With shivering heart the strife we saw
Of passion with eternal law;

And yet with reverential awe
We watched the fount of fiery life
Which served for that Titanic strife.

When Goethe's death was told, we said,—
Sunk, then, is Europe's sagest head.
Physician of the iron age,
Goethe had done his pilgrimage,
He took the suffering human race,
   He read each wound, each weakness clear;
And struck his finger on the place,
   And said: Thou ailest here, and here!
He looked on Europe's dying hour
Of fitful dream and feverish power;
His eye plunged down the weltering strife,
The turmoil of expiring life—
He said, The end is everywhere,
Art still has truth, take refuge there!
And he was happy, if to know
Causes of things, and far below
His feet to see the lurid flow
Of terror, and insane distress,
And headlong fate, be happinesss.

And Wordsworth!—Ah, pale ghosts, rejoice!
For never has such soothing voice
Been to your shadowy world conveyed,
Since erst, at morn, some wandering shade
Heard the clear song of Orpheus come
Through Hades, and the mournful gloom.
Wordsworth has gone from us—and ye,
Ah, may ye feel his voice as we!
He too upon a wintry clime
Had fallen—on this iron time
   Of doubts, disputes, distractions, fears.
He found us when the age had bound
Our souls in its benumbing round;
   He spoke, and loosed our heart in tears.

He laid us as we lay at birth,
On the cool, flowery lap of earth.
Smiles broke from us and we had ease;
The hills were round us, and the breeze
Went o'er the sunlit fields again;
Our foreheads felt the wind and rain,
Our youth returned; for there was shed
On spirits that had long been dead,
Spirits dried up and closely furled,
The freshness of the early world.

Ah! since dark days still bring to light
Man's prudence and man's fiery might,
Time may restore us in his course
Goethe's sage mind and Byron's force;
But where will Europe's latter hour
Again find Wordsworth's healing power?
Others will teach us how to dare,
    And against fear our breast to steel;
Others will strengthen us to bear—
    But who, ah! who, will make us feel?
The cloud of mortal destiny,
Others will front it fearlessly—
But who, like him, will put it by?
Keep fresh the grass upon his grave,
O Rotha, with thy living wave!
Sing him thy best! for few or none
Hears thy voice right, now he is gone.

A FINAL WORD ON AMERICA
(From an essay in the Nineteenth Century)

SIR HENRY MAINE, in an admirable essay
which, though not signed, betrays him for its
author by its rare and characteristic qualities of
mind and style—Sir Henry Maine in the *Quarterly
Review* adopts and often reiterates a phrase of M.
Scherer, to the effect that "democracy is only a form

of government." He holds up to ridicule a sentence of Mr. Bancroft's "History," in which the American democracy is told that its ascent to power "proceeded as uniformly and majestically as the laws of being, and was as certain as the degrees of eternity." Let us be willing to give Sir Henry Maine his way and to allow no magnificent claim of this kind on behalf of the American democracy. Let us treat as not more solid the assertion in the Declaration of Independence, that "all men are created equal, are endowed by their Creator with certain inalienable rights, among them life, liberty, and the pursuit of happiness." Let us concede that these natural rights are a figment; that chance and circumstance, as much as deliberate foresight and design, have brought the United States into their present condition, that moreover the British rule which they threw off was not the rule of oppressors and tyrants which declaimers suppose; and that the merit of the Americans was not that of oppressed men rising against tyrants, but rather of sensible young people getting rid of stupid and overweening guardians who misunderstood and mismanaged them.

All this let us concede, if we will; but in conceding it let us not lose sight of the really important point, which is this: that their institutions do in fact suit the people of the United States so well, and that from this suitableness they do derive so much actual benefit. As one watches the play of their institutions, the image suggests itself to one's mind of a man in a suit of clothes which fits him to perfection, leaving all his movements unimpeded and easy. It is loose where it ought to be loose, and it sits close where its sitting close is an advantage. The central government of the United States keeps in its own hands those functions which, if the nation is to have real unity, ought to be kept there; those functions it takes to itself and no others.

The State governments and the municipal governments provide people with the fullest liberty of managing their own affairs, and afford, besides, a constant and invaluable school of practical experience. This wonderful suit of clothes, again (to recur to our image), is found also to adapt itself naturally to the wearer's growth, and to admit of all enlargements as they successively arise. I speak of the state of things since the suppression of slavery, of the state of things which meets a spectator's eye at the present time in America. There are points in which the institutions of the United States may call forth criticism. One observer may think that it would be well if the President's term of office were longer, if his ministers sat in Congress or must possess the confidence of Congress. Another observer may say that the marriage laws for the whole nation ought to be fixed by Congress, and not to vary at the will of the legislatures of the several States. I myself was much struck with the inconvenience of not allowing a man to sit in Congress except for his own district; a man like Wendell Phillips was thus excluded, because Boston would not return him. It is as if Mr. Bright could have no other constituency open to him if Rochdale would not send him to Parliament. But all these are really questions of machinery (to use my own term), and ought not so to engage our attention as to prevent our seeing that the capital fact as to the institutions of the United States is this: their suitableness to the American people and their natural and easy working. If we are not to be allowed to say, with Mr. Beecher, that this people has " a genius for the organization of States," then at all events we must admit that in its own organization it has enjoyed the most signal good fortune.

THE REAL BURNS

BY his English poetry Burns in general belongs to the eighteenth century, and has little importance for us.

" Mark ruffian violence, distain'd with crimes,
  Rousing elate in these degenerate times;
  View unsuspecting Innocence a prey,
  As guileful Fraud points out the erring way;
  While subtle Litigation's pliant tongue
  The lifeblood equal sucks of Right and Wrong !"

Evidently this is not the real Burns, or his name and fame would have disappeared long ago. Nor is Clarinda's love poet, Sylvander, the real Burns either. But he tells us himself: " These English songs gravel me to death. I have not the command of the language that I have of my native tongue. In fact, I think that my ideas are more barren in English than in Scotch. I have been at ' Duncan Gray ' to dress it in English, but all I can do is desperately stupid." We English turn naturally, in Burns, to the poems in our own language, because we can read them easily; but in those poems we have not the real Burns.

The real Burns is of course in his Scotch poems. Let us boldly say that of much of this poetry, a poetry dealing perpetually with Scotch drink, Scotch religion, and Scotch manners, a Scotchman's estimate is apt to be personal. A Scotchman is used to this world of Scotch drink, Scotch religion, and Scotch manners; he has a tenderness for it; he meets his poet half way. In this tender mood he reads pieces like the " Holy Fair " or " Hallowe'en." But this world of Scotch drink, Scotch religion, and Scotch manners is against a poet, not for him, when it is not a partial countryman who reads him; for in itself it is not a beautiful world, and no one can deny that it is of advantage to a poet to deal with a beautiful world. Burns's world of Scotch drink, Scotch religion, and Scotch manners is often a harsh, a sordid, a repulsive world; even the world of his "Cotter's Saturday Night" is not a beautiful world. No doubt a poet's criticism of life may have such truth and power that it triumphs over its world and delights us. Burns may triumph over his world; often he does triumph over his world, but let us observe how and where. Burns is the first case we have had where the bias of the personal estimate tends to mislead; let us look at him closely, he can bear it.

Many of his admirers will tell us that we have Burns, convivial, genuine, delightful, here:

> "Leeze me on drink! it gies us mair
>   Than either school or college;
> It kindles wit, it waukens lair,
>   It pangs us fou o' knowledge.
> Be't whisky gill or penny wheep
>   Or any stronger potion,
> It never fails, on drinking deep,
>   To kittle up our notion
>   By night or day."

There is a great deal of that sort of thing in Burns, and it is unsatisfactory, not because it is bacchanalian poetry, but because it has not that accent of sincerity which bacchanalian poetry, to do it justice, very often has. There is something in it of bravado, something which makes us feel that we have not the man speaking to us with his real voice; something, therefore, poetically unsound.

With still more confidence will his admirers tell us that we have the genuine Burns, the great poet, when his strain asserts the independence, equality, dignity, of men, as in the famous song, "For a' that and a' that":

> " A prince can mak' a belted knight,
>   A marquis, duke, and a' that;
> But an honest man's aboon his might
>   Guid faith he mauna fa' that !
>   For a' that and a' that
>   Their dignities and a' that,
> The pith o' sense and pride o' worth
>   Are higher ranks than a' that."

Here they find his grand, genuine touches; and still more, when this puissant genius, who so often set morality at defiance, falls moralizing:

> " The sacred lowe o' weel-placed love
>   Luxuriantly indulge it;
> But never tempt th' illicit rove,
>   Tho' naething should divulge it.
> I waive the quantum o' the sin,
>   The hazard o' concealing,
> But och ! it hardens a' within,
>   And petrifies the feeling."

Or in a higher strain:

> " Who made the heart, 'tis He alone
>   Decidedly can try us;
> He knows each chord, its various tone;
>   Each spring, its various bias.
> Then at the balance let's be mute,
>   We never can adjust it;
> What's done we partly may compute,
>   But know not what's resisted."

Or in a better strain yet, a strain, his admirers will say, unsurpassable:

> " To make a happy fireside clime
>   To weans and wife,
> That's the true pathos and sublime
>   Of human life."

There is criticism of life for you, the admirers of Burns will say to us; there is the application of ideas to life! There is, undoubtedly. The doctrine of the last-quoted lines coincides almost exactly with what was the aim and end, Xenophon tells us, of all the teaching of Socrates. And the application is a powerful one; made by a man of vigorous understanding, and (need I say?) a master of language.

But for supreme poetical success more is required than the powerful application of ideas to life; it must be an application under the conditions fixed by the laws of poetic truth and poetic beauty. Those laws fix as an essential condition, in the poet's treatment of such matters as are here in question, high seriousness—the high seriousness which comes from absolute sincerity. The accent of high seriousness, born of absolute sincerity, is what gives to such verse as

" In la sua volontade e nostra pace. . . ."

to such criticism of life as Dante's its power. Is this accent felt in the passages which I have been quoting from Burns? Surely not; surely; if our sense is quick, we must perceive that we have not in those passages a voice from the very inmost soul of the genuine Burns; he is not speaking to us from these depths, he is more or less preaching. And the compensation for admiring such passages less, from missing the perfect poetic accent in them, will be that we shall admire more the poetry where that accent is found.

No; Burns, like Chaucer, comes short of the high seriousness of the great classics, and the virtue of matter and manner which goes with that high seriousness is wanting to his work. At moments he touches it in a profound and passionate melancholy, as in those four immortal lines taken by Byron as a motto for " The Giaour," but which have in them

a depth of poetic quality such as resides in no verse
of Byron's own:

> "Had we never loved sae kindly,
> Had we never loved sae blindly,
> Never met, or never parted,
> We had ne'er been broken-hearted."

But a whole poem of that quality Burns cannot
make; the rest, in the "Farewell to Nancy," is ver-
biage.

We arrive best at the real estimate of Burns, I
think, by conceiving his work as having truth of matter and truth of manner, but not the accent of the
poetic virtue of the highest masters. His genuine
criticism of life, when the sheer poet in him speaks,
is ironic; it is not:

> "Thou Power Supreme whose mighty scheme
> These woes of mine fulfil,
> Here firm I rest, they must be best
> Because they are Thy will!"

It is far rather, "Whistle owre the lave o't!" Yet
we may say of him as of Chaucer, that of life and
the world, as they come before him, his view is
large, free, shrewd, benignant—truly poetic, therefore; and his manner of rendering what he sees is
to match. But we must note, at the same time, his
great difference from Chaucer. The freedom of
Chaucer is heightened, in Burns, by a fiery, reckless
energy; the benignity of Chaucer deepens, in Burns,
into an overwhelming sense of the pathos of things—
of the pathos of human nature, the pathos, also, of
non-human nature. Instead of the fluidity of Chaucer's manner, the manner of Burns has spring, bound-
ing swiftness. Burns is by far the greater force,
though he has perhaps less charm. The world of
Chaucer is fairer, richer, more significant than that
of Burns; but when the largeness and freedom of

Burns get full sweep, as in "Tam o' Shanter," or still more in that puissant and splendid production, "The Jolly Beggars," his world may be what it will, his poetic genius triumphs over it. In the world of "The Jolly Beggars" there is more than hideousness and squalor, there is bestiality; yet the piece is a superb poetic success. It has a breadth, truth, and power which make the famous scene in Auerbach's cellar, of Goethe's "Faust," seem artificial and tame beside it, and which are only matched by Shakespeare and Aristophanes.

Here, where his largeness and freedom serve him so admirably, and also in those poems and songs, where to shrewdness he adds infinite archness and wit, and to benignity infinite pathos, where his manner is flawless, and a perfect poetic whole is the result—in things like the addresss to the mouse whose home he had ruined; in things like "Duncan Gray," "Tam Glen," "Whistle, and I'll Come to You, My Lad," "Auld Lang Syne" (the list might be made much longer)—here we have the genuine Burns, of whom the real estimate must be high indeed. Not a classic, nor with the excellent *spondaiotas* of the great classics, nor with a verse rising to a criticism of life and a virtue like theirs; but a poet with thorough truth of substance and an answering truth of style, giving us a poetry sound to the core. We all of us have a leaning toward the pathetic, and may be inclined perhaps to prize Burns most for his touches of piercing, sometimes almost intolerable, pathos; for verse like:

> "We twa hae paidl't i' the burn
>   From mornin' sun till dine;
> But seas between us braid hae roar'd
>   Sin auld lang syne. . . ."

—where he is as lovely as he is sound. But perhaps it is by the perfection of soundness of his lighter

and archer masterpieces that he is poetically most
wholesome for us. For the votary misled by a personal estimate of Shelley, as so many of us have
been, are, and will be,—of that beautiful spirit building his many-colored haze of words and images

> "Pinnacled dim in the intense inane"—

no contact can be wholesomer than the contact with
Burns at his archest and soundest. Side by side
with the

> "On the brink of the night and the morning
> My courses are wont to respire,
> But the earth has just whispered a warning
> That their flight must be swifter than fire."

of "Prometheus Unbound," how salutary, how very
salutary, to place this from "Tam Glen":

> "My minnie does constantly deave me
> And bids me beware o' young men;
> They flatter, she says, to deceive me;
> But wha can think sae o' Tam Glen?"

But we enter on burning ground as we approach
the poetry of times so near to us, poetry like that
of Byron, Shelley, and Wordsworth, of which the
estimates are so often not only personal, but personal with passion. For my purpose, it is enough
to have taken the single case of Burns, the first
poet we come to of whose work the estimate formed
is evidently apt to be personal, and to have suggested how we may proceed, using the poetry of the
great classics, as a sort of touchstone, to correct this
estimate, as we had previously corrected by the same
means the historic estimate where we met with it.

MARCUS AURELIUS

Marcus Aurelius Antoninus was a Roman emperor of the second century after Christ. He was one of the most noted men of antiquity, and his character was exemplified in his reign, which was in marked contrast to that of other rulers of the empire. His "Meditations," from which the subjoined passages were selected, is perhaps the most striking expression of the best pagan thought.

THE BEAUTY OF THE WORLD

To him who hath a true insight into the real nature of the Universe, every change in everything therein that is a part thereof seems appropriate and delightful. The bread that is over-baked so that it cracks and bursts asunder hath not the form desired by the baker; yet none the less it hath a beauty of its own, and is most tempting to the palate. Figs bursting in their ripeness, olives near even unto decay, have yet in their broken ripeness a distinctive beauty. Shocks of corn bending down in their fulness, the lion's mane, the wild boar's mouth all flecked with foam, and many other things of the same kind, though perhaps not pleasing in and of themselves, yet as necessary parts of the Universe created by the Divine Being they add to the beauty of the Universe, and inspire a feeling of pleasure. So that if a man hath appreciation of and an insight into the purpose of the Universe, there is scarcely a portion thereof that will not to him in a sense seem adapted to give delight. In this sense the open jaws of wild beasts will appear no less pleasing than their prototypes in the realm of art. Even in old men and women he will be able to perceive a distinctive maturity and seemliness, while the winsome bloom of youth he can contemplate with eyes free from lascivious desire. And in like manner it will be with very many things which to every one may not seem pleasing, but which will certainly rejoice the man who is a true student of Nature and her works.

TO THE PURE ALL THINGS ARE PURE

IN the mind of him who is pure and good will be found neither corruption nor defilement nor any malignant taint. Unlike the actor who leaves the stage before his part is played, the life of such a man is complete whenever death may come. He is neither cowardly nor presuming; not enslaved to life nor indifferent to its duties; and in him is found nothing worthy of condemnation nor that which putteth to shame.

Test by a trial how excellent is the life of the good man;—the man who rejoices at the portion given him in the universal lot and abides therein content; just in all his ways and kindly minded toward all men.

This is moral perfection: to live each day as though it were the last; to be tranquil, sincere, yet not indifferent to one's fate.

THE GODS BE THANKED

TO the gods I am indebted for having good grandfathers, good parents, a good sister, good teachers, good associates, good kinsmen and friends. Further, I owe it to the gods that I was not hurried into any offence against any of them, though I had a disposition which, if opportunity had offered, might have led me to do something of this kind. But, through their favor, there never was such a convenience of circumstances as put me to the trial. . . .

Further, I am thankful to the gods that I was subjected to a ruler and [adoptive] father who was able to take away all pride from me, and to bring me to the knowledge that it was possible for a man to live in a palace without wanting either guards or embroidered dresses, or torches and statues, and suchlike show; but that it is in such a man's power to bring himself very near to the fashion of a private person, without being for this reason either mean in thought, or more remiss in action, with respect to the things which must be done for the public interest in a manner that befits a ruler. . . .

I thank the gods that I did not make more proficiency in rhetoric, poetry, and the other studies in which I should perhaps have been completely engaged if I had seen that I was making progress in them; that I made haste to place those who brought me up in the station of honor which they seemed to desire, without putting them off with the hope of my doing it some time after.

I thank the gods that I received clear and frequent impressions about living in accordance with Nature, and what kind of a life that is; so that, so far as dependent on the gods, and their gifts and help and inspiration, nothing hindered me from forthwith living according to Nature; though I still fall short of it through my own fault, and not observing the admonition of the gods, and, I may almost say, their direct instructions.

I thank the gods that though it was my mother's fate to die young, she spent the last years of her life with me; that I have such a wife, so obedient, and so affectionate, and so simple; that I had abundance of good masters for my children; and that when I had an inclination to philosophy, I did not waste my time on scribblers, or in the resolution of syllogisms, or occupy myself about the investigations of appearances in the heavens: for all these things require the help of the gods and fortune.

JANE AUSTEN

JANE AUSTEN, novelist, was born at Steventon, England, in 1775; died in 1817. She was the daughter of a clergyman, and early availed herself of all opportunities to study ancient and modern writers. "Pride and Prejudice," her best work, stands to-day as one of the English classics, and its reading is considered essential by those who wish to be acquainted with the best literature of the past one hundred years.

MR. COLLINS PROPOSES AND ELIZABETH DISPOSES

(From "Pride and Prejudice")

MR. COLLINS was not left long to the silent contemplation of his successful love; for Mrs. Bennet, having dawdled about in the vestibule to watch for the end of the conference, no sooner saw Elizabeth open the door and with quick step pass her toward the staircase, than she entered the breakfast room, and congratulated both him and herself in warm terms on the happy prospect of their nearer connection. Mr. Collins received and returned these felicitations with equal pleasure, and then proceeded to relate the particulars of their interview, with the result of which he trusted he had every reason to be satisfied, since the refusal which his cousin had steadfastly given him would naturally flow from her bashful modesty and the genuine delicacy of her character.

This information, however, startled Mrs. Bennet; she would have been glad to be equally satisfied that her daughter had meant to encourage him by protesting against his proposals, but she dared not believe it, and could not help saying so.

"But depend upon it, Mr. Collins," she added, "that Lizzy shall be brought to reason. I will speak to her about it myself directly. She is a very headstrong, foolish girl, and does not know her own interest; but I will make her know it!"

"Pardon me for interrupting you, madam," cried Mr. Collins; "but if she is really headstrong and foolish, I know not whether she would altogether be a very desirable wife to a man in my situation, who naturally looks for happiness in the marriage state. If, therefore, she actually persists in rejecting my suit, perhaps it were better not to force her into accepting me, because, if liable to such defects of temper, she could not add much to my felicity."

"Sir, you quite misunderstand me," said Mrs. Bennet, alarmed. "Lizzy is only headstrong in such matters as these. In everything else she is as good-natured a girl as ever lived. I will go directly to Mr. Bennet, and we shall very soon settle it with her, I am sure."

She would not give him time to reply, but hurrying instantly to her husband, called out, as she entered the library:—

"Oh, Mr. Bennet, you are wanted immediately; we are all in an uproar! You must come and make Lizzy marry Mr. Collins, for she vows she will not have him; and if you do not make haste he will change his mind and not have her!"

Mr. Bennet raised his eyes from his book as she entered, and fixed them on her face with a calm unconcern, which was not in the least altered by her communication.

"I have not the pleasure of understanding you," said he, when she had finished her speech. "Of what are you talking?"

"Of Mr. Collins and Lizzy. Lizzy declares she will not have Mr. Collins, and Mr. Collins begins to say that he will not have Lizzy.

"And what am I to do on the occasion? It seems a hopeless business."

"Speak to Lizzy about it yourself. Tell her that you insist upon her marrying him."

"Let her be called down. She shall hear my opinion."

Mrs. Bennet rang the bell, and Miss Elizabeth was summoned to the library.

"Come here, child," cried her father, as she appeared. "I have sent for you on an affair of importance. I understand that Mr. Collins has made you an offer of marriage. Is it true?" Elizabeth replied that it was. "Very well—and this offer of marriage you have refused?"

"I have, sir?"

"Very well. We now come to the point. Your mother insists upon your accepting it. Is it not so, Mrs. Bennet?"

"Yes, or I will never see her again."

"An unhappy alternative is before you, Elizabeth. From this day you must be a stranger to one of your parents. Your mother will never see you again if you do not marry Mr. Collins, and I will never see you again if you do!"

Elizabeth could not but smile at such a conclusion of such a beginning; but Mrs. Bennet, who had persuaded herself that her husband regarded the affair as she wished, was excessively disappointed.

"What do you mean, Mr. Bennet, by talking in this way? You promised me to insist upon her marrying him."

"My dear," replied her husband, "I have two small favors to request. First, that you will allow me the free use of my understanding on the present occasion; and, secondly, of my room. I shall be glad to have the library to myself as soon as may be."

Not yet, however, in spite of her disappointment in her husband, did Mrs. Bennet give up the point. She talked to Elizabeth again and again; coaxed and threatened her by turns. She endeavored to secure Jane in her interest, but Jane, with all possible mildness, declined interfering; and Elizabeth, sometimes with real earnestness, and sometimes with playful gayety, replied to her attacks. Though her manner varied, however, her determination never did.

Mr. Collins, meanwhile, was meditating in solitude on what had passed. He thought too well of himself to comprehend on what motive his cousin could refuse him; and though his pride was hurt, he suffered in no other way. His regard for her was quite imaginary, and the possibility of her deserving her mother's reproach prevented his feeling any regret.

While the family were in this confusion Charlotte Lucas came to spend the day with them. She was met in the vestibule by Lydia, who, flying to her, cried, in a half whisper, "I am glad you are come, for there is such fun here! What do you think has happened this morning? Mr. Collins has made an offer to Lizzy, and she will not have him."

Charlotte had hardly time to answer before they were joined by Kitty, who came to tell the same news: and no sooner had they entered the breakfast room where Mrs. Bennet was alone than she likewise began on the subject, calling on Miss Lucas for her compassion, and entreating her to persuade her friend Lizzy to comply with the wishes of all her family. "Pray do, my dear Miss Lucas," she added, in a melancholy tone, "for nobody is on my side, nobody takes part with me; I am cruelly used; nobody feels for my poor nerves."

Charlotte's reply was spared by the entrance of Jane and Elizabeth.

"Ay, there she comes," continued Mrs. Bennet, "looking as unconcerned as may be, and caring no more for us than if we were at York, provided she can have her own way. But I tell you what, Miss Lizzy, if you take it into your head to go on refusing every offer of marriage in this way, you will never get a husband at all; and I am sure I do not know who is to maintain you when your father is dead. *I* shall not be able to keep you—and so I warn you. I have done with you from this very day. I told you in the library, you know, that I should never speak to you again, and you will find me as good as my word. I have no pleasure in talking to undutiful children. Not that I have much pleasure, indeed, in talking to anybody. People who suffer as I do from nervous complaints can have no great inclination for talking. Nobody can tell what I suffer! But it is always so: those who do not complain are never pitied."

Her daughters listened in silence to this effusion, sensible that any attempt to reason with or soothe her would only increase the irritation. She talked on, therefore, without interruption from any of them, till they were joined by Mr. Collins, who entered with an air more stately than usual, and on perceiving whom she said to the girls:—

"Now I do insist upon it that you, all of you, hold your tongues and let Mr. Collins and me have a little conversation together."

Elizabeth passed quietly out of the room, Jane and Kitty followed, but Lydia stood her ground, determined to hear all she could; and Charlotte detained first by the civility of Mr. Collins, whose inquiries after herself and all her family were very minute, and then by a little curiosity, satisfied herself with walking to the window and pretending not to hear. In a doleful voice Mrs. Bennet thus began the projected conversation: "Oh, Mr. Collins!"

"My dear madam," replied he, "let us be forever silent on this point. Far be it from me," he presently continued, in a voice that marked his displeasure, "to resent the behavior of your daughter. Resignation to inevitable evils is the duty of us all—the peculiar duty of a young man who has been so fortunate as I have been, in early preferment; and, I trust I am resigned. Perhaps not the less so from feeling a doubt of my positive happiness had my fair cousin honored me with her hand; for I have often observed that resignation is never so perfect as when the blessing denied begins to lose somewhat of its value in our estimation. You will not, I hope, consider me as showing any disrespect to your family, my dear madam, by thus withdrawing my pretensions to your daughter's favor, without having paid yourself and Mr. Bennet the compliment of requesting you to interpose your authority in my behalf. My conduct may, I fear, be objectionable in having accepted my dismissal from your daughter's lips instead of your own; but we are all liable to error. I have certainly meant well through the whole affair. My object has been to secure an amiable companion for myself, with due consideration for the advantage of all your family; and if my manner has been at all reprehensible, I here beg leave to apologize."

ELIZABETH DEFIES LADY CATHERINE

(From "Pride and Prejudice")

ONE morning, about a week after Bingley's engagement with Jane had been formed, as he and the females of the family were sitting together in the dining room, their attention was suddenly drawn to the window by the sound of a carriage, and they perceived a chaise and four driving up the lawn. It was too early in the morning for visitors, and besides, the equipage did not answer to that of any of their neighbors. The horses were post; and neither the carriage nor the livery of the servant who preceded it was familiar to them. As it was certain, however, that somebody was coming, Bingley instantly prevailed on Miss Emmet to avoid the confinement of such an intrusion and walk away with him into the shrubbery. They both set off, and the conjectures of the remaining three continued, though with little satisfaction, till the door was thrown open and their visitor entered. It was Lady Catherine De Bourgh.

They were of course all intending to be surprised, but their astonishment was beyond their expectation; and on the part of Mrs. Bennet and Kitty, though she was perfectly unknown to them, even inferior to what Elizabeth felt.

She entered the room with an air more than usually ungracious, made no other reply to Elizabeth's salutation than a slight inclination of the head, and sat down without saying a word. Elizabeth had mentioned her name to her mother on her ladyship's entrance, though no request of introduction had been made.

Mrs. Bennet, all amazement, though flattered by having a guest of such high importance, received her with the utmost politeness. After sitting for a moment in silence she said, very stiffly, to Elizabeth:—

"I hope you are well, Miss Bennet. That lady, I suppose, is your mother?"

Elizabeth replied very concisely that she was.

"And that, I suppose, is one of your sisters?"

"Yes, madam," said Mrs. Bennet, delighted to speak to a Lady Catherine; "she is my youngest girl but one. My youngest of all is lately married, and my eldest is somewhere about the ground, walking with a young man, who, I believe, will soon become a part of the family."

"You have a very small park here," returned Lady Catherine, after a short silence.

"It is nothing in comparison with Rosings, my lady, I dare say; but I assure you it is much larger than Sir William Lucas'."

"This must be a most inconvenient sitting room for the evening in summer; the windows are full west."

Mrs. Bennet assured her that they never sat there after dinner; and then added:—

"May I take the liberty of asking your ladyship whether you left Mr. and Mrs. Collins well?"

"Yes, very well. I saw them the night before last."

Elizabeth now expected that she would produce a letter for her from Charlotte, as it seemed the only probable motive for her calling. But no letter appeared, and she was completely puzzled.

Mrs. Bennet with great civility begged her ladyship to take some refreshment; but Lady Catherine very resolutely, and not very politely, declined eating anything; and then, rising up, said to Elizabeth:—

"Miss Bennet, there seemed to be a prettyish kind of a little wilderness on one side of your lawn. I should be glad to take a turn in it, if you will favor me with your company."

"Go, my dear," cried her mother, "and show her ladyship about the different walks. I think she will be pleased with the hermitage."

Elizabeth obeyed; and, running into her own room for her parasol, attended her noble guest downstairs. As they passed through the hall, Lady Catherine opened the doors into the dining parlor and drawing-room, and pronouncing them, after a short survey, to be decent-looking rooms, walked on.

Her carriage remained at the door, and Elizabeth saw that her waiting woman was in it. They proceeded in silence along the gravel walk that led to the copse; Elizabeth was determined to make no effort for conversation with a woman who was now more than usually insolent and disagreeable.

"How could I ever think her like her nephew?" said she, as she looked in her face.

As soon as they entered the copse, Lady Catherine began in the following manner:—

"You can be at no loss, Miss Bennet, to understand the reason of my journey hither. Your own heart, your own conscience, must tell you why I come."

Elizabeth looked with unaffected astonishment.

"Indeed you are mistaken, madam; I have not been at all able to account for the honor of seeing you here."

"Miss Bennet," replied her ladyship, in an angry tone, "you ought to know that I am not to be trifled with. But however insincere you may choose to be, you shall not find me so. My character has ever been celebrated for its sincerity and frankness; and in a cause of such moment as this I shall certainly not depart from it. A report of a most alarming nature reached me two days ago. I was told that not only your sister was on the point of being most advantageously married, but that you, that Miss Elizabeth Bennet, would, in all likelihood, be soon united afterward to my nephew, my own nephew, Mr. Darcy. Though I know it must be a scandalous falsehood, though I would not injure him so much as to suppose the truth of it possible, I instantly resolved on setting off for this place that I might make my sentiments known to you."

"If you believed it impossible to be true," said Elizabeth, coloring with astonishment and disdain,

"I wonder you took the trouble of coming so far. What could your ladyship propose by it?"

"At once to insist upon having such a report universally contradicted."

"Your coming to Longbourn to see me and my family," said Elizabeth, coolly, "will be rather a confirmation of it,—if, indeed, such a report is in existence."

"If! Do you, then, pretend to be ignorant of it? Has it not been industriously circulated by yourselves? Do you not know that such a report is spread about?"

"I never heard that it was."

"And you can likewise declare that there is no foundation for it?"

"I do not pretend to possess equal frankness with your ladyship. You may ask questions which I shall not choose to answer."

"This is not to be borne! Miss Bennet, I insist on being satisfied. Has he, my nephew, made you an offer of marriage?"

"Your ladyship has declared it to be impossible."

"It ought to be so; it must be so, while he retains the use of his reason. But your arts and allurements may, in a moment of infatuation, have made him forget what he owes to himself and to all his family. You may have drawn him in."

"If I have, I shall be the last person to confess it."

"Miss Bennet, do you know who I am? I have not been accustomed to such language as this. I am almost the nearest relation he has in the world, and am entitled to know all his dearest concerns."

"But you are not entitled to know mine; nor will such behavior as this ever induce me to be explicit."

"Let me be rightly understood. This match, to which you have the presumption to aspire, can never take place—no, never. Mr. Darcy is engaged to my daughter. Now, what have you to say?"

"Only this—that if he is so, you can have no reason to suppose he will make an offer to me."

Lady Catherine hesitated a moment, and then replied:—

"The engagement between them is of a peculiar kind. From their infancy they have been intended for each other. It was the favorite wish of his mother, as well as of hers. While in their cradles we planned the union and now, at the moment when the wishes of both sisters would be accomplished in their marriage, to be prevented by a young woman of inferior birth, of no importance in the world, and wholly unallied to the family! Do you pay no regard to the wishes of his friends? to his tacit engagement with Miss De Bourgh? Are you lost to every feeling of propriety and delicacy? Have you not heard me say that from his earliest hours, he was destined for his cousin?"

"Yes; and I had heard it before. But what is that to me? If there is no other objection to my marrying your nephew, I shall certainly not be kept from it by knowing that his mother and aunt wished him to marry Miss De Bourgh. You both did as much as you could in planning the marriage; its completion depended on others. If Mr. Darcy is neither by honor nor inclination confined to his cousin, why is not he to make another choice? and if I am that choice, why may not I accept him?"

"Because honor, decorum, prudence, nay interest, forbid it. Yes, Miss Bennet, interest, for do not expect to be noticed by his family or friends, if you wilfully act against the inclinations of all. You will be censured, slighted, and despised by every one connected with him. Your alliance will be a disgrace; your name will never even be mentioned by any of us."

"These are heavy misfortunes!" replied Elizabeth. "But the wife of Mr. Darcy must have such extraordinary sources of happiness necessarily attached to her situation that she could, upon the whole, have no cause to repine."

"Obstinate, headstrong girl! I am ashamed of you! Is this your gratitude for my attentions to you last spring? Is nothing due to me on that score? Let us sit down. You are to understand, Miss Bennet, that I came here with the determined resolution of carrying out my purpose; nor will I be dissuaded from it. I have not been used to submit to any person's whims. I have not been in the habit of brooking disappointment."

"That will make your ladyship's situation at present more pitiable but it will have no effect on me."

"I will not be interrupted. Hear me in silence. My daughter and my nephew are formed for each other. They are descended, on the maternal side, from the same noble line; and, on the father's from respectable, honorable, and ancient, though untitled, families. Their fortune on both sides is splendid. They are destined for each other by the voice of every member of their respective houses; and what is to divide them?—the upstart pretensions of a young woman without family, connections, or fortune! Is this to be endured? But it must not, shall not be! If you were sensible of your own good, you would not wish to quit the sphere in which you have been brought up."

"In marrying your nephew, I should not consider myself as quitting that sphere. He is a gentleman; I am a gentleman's daughter; so far we are equal."

"True. You are a gentleman's daughter. But what was your mother? Who are your uncles and aunts? Do not imagine me ignorant of their condition."

"Whatever my connections may be," said Elizabeth, "if your nephew does not object to them, they can be nothing to you."

"Tell me, once for all, are you engaged to him?"

Though Elizabeth would not, for the mere purpose of obliging Lady Catherine, have answered this question, she could not but say, after a moment's deliberation:—

"I am not."

Lady Catherine seemed pleased.

"And will you promise me never to enter into such an engagement?"

"I will make no promise of the kind."

"Miss Bennet, I am shocked and astonished. I expected to find a more reasonable young woman. But do not deceive yourself into a belief that I will ever recede. I shall not go away till you have given me the assurance I require."

"And I certainly never shall give it. I am not to be intimidated into anything so wholly unreasonable. Your ladyship wants Mr. Darcy to marry your daughter; but would my giving you the wished-for promise make their marriage at all more probable? Supposing him to be attached to me, would my refusing to accept his hand make him wish to bestow it on his cousin? Allow me to say, Lady Catherine, that the arguments with which you have supported this extraordinary application have been as frivolous as the application was ill-judged. You have widely mistaken my character, if you think I can be worked on by such persuasions as these. How far your nephew might approve of your interference in his affairs I cannot tell, but you have certainly no right to concern yourself in mine. I must beg, therefore, to be importuned no further on the subject."

"Not so hasty, if you please; I have by no means done. To all the objections I have already urged I have still another to add. I am no stranger to the particulars of your younger sister's infamous elopement: I know it all—that the young man's marrying her was a patched-up business at the expense of your father and uncle. And is such a girl to be my nephew's sister? Is her husband, who is the son of his late father's steward, to be his brother? Heaven and earth! of what are you thinking? Are the shades of Pemberley to be thus polluted?"

"You can now have nothing further to say," she resentfully answered. "You have insulted me in every possible method. I must beg to return to the house."

And she rose as she spoke. Lady Catherine rose also, and they turned back. Her ladyship was highly incensed.

"You have no regard, then, for the honor and credit of my nephew? Unfeeling, selfish girl! Do you not consider that a connection with you must disgrace him in the eyes of everybody?"

"Lady Catherine, I have nothing further to say. You know my sentiments."

"You are, then, resolved to have him?"

"I have said no such thing. I am only resolved to act in that manner which will, in my own opinion, constitute my happiness, without reference to you, or to any person so wholly unconnected with me."

"It is well. You refuse, then, to oblige me; you refuse to obey the claims of duty, honor and gratitude. You are determined to ruin him in the opinion of all his friends, and make him the contempt of the world."

"Neither duty, nor honor, nor gratitude," replied Elizabeth, "has any possible claim on me, in the present instance. No principle of either would be violated by my marriage with Mr. Darcy. And with regard to the resentment of his family, or the indignation of the world, if the former were excited by his marrying me, it would not give me one moment's concern; and the world in general would have too much sense to join in the scorn."

"And this is your real opinion! This is your final resolve! Very well! I shall now know how to act. Do not imagine, Miss Bennet, that your ambition will ever be gratified. I came to try you. I hoped to find you reasonable, but depend upon it, I will carry my point."

In this manner Lady Catherine talked on till they were at the door of the carriage, when, turning hastily round, she added:

"I take no leave of you, Miss Bennet. I send no compliments to your mother; you deserve no such attention. I am most seriously displeased."

Elizabeth made no answer; and without attempting to persuade her ladyship to return into the house, walked quietly into it herself. She heard the carriage drive away as she proceeded upstairs. Her mother impatiently met her at the door of her dressing-room, to ask why Lady Catherine would not come in again and rest herself.

"She did not choose it," said her daughter; "she would go."

"She is a very fine-looking woman, and her calling here was prodigiously civil; for she only came, I suppose, to tell us the Collinses were well. She is on her road somewhere, I dare say; and so, passing through Meryton, thought she might as well call on you. I suppose she had nothing particular to say to you, Lizzy?"

Elizabeth was forced to give in to a little falsehood here; for to acknowledge the substance of their conversation was impossible.

LYDIA BENNET'S WEDDING

(From "Pride and Prejudice")

THEIR sister's wedding-day arrived, and Jane and Elizabeth felt for her probably more than she felt for herself. The carriage was sent to meet them at ——, and they were to return in it by dinner-time. Their arrival was dreaded by the elder Miss Bennets, and Jane more especially, who gave Lydia the feelings which would have attended herself had she been the culprit, and was wretched in the thought of what her sister must endure.

They came. The family were assembled in the breakfast-room to receive them. Smiles decked the face of Mrs. Bennet as the carriage drove up to the door; her husband looked impenetrably grave; her daughters alarmed, anxious, uneasy.

Lydia's voice was heard in the vestibule; the door was thrown open, and she ran into the room. Her mother stepped forward, embraced her, and welcomed her with rapture; gave her hand, with an affectionate smile, to Wickham, who followed his lady; and wished them both joy with an alacrity which showed no doubt of their happiness.

Their reception from Mr. Bennet, to whom they then turned, was not quite so cordial. His countenance rather gained in austerity, and he scarcely opened his lips. The easy assurance of the young couple, indeed, was enough to provoke him. Elizabeth was disgusted, and even Miss Bennet was shocked. Lydia was Lydia still—untamed, unabashed, wild, noisy, and fearless. She turned from sister to sister, demanding their congratulations; and, when at length they all sat down, looked eagerly round the room, took notice of some little alteration in it, and observed, with a laugh, that it was a great while since she had been there.

Wickham was not at all more distressed than herself; but his manners were always so pleasing, that had his character and his marriage been exactly what they ought, his smiles and easy address, while he claimed their relationship, would have delighted them all. Elizabeth had not before believed him quite equal to such assurance; but she sat down, resolving within herself to draw no limits in future to the impudence of an impudent man. She blushed, and Jane blushed; but the cheeks of the two who caused their confusion suffered no variation of color. There was no want of discourse. The bride and her mother could neither of them talk fast enough; and Wickham, who happened to sit near Elizabeth, began inquiring after his acquaintance in that neighborhood with a good-humored ease which she felt very unable to equal in her replies. They seemed each of them to have the happiest memories in the world. Nothing of the past was recollected with pain; and Lydia led voluntarily to subjects which her sisters would not have alluded to for the world.

"Only think of its being three months," she cried, "since I went away! it seems but a fortnight, I declare! and yet there have been things enough happened in the time. Good gracious! when I went away I am sure I had no more idea of being married till I came back again! though I thought it would be very good fun if I was."

Her father lifted up his eyes; Jane was distressed; Elizabeth looked expressively at Lydia; but she, who never saw or heard anything of which she chose to be insensible, gayly continued: "Oh, mamma, do the people hereabouts know I am married to-day? I was afraid they might not; and we overtook William Goulding in his curricle, so I was determined he should know it; and so I let down the side-glass next to him, and took off my glove and let my hand just rest upon the window-frame, so that he might see the ring, and then I bowed and smiled like anything."

Elizabeth could bear it no longer. She got up and ran out of the room; and returned no more till she heard them passing through the hall to the dining parlor. She then joined them soon enough to see Lydia, with anxious parade, walk up to her mother's right hand, and hear her say to her eldest sister, "Ah, Jane, I take your place now, and you must go lower, because I am a married woman."

It was not to be supposed that time would give Lydia that embarrassment from which she had been so wholly free at first. Her ease and good spirits increased. She longed to see Mrs. Philips, the Lucases, and all their other neighbors, and to hear herself called "Mrs. Wickham" by each of them; and in the meantime she went after dinner to show her ring, and boast of being married, to Mrs. Hill and the two housemaids.

"Well, mamma," said she, when they were all returned to the breakfast-room, "and what do you think of my husband? Is not he a charming man? I am sure my sisters must all envy me. I only hope they may have half my good-luck. They must all go to Brighton—that is the place to get husbands. What a pity it is, mamma, we did not all go."

"Very true; and if I had my will we should. But, my dear Lydia, I don't at all like your going such a way off. Must it be so?"

"O Lord! yes; there is nothing in that. I shall like it of all things. You and papa, and my sisters, must come down and see us. We shall be at Newcastle all the winter, and I dare say there will be some balls, and I will take care to get good partners for them all."

"I should like it beyond anything," said her mother.

"And then when you go away you may leave one or two of my sisters behind you, and I dare say I shall get husbands for them before the winter is over."

"I thank you for my share of the favor," said Elizabeth; "but I do not particularly like your way of getting husbands."

Their visitors were not to remain above ten days

with them. Mr. Wickham had received his commission before he left London, and he was to join his regiment at the end of a fortnight.

No one but Mrs. Bennet regretted that their stay would be so short; and she made the most of her time by visiting about with her daughter, and having very frequent parties at home. These parties were acceptable to all; to avoid a family circle was even more desirable to such as did think than such as did not.

Wickham's affection for Lydia was just what Elizabeth had expected to find it—not equal to Lydia's for him. She had scarcely needed her present observation to be satisfied, from the reason of things, that their elopement had been brought on by the strength of her love rather than by his; and she would have wondered why, without violently caring for her, he chose to elope with her at all, had she not felt certain that his flight was rendered necessary by distress of circumstances; and if that were the case, he was not the young man to resist the opportunity of having a companion.

Lydia was exceedingly fond of him. He was her dear Wickham on every occasion; no one was to be put in competition with him. He did everything best in the world; and she was sure he would kill more birds on the first of September than anybody else in the country.

One morning, soon after their arrival, as she was sitting with her two elder sisters, she said to Elizabeth:

"Lizzy, I never gave you an account of my wedding, I believe. You were not by when I told mamma and the others all about it. Are not you curious to hear how it was managed?"

"No, really," replied Elizabeth; "I think there cannot be too little said on the subject."

"La! You are so strange! But I must tell you

how it went off. We were married, you know, at St. Clement's, because Wickham's lodgings were in that parish. And it was settled that we should all be there by eleven o'clock. My uncle and aunt and I were to go together, and the others were to meet us at the church. Well, Monday morning came, and I was in such a fuss! I was so afraid, you know, that something would happen to put it off, and then I should have gone quite distracted. And there was my aunt, all the time I was dressing, preaching and talking away just as if she was reading a sermon. However, I did not hear above one word in ten, for I was thinking, you may suppose, of my dear Wickham. I longed to know whether he would be married in his blue coat.

"Well, and so we breakfasted at ten, as usual. I thought it would never be over, for, by the bye, you are to understand that my uncle and aunt were horrid unpleasant all the time I was with them. If you'll believe me, I did not once put my foot out-of-doors, though I was there a fortnight. Not one party, or scheme, or anything. To be sure, London was rather thin; but, however, the Little Theater was open. Well, and so just as the carriage came to the door, my uncle was called away upon business to that horrid man, Mr. Stone. And then, you know, when once they get together there is no end of it. Well, I was so frightened I did not know what to do, for my uncle was to give me away; and if we were beyond the hour we could not be married all day. But, luckily, he came back again in ten minutes' time, and then we all set out. However, I recollected afterward that if he had been prevented going, the wedding need not be put off, for Mr. Darcy might have done as well."

"Mr. Darcy!" repeated Elizabeth, in utter amazement.

"Oh, yes! he was to come there with Wickham, you

know. But, gracious me! I quite forgot. I ought
not to have said a word about it: I promised them so
faithfully! What will Wickham say? It was to be
such a secret!"

"If it was to be a secret," said Jane, "say not
another word on the subject. You may depend upon
my seeking no farther."

"Oh, certainly," said Elizabeth, though burning
with curiosity; "we will ask you no questions."

"Thank you," said Lydia; "for if you did, I
should certainly tell you all, and then Wickham
would be so angry!"

On such encouragement to ask, Elizabeth was
forced to put it out of her power by running away.

But to live in ignorance on such a point was impossible; or at least it was impossible not to try for
information. Mr. Darcy had been at her sister's wedding. It was exactly a scene, and exactly among
people, where he had apparently least to do, and
least temptation to go. Conjectures as to the meaning of it, rapid and wild, hurried into her brain, but
she was satisfied with none. Those that best pleased
her, as placing his conduct in the noblest light,
seemed almost improbable. She could not bear such
suspense; and hastily seizing a sheet of paper, wrote
a short letter to her aunt, to request an explanation
of what Lydia had dropped, if it were compatible
with the secrecy which had been intended.

"You may readily comprehend," she added, "what
my curiosity must be to know how a person unconnected with any of us, and, comparatively speaking,
a stranger to our family, should have been among
you at such a time. Pray write instantly, and let me
understand it—unless it is, for very cogent reasons,
to remain in the secrecy which Lydia seems to think
necessary; and then I must endeavor to be satisfied
with ignorance.

"Not that I shall, though," she added to herself,

and she finished the letter: "and, my dear aunt, if you do not tell me in an honorable manner, I shall certainly be reduced to tricks and stratagems to find it out."

Jane's delicate sense of honor would not allow her to speak to Elizabeth privately of what Lydia had let fall; Elizabeth was glad of it; till it appeared whether her inquiries would receive any satisfaction, she had rather be without a confidante.

MR. BENNET AND MR. COLLINS PLAY BACKGAMMON

(From " Pride and Prejudice ")

DURING dinner, Mr. Bennet scarcely spoke at all; but when the servants were withdrawn he thought it time to have some conversation with his guest, and therefore started a subject in which he expected him to shine, by observing that he seemed very fortunate in his patroness. Lady Catherine de Bourgh's attention to his wishes, and consideration for his comfort, appeared very remarkable. Mr. Bennet could not have chosen better. Mr. Collins was eloquent in her praise. The subject elevated him to more than usual solemnity of manner; and with a most important aspect he protested that " he had never in his life witnessed such behavior in a person of rank, such affability and condescension, as he had himself experienced from Lady Catherine. She had been graciously pleased to approve of both the discourses which he had already had the honor of preaching before her. She had also asked him twice to dine at Rosings, and had sent for him only the Saturday before, to make up her pool of quadrille in the evening. Lady Catherine was reckoned proud by many people, he knew, but he had never seen anything but affability in her. She had always spoken to him as she would to any other gentleman; she made not the smallest objection to his joining in the society of the neighborhood, nor to his leaving his parish occasionally for a week or two to visit his relations. She had even condescended to advise him to marry as soon as he could, provided he chose with discretion; and had once paid him a visit in his humble parsonage, where she had perfectly approved all the alterations he had been making, and had even vouchsafed to suggest some herself—some shelves in the closets upstairs.

"That is all very proper and civil, I am sure," said Mrs. Bennet, and I dare say she is a very agreeable woman. It is a pity that great ladies in general are not more like her. Does she live near you, sir?"

"The garden in which stands my humble abode is separated only by a lane from Rosings Park, her ladyship's residence."

"I think you said she was a widow, sir; has she any family?"

"She has only one daughter, the heiress of Rosings, and of very extensive property."

"Ah," cried Mrs. Bennet, shaking her head, "then she is better off than many girls. And what sort of young lady is she? Is she handsome?"

"She is a most charming young lady indeed. Lady Catherine herself says that, in point of true beauty, Miss de Bourgh is far superior to the handsomest of her sex, because there is that in her features which marks the young woman of distinguished birth. She is unfortunately of a sickly constitution, which has prevented her making that progress in many accomplishments which she could not otherwise have failed of, as I am informed by the lady who superintended her education, and who still resides with them. But she is perfectly amiable, and often condescends to drive by my humble abode in her little phaeton and ponies."

"Has she been presented? I do not remember her name among the ladies at court."

"Her indifferent state of health unhappily prevents her being in town; and by that means, as I told Lady Catherine myself one day, has deprived the British court of its brightest ornament. Her ladyship seemed pleased with the idea; and you may imagine that I am happy on every occasion to offer those little delicate compliments which are always acceptable to ladies. I have more than once observed to Lady Catherine that her charming daughter seemed born to be a duchess, and that the most elevated rank, instead of giving her consequence, would be adorned by her. These are the kind of little things which please her ladyship, and it is a sort of attention which I conceive myself peculiarly bound to pay."

"You judge very properly," said Mr. Bennet; "and it is happy for you that you possess the talent of flattering with delicacy. May I ask whether these pleasing attentions proceed from the impulse of the moment, or are the result of previous study?"

"They arise chiefly from what is passing at the time; and though I sometimes amuse myself with suggesting and arranging such little elegant compliments as may be adapted to ordinary occasions, I always wish to give them as unstudied an air as possible."

Mr. Bennet's expectations were fully answered. His cousin was as absurd as he had hoped; and he listened to him with the keenest enjoyment, maintaining at the same time the most absolute composure of countenance, and, except in an occasional glance at Elizabeth, requiring no partner in his pleasure.

By tea-time, however, the dose had been enough, and Mr. Bennet was glad to take his guest into the drawing-room again, and when tea was over, glad to invite him to read aloud to the ladies. Mr. Collins readily assented, and a book was produced; but on beholding it (for everything announced it to be from a circulating library) he started back, and, begging pardon, protested that he never read novels. Kitty stared at him, and Lydia exclaimed. Other books were produced, and after some deliberation he chose "Fordyce's Sermons." Lydia gaped as he opened the volume; and before he had, with very monotonous solemnity, read three pages, she interrupted him with—

"Do you know, mamma, that my Uncle Philips talks of turning away Richard? and if he does, Colonel Forster will hire him. My aunt told me so herself on Saturday. I shall walk to Meryton to-morrow to hear more about it, and to ask when Mr. Denny comes back from town.

Lydia was bid by her two eldest sisters to hold her tongue; but Mr. Collins, much offended, laid aside his book, and said:

"I have often observed how little young ladies are interested by books of a serious stamp, though solely written for their benefit. It amazes me, I confess; for certainly there can be nothing so advantageous to them as instruction. But I will no longer importune my young cousin."

Then, turning to Mr. Bennet, he offered himself as his antagonist at backgammon. Mr. Bennet accepted the challenge, observing that he acted very wisely in leaving the girls to their own trifling amusements. Mrs. Bennet and her daughters apologized most civilly for Lydia's interruption, and promised that it should not occur again, if he would resume his book; but Mr. Collins, after assuring them that he bore his young cousin no ill-will, and should never resent her behavior as any affront, seated himself at another table with Mr. Bennet, and prepared for backgammon.

IRVING BACHELLER

IRVING BACHELLER was born at Pierpont, N. Y., in 1859. For many years he was in active newspaper work in New York City, and until recently an editor of the *World*. He has written several novels, the most popular being "Eben Holden" and "D'ri and I."

THE SEA FIGHT

(From "D'ri and I." Copyright by Lothrop Publishing Company, and used by permission)

THE cry of "Sail ho!" woke me early one morning. It was the 10th of September. The enemy was coming. Sails were sticking out of the misty dawn a few miles away. In a moment our decks were black and noisy with the hundred and two that manned the vessel. It was every hand to rope and windlass then. Sails went up with a snap all around us, and the creak of blocks sounded far and near. In twelve minutes we were under way, leading the van to battle. The sun came up, lighting the great towers of canvas. Every vessel was now feeling for the wind, some with oars and sweeps to aid them. A light breeze came out of the southwest. Perry stood near me, his hat in his hand. He was looking back at the *Niagara*.

"Run to the leeward of the islands," said he to the sailing-master.

"Then you'll have to fight to the leeward," said the latter.

"Don't care, so long as we fight," said Perry. "Windward or leeward, we want to fight."

Then came the signal to change our course. The wind shifting to the southeast, we were all able to clear the islands and keep the weather-gage. A cloud came over the sun; far away the mist thickened. The enemy wallowed to the topsails, and went out of sight. We had lost the wind. Our sails went limp; flag and pennant hung lifeless. A light rain drizzled down, breaking the smooth plane of water into crowding rings and bubbles. Perry stood out in the drizzle as we lay waiting. All eyes were turning to the sky and to Perry. He had a look of worry and disgust. He was out for a quarrel, though the surgeon said he was in more need of physic, having the fever of malaria as well as that of war. He stood there, tall and handsome, in a loose jacket of blue nankeen, with no sign of weakness in him, his eyes flashing as he looked up at the sky.

D'ri and I stood in the squad at the bow gun. D'ri was wearing an old straw hat; his flannel shirt was open at the collar.

"Ship stan's luk an ol' cow chawin' 'er cud," said he, looking off at the weather. "They's a win' comin' over there. It'll give 'er a slap 'n th' side purty soon, mebbe. Then she'll switch 'er tail 'n' go on 'bout 'er business."

In a moment we heard a roaring cheer back amidships. Perry had come up the companionway with his blue battle-flag. He held it before him at arm's-length. I could see a part of its legend, in white letters, "Don't give up the ship."

"My brave lads," he shouted, "shall we hoist it?"

Our "Ay, ay, sir!" could have been heard a mile away, and the flag rose, above tossing hats and howling voices, to the mainroyalmasthead.

The wind came; we could hear the sails snap and stiffen as it overhauled the fleet behind us. In a jiffy it bunted our own hull and canvas, and again we began to plough the water. It grew into a smart breeze, and scattered the fleet of clouds that hovered over us. The rain passed; sunlight sparkled on the rippling plane of water. We could now see the enemy; he had hove to, and was waiting for us in a line. A crowd was gathering on the high shores we had left to see the battle. We were well in advance, crowding our canvas in a good breeze. I could hear only the roaring furrows of water on each side of the prow. Every man of us held his tongue, mentally trimming ship, as they say, for whatever might come. Three men scuffled by, sanding the decks. D'ri was leaning placidly over the big gun. He looked off at the white line, squinted knowingly, and spat over the bulwarks. Then he straightened up, tilting his hat to his right ear.

"They're p'intin' their guns," said a swabber.

"Fust they know they'll git spit on," said D'ri, calmly.

Well, for two hours it was all creeping and talking under the breath, and here and there an oath as some nervous chap tightened the ropes of his resolution. Then suddenly, as we swung about, a murmur went up and down the deck. We could see with our naked eyes the men who were to give us battle. Perry shouted sternly to some gunners who thought it high time to fire. Then word came: there would be no firing until we got close. Little gusts of music came chasing over the water faint-footed to our decks—a band playing "Rule Britannia." I was looking at a brig in the line of the enemy when a bolt of fire leaped out of her and thick belches of smoke rushed to her topsails. Then something hit the sea near by with a great hissing slap, and we turned quickly to see chunks of the shattered lake surface fly up in nets of spray and fall roaring on our deck. We were all drenched there at the bow gun. I remember some of those water-drops had the sting of hard-flung pebbles, but we only bent our heads, waiting eagerly for the word to fire.

"We was th' ones 'at got spit on," said a gunner, looking at D'ri.

"Wish they'd let us holler back," said the latter, placidly. "Sick o' holdin' in."

We kept fanning down upon the enemy, now little more than a mile away, signalling the fleet to follow.

"My God! see there!" a gunner shouted.

The British line had turned into a reeling, whirling ridge of smoke lifting over spurts of flame at the bottom. We knew what was coming. Untried in the perils of shot and shell, some of my gunners stooped to cover under the bulwarks.

"Pull 'em out o' there," I called, turning to D'ri, who stood beside me.

The storm of iron hit us. A heavy ball crashed into the after bulwarks, tearing them away and slamming over gun and carriage, that slid a space, grinding the gunners under it. One end of a bowline whipped over us; a jib dropped; a brace fell crawling over my shoulders like a big snake; the foremast went into splinters a few feet above the deck, its top falling over, its canvas sagging in great folds. It was all the work of a second. That hasty flight of iron, coming out of the air, thick as a flock of pigeons, had gone through hull and rigging in a wink of the eye. And a fine mess it had made. Men lay scattered along the deck, bleeding, yelling, struggling. There were two lying near us with blood spurting out of their necks. One rose upon a knee, choking horribly, shaken with the last throes of his flooded heart, and reeled over. The *Scorpion* of our fleet had got her guns in action; the little *Ariel* was also firing. D'ri leaned over, shouting in my ear.

"Don't like th' way they're whalin' uv us," he said, his cheeks red with anger.

"Nor I," was my answer.

"Don't like t' stan' here an' dew nuthin' but git licked," he went on. "'T ain' no way nat'ral."

Perry came hurrying forward.

"Fire!" he commanded, with a quick gesture, and we began to warm up our big twenty-pounder there in the bow. But the deadly scuds of iron kept flying over and upon our deck, bursting into awful showers of bolt and chain and spike and hammerheads. We saw shortly that our brig was badly out of gear. She began to drift to leeward, and being unable to aim at the enemy, we could make no use of the bow gun. Every brace and bowline cut away, her canvas torn to rags, her hull shot through, and half her men dead or wounded, she was, indeed, a sorry sight. The *Niagara* went by on the safe side of us, heedless of our plight. Perry stood near, cursing as he looked off at her. Two of my gunners had been hurt by bursting canister. D'ri and I picked them up, and made for the cockpit. D'ri's man kept howling and kicking. As we hurried over the bloody deck, there came a mighty crash beside us and a burst of old iron that tumbled me to my knees.

A cloud of smoke covered us. I felt the man I bore struggle and then go limp in my arms; I felt my knees getting warm and wet. The smoke rose; the tall, herculean back of D'ri was just ahead of me. His sleeve had been ripped away from shoulder to elbow, and a spray of blood from his upper arm was flying back upon me. His hat crown had been torn off, and there was a big rent in his trousers, but he kept going. I saw my man had been killed in my arms by a piece of chain, buried to its last link in his breast. I was so confused by the shock of it all that I had not the sense to lay him down, but followed D'ri to the cockpit. He stumbled on the stairs, falling heavily with his burden. Then I dropped my poor gunner and helped them carry D'ri to a table, where they bade me lie down beside him.

"It is no time for jesting," said I, with some dignity.

"My dear fellow," the surgeon answered, "your wound is no jest. You are not fit for duty."

I looked down at the big hole in my trousers and the cut in my thigh, of which I had known nothing until then. I had no sooner seen it and the blood than I saw that I also was in some need of repair, and lay down with a quick sense of faintness. My wound was no pretty thing to see, but was of little consequence, a missile having torn the surface only. I was able to help Surgeon Usher as he caught the severed veins and bathed the bloody strands of muscle in D'ri's arm, while another dressed my thigh. That room was full of the wounded, some lying on the floor, some standing, some stretched upon cots and tables. Every moment they were crowding down the companionway with others. The cannonading was now so close and heavy that it gave me an ache in the ears, but above its quaking thunder I could hear the shrill cries of men sinking to hasty death in the grip of pain. The brig was in sore distress, her timbers creaking, snapping, quivering, like one being beaten to death, his bones cracking, his muscles pulping under heavy blows. We were above water-line there in the cockpit; we could feel her flinch and stagger. On her side there came suddenly a crushing blow, as if some great hammer, swung far in the sky, had come down upon her. I could hear the split and break of heavy timbers; I could see splinters flying over me in a rush of smoke, and the legs of a man go bumping on the beams above. Then came another crash of timbers on the port side. I leaped off the table and ran, limping, to the deck, I do not know why; I was driven by some quick and irresistible impulse. I was near out of my head, anyway, with the rage of battle in me and no chance to fight. Well, suddenly, I found myself stumbling, with drawn sabre, over heaps of the hurt and dead there on our reeking deck. It was a horrible place: everything tipped over, man and gun and mast and bulwark. The air was full of smoke, but near me I could see a topsail of the enemy. Balls were now plunging in the water alongside, the spray drenching our deck. Some poor man lying low among the dead caught me by the boot-leg with an appealing gesture. I took hold of his collar, dragging him to the cockpit. The surgeon had just finished with D'ri. His arm was now in sling and bandages. He was lying on his back, the good arm over his face. There was a lull in the cannonading. I went quickly to his side.

"How are you feeling?" I asked, giving his hand a good grip.

"Nuthin' t' brag uv," he answered. "Never see nobody git hell rose with 'em 's quick es we did—never."

Just then we heard the voice of Perry. He stood on the stairs calling into the cockpit.

"Can any wounded man below there pull a rope?" he shouted.

D'ri was on his feet in a jiffy, and we were both clambering to the deck as another scud of junk went over us. Perry was trying, with block and tackle, to mount a carronade. A handful of men were helping him. D'ri rushed to the ropes, I following, and we both pulled with a will. A sailor who had been hit in the legs hobbled up, asking for room on the rope. I told him he could be of no use, but he spat an oath, and pointing at my leg, which was now bleeding, swore he was sounder than I, and put up his fists to prove it. I have seen no better show of pluck in all my fighting, nor any that ever gave me a greater pride of my own people and my country. War is a great evil, I begin to think, but there is nothing finer than the sight of a man who, forgetting himself, rushes into the shadow of death for the sake of something that is better. At every heave on the rope our blood came out of us, until a ball shattered a pulley, and the gun fell. Perry had then a fierce look, but his words were cool, his manner dauntless. He peered through lifting clouds of smoke at our line. He stood near me, and his head was bare. He crossed the littered deck, his battle-flag and broad pennant that an orderly had brought him trailing from his shoulder. He halted by a boat swung at the davits on the port side—the only one that had not gone to splinters. There he called a crew about him, and all got quickly aboard the boat— seven besides the younger brother of Captain Perry —and lowered it. Word flew that he was leaving to take command of the sister brig, the *Niagara*, which lay off a quarter of a mile or so from where we stood. We all wished to go, but he would have only sound men; there were not a dozen on the ship who had all their blood in them. As they pulled away, Perry standing in the stern, D'ri lifted a bloody, tattered flag, and leaning from the bulwarks, shook it over them, cheering loudly.

"Give it to 'em!" he shouted. "We'll tek care o' the ol' brig."

We were all crying, we poor devils that were left behind. One, a mere boy, stood near me swinging his hat above his head, cheering. Hat and hand fell to the deck as I turned to him. He was reeling, when D'ri caught him quickly with his good arm and bore him to the cockpit.

The little boat was barely a length off when heavy shot fell splashing in her wake. Soon they were dropping all around her. One crossed her bow, ripping a long furrow in the sea. A chip flew off her stern; a lift of splinters from an oar scattered behind her. Plunging missiles marked her course with a plait of foam, but she rode on bravely. We saw her groping under the smoke clouds; we saw her nearing the other brig, and were all on tiptoe. The air cleared a little, and we could see them ship oars and go up the side. Then we set our blood dripping with cheers again, we who were wounded there on the deck of the *Lawrence.* Lieutenant Yarnell ordered her one flag down. As it sank fluttering, we groaned. Our dismay went quickly from man to man. Presently we could hear the cries of the wounded there below. A man came staggering out of the cockpit, and fell to his hands and knees, creeping toward us and protesting fiercely, the blood dripping from his mouth between curses.

" Another shot would sink her," Yarnell shouted.

" Let 'er sink," said D'ri. " Wish t' God I c'u'd put my foot through 'er bottom. When the flag goes down I wan't t' go tew.'

The British turned their guns; we were no longer in the smoky paths of thundering canister. The *Niagara* was now under fire. We could see the dogs of war rushing at her in leashes of flame and smoke. Our little gunboats, urged by oar and sweep, were hastening to the battle front. We could see their men, waist-high above bulwarks, firing as they came. The *Detroit* and the *Queen Charlotte,* two heavy brigs of the British line, had run afoul of each other. The *Niagara,* signalling for close action, bore down upon them. Crossing the bow of one ship and the stern of the other, she raked them with broadsides. We saw braces fly and masts fall in the volley. The *Niagara* sheered off, pouring shoals of metal on a British schooner, stripping her bare. Our little boats had come up, and were boring into the brigs. In a brief time—it was then near three o'clock —a white flag, at the end of a boarding-pike, fluttered over a British deck. D'ri, who had been sitting awhile, was now up and cheering as he waved his crownless hat. He had lent his flag, and, in the flurry, some one dropped it overboard. D'ri saw it fall, and before we could stop him he had leaped into the sea. I hastened to his help, tossing a rope's end as he came up, swimming with one arm, the flag in his teeth. I towed him to the landing-stair and helped him over. Leaning on my shoulder, he shook out the tattered flag, its white laced with his own blood.

Each grabbed a tatter of the good flag, pressing hard upon D'ri, and put it to his lips and kissed it proudly. Then we marched up and down, D'ri waving it above us—a bloody squad as ever walked, shouting loudly. D'ri had begun to weaken with loss of blood, so I coaxed him to go below with me.

The battle was over; a Yankee band was playing near by.

"Perry is coming! Perry is coming!" we heard them shouting.

A feeble cry that had in it pride and joy and inextinguishable devotion passed many a fevered lip in the cockpit.

There were those near who had won a better peace, and they lay as a man that listens to what were now the merest vanity.

Perry came, when the sun was low, with a number of British officers, and received their surrender on his own bloody deck. I remember, as they stood by the ruined bulwarks and looked down upon tokens of wreck and slaughter, a dog began howling dismally in the cockpit.

LORD BACON

FRANCIS BACON (Viscount St. Alban), jurist and philosopher, born in London, 1561; died 1626. He studied three years at Cambridge University and then entered the diplomatic service. In 1618 he was made Lord Chancellor. His essays appeared in 1597. His histories of Henry VII, Henry VIII and Elizabeth rank next in importance. His philosophical works have received the commendation of the scholars of four centuries.

TRANSLATION OF THE 137TH PSALM

WHENAS we sat all sad and desolate,
   By Babylon upon the river's side,
Eased from the tasks which in our captive state
   We were enforcèd daily to abide,
     Our harps we had brought with us to the field,
     Some solace to our heavy souls to yield.

But soon we found we failed of our account,
   For when our minds some freedom did obtain,
Straightways the memory of Sion Mount
   Did cause afresh our wounds to bleed again;
     So that with present gifts, and future fears,
     Our eyes burst forth into a stream of tears.

As for our harps, since sorrow struck them dumb,
   We hanged them on the willow-trees were near;
Yet did our cruel masters to us come,
   Asking of us some Hebrew songs to hear:
     Taunting us rather in our misery,
     Than much delighting in our melody.

Alas (said we) who can once force or frame
  His grievèd and oppressèd heart to sing
The praises of Jehovah's glorious name,
  In banishment, under a foreign king?
    In Sion is his seat and dwelling-place,
    Thence doth he show the brightness of his face.

Hierusalem, where God his throne hath set,
  Shall any hour absent thee from my mind?
Then let my right hand quite her skill forget,
  Then let my voice and words no passage find;
    Nay, if I do not thee prefer in all
    That in the compass of my thoughts can fall.

Remember thou, O Lord, the cruel cry
  Of Eden's children, which did ring and sound,
Inciting the Chaldean's cruelty,
  "Down with it, down with it, even unto the ground."
    In that good day repay it unto them,
    When thou shalt visit thy Hierusalem.

And thou, O Babylon, shalt have thy turn
  By just revenge, and happy shall he be,
That thy proud walls and towers shall waste and burn,
  And as thou didst by us, so do by thee.
    Yea, happy he that takes thy children's bones,
    And dasheth them against the pavement stones.

LIFE

THE World's a bubble, and the Life of Man
      Less than a span:
In his conception wretched, from the womb,
      So to the tomb;
Curst from his cradle, and brought up to years
      With cares and fears.
Who then to frail mortality shall trust,
But limns on water, or but writes in dust.

Yet whilst with sorrow here we live opprest,
    What life is best?
Courts are but only superficial schools
    To dandle fools:
The rural parts are turn'ed into a den
    Of savage men:
And where's a city from foul vice so free,
But may be term'd the worst of all the three?

Domestic cares afflict the husband's bed,
    Or pains his head:
Those that live single, take it for a curse,
    Or do things worse:
Some would have children: those that have them,
      moan
    Or wish them gone:
What is it, then, to have, or have no wife,
But single thraldom, or a double strife?

Our own affection still at home to please
    Is a disease:
To cross the seas to any foreign soil,
    Peril and toil:
Wars with their noise affright us; when they cease
    We are worse in peace;
What then remains, but that we still should cry
For being born, or, being born, to die?

OF LOVE

THE stage is more beholding to love than the life
of men; for as to the stage, love is even matter of comedies, and now and then of tragedies;
but in life it doth much mischief; sometimes like a
siren, sometimes like a fury. You may observe that
amongst all the great and worthy persons (whereof
the memory remaineth, either ancient or recent)

there is not one that hath been transported to the mad degree of love, which shows that great spirits and great business do keep out this weak passion. You must except, nevertheless, Marcus Antonius, the half partner of the empire of Rome, and Appius Claudius, the decemvir and law-giver; whereof the former was indeed a voluptuous man, and inordinate; but the latter was an austere and wise man; and therefore it seems (though rarely) that love can find entrance, not only into an open heart, but also into a heart well fortified, if watch be not well kept. It is a poor saying of Epicurus, "Satis magnum alter alteri theatrum sumus"; as if man, made for the contemplation of heaven, and all noble objects, should do nothing but kneel before a little idol, and make himself a subject, though not of the mouth (as beasts are), yet of the eye, which was given him for higher purposes. It is a strange thing to note the excess of this passion, and how it braves the nature and value of things by this, that the speaking in a perpetual hyperbole is comely in nothing but love; neither is it merely in the phrase; for whereas it hath been well said, "That the arch flatterer, with whom all the pretty flatterers have intelligence, is a man's self"; certainly the lover is more; for there was never a proud man thought so absurdly well of himself as the lover doth of the person loved; and therefore it was well said, "That it is impossible to love and to be wise." Neither doth this weakness appear to others only, and not to the party loved, but to the loved most of all, except the love be reciprocal; for it is a true rule, that love is ever rewarded, either with the reciprocal or with an inward or secret contempt; by how much more the men ought to beware of this passion, which loseth not only other things, but itself. As for the other losses, the poet's relation doth well figure them: "That he that preferred Helena quitted the gifts of Juno and Pallas"; for whosoever esteemeth too much of amorous affection quitteth both riches and wisdom. This passion hath its floods in the very times of weakness, which are great prosperity and great adversity, though this latter hath been less observed; both which times kindle love, and make it more fervent, and therefore show it to be the child of folly. They do best who, if they cannot but admit love, yet make it keep quarter, and sever it wholly from their serious affairs and actions of life; for if it check once with business, it troubleth men's fortunes, and maketh men that they can no ways be true to their own ends. I know not how, but martial men are given to love; I think it is but as they are given to wine; for perils commonly ask to be paid in pleasures.

There is in man's nature a secret inclination and motion towards love of others, which, if it be not spent upon some one or a few, doth naturally spread itself towards many, and maketh men become humane and charitable, as it is seen sometimes in friars. Nuptial love maketh mankind; friendly love perfecteth it; but wanton love corrupteth and embasseth it.

OF DEATH

MEN fear death as children fear to go in the dark; and as that natural fear in children is increased with tales, so is the other. Certainly, the contemplation of death, as the wages of sin, and the passage to another world, is holy and religious; but the fear of it, as a tribute due unto nature, is weak. Yet in religious meditations there is sometimes mixture of vanity and of superstition. And by him that spake only as a philosopher and natural man, it was well said, "The surroundings of death terrify more than death itself." It is worthy the

observing that there is no passion of the mind of
man so weak but it mates and masters the fear of
death; and therefore death is no such terrible enemy, when a man hath so many attendants about
him that can win the combat of him. Revenge triumphs over death; love slights it; honor aspireth
to it; grief flieth to it; fear preoccupieth it—nay,
we read, after Otho the emperor had slain himself,
pity (which is the tenderest of affections) provoked
many to die out of mere compassion to their sovereign, and as the truest sort of followers. It is
as natural to die as to be born; and to a little
infant, perhaps, the one is as painful as the other.
He that dies in an earnest pursuit is like one that
is wounded in hot blood, who, for the time, scarce
feels the hurt; and therefore a mind fixed and bent
upon somewhat that is good doth avert the dolors
of death. But, above all, believe it, the sweetest
canticle is *Nunc dimittis,* when a man hath obtained
worthy ends and expectations. Death hath this also,
that it openeth the gate to good fame and extin-
guisheth envy. "The same person shall be beloved
when dead."

OF MARRIAGE AND SINGLE LIFE

HE that hath wife and children hath given host-
ages to fortune; for they are impediments to
great enterprises, either of virtue or mischief. Certainly the best works, and of greatest merit for the
public, have proceeded from the unmarried or child-
less men, which both in affection and means have
married and endowed the public. Yet it were great
reason that those that have children should have
greatest care of future times, unto which they
know they must transmit their dearest pledges. Unmarried men are best friends, best masters, best

servants; but not always best subjects; for they are light to run away—and almost all fugitives are of that condition. A single life doth well with churchmen, for charity will hardly water the ground where it must first fill a pool. It is indifferent for judges and magistrates; for if they be facile and corrupt, you shall have a servant five times worse than a wife. For soldiers, I find generals commonly, in their hortatives, put men in mind of their wives and their children, and I think the despising of marriage amongst the Turks maketh the vulgar soldier more base. Certainly, wife and children are a kind of discipline of humanity; and single men, though they be many times more charitable, because their means are less exhaust, yet, on the other side, they are more cruel and hard-hearted (good to make severe inquisitors), because their tenderness is not so oft called upon. Wives are young men's mistresses; companions for middle age, and old mens' nurses; so that a man may have a quarrel to marry when he will. But yet he was reputed one of the wise men that made answer to the question when a man should marry: " A young man, not yet; an elder man, not at all."

JOANNA BAILLIE

JOANNA BAILLIE, a Scottish poetess, born in Both-well, Lanarkshire, 1762; died in England in 1851. She was encouraged in her literary aspirations by Sir Walter Scott, and "The Family Legend," from her "Plays on the Passions," was presented at Edin-burgh under his auspices. She is known to our day through a number of short poems.

WOO'D AND MARRIED AND A'

THE bride she is winsome and bonny,
 Her hair it is snooded sae sleek,
And faithfu' and kind is her Johnny,
 Yet fast fa' the tears on her cheek.
New pearlins are cause of her sorrow,
 New pearlins and plenishing, too:
The bride that has a' to borrow
 Has e'en right mickle ado.
  Woo'd and married and a'!
  Woo'd and married and a'!
  Isna she very weel aff
   To be woo'd and married at a'?

Her mither then hastily spak':
 "The lassie is glaikit wi' pride;
In my pouch I had never a plack
 On the day when I was a bride.
E'en tak' to your wheel, and be clever,
 And draw out your thread in the sun;
The gear that is gifted, it never
 Will last like the gear that is won.

Woo'd and married and a'!
Wi' havins and tocher sae sma'!
I think ye are very weel aff
To be woo'd and married at a'!"

"Toot, toot!" quo' her gray-headed faither,
"She's less o' a bride than a bairn;
She's ta'en like a cout frae the heather,
Wi' sense and discretion to learn.
Half husband, I trow, and half daddy,
As humor inconstantly leans,
The chiel maun be patient and steady,
That yokes wi' a mate in her teens.
A kerchief sae douce and sae neat,
O'er her locks that the wind used to blaw!
I'm baith like to laugh and to greet,
When I think o' her married at a'!"

Then out spak' the wily bridegroom,
Weel waled were his wordies, I ween:—
"I'm rich, though my coffer be toom,
Wi' the blinks o' your bonny blue een.
I'm prouder o' thee by my side,
Though thy ruffles or ribbons be few,
Than if Kate o' the Croft were my bride,
Wi' purfles and pearlins enow.
Dear and dearest of ony!
Ye're woo'd and buikit and a'!
And do ye think scorn o' your Johnny,
And grieve to be married at a', ?"

She turn'd and she blush'd and she smil'd,
And she looket sae bashfully down;
The pride o' her heart was beguil'd,
And she played wi' the sleeves o' her gown;

She twirled the tag o' her lace,
  And she nippet her bodice sae blue,
Syne blinket sae sweet in his face,
  And aff like a maukin she flew.
    Woo'd and married and a' !
    Wi' Johnny to roose her and a' !
  She thinks hersel' very weel aff,
    To be woo'd and married and a' !

IT WAS ON A MORN

IT was on a morn, when we were thrang,
  The kirn it crooned, the cheese was making,
  And bannocks on the girdle baking,
When ane at the door chappt ioud and lang.

Yet the auld gudewife and her mays sae tight,
  Of a' this bauld din took sma' notice, I ween;
For a chap at the door in braid daylight
  Is no like a chap that's heard at e'en.

But the docksy auld laird of the Warlock glen,
  Wha waited without, half blate, half cheery,
  And langed for a sight o' his winsome deary,
Raised up the latch, and came crousely ben.

His coat it was new and his o'erlay was white,
  His mittens and hose were cozie and bien;
But a wooer that comes in braid daylight
  Is no like a wooer that comes at e'en.

He greeted the carline and lasses sae braw,
  And his bare lyart pow sae smoothly he straikit
  And he looket about, like a body half glaikit,
On bonny sweet Nanny, the youngest o' a'.

" Ha, laird!" quo' the carline, "and look ye that
way?
Fye, let na' sic fancies bewilder you clean:
An elderlin man, in the noon o' the day,
Should be wiser than youngsters that come at e'en."

" Na, na," quo' the pawky auld wife, " I trow,
You'll no' fash your head wi' a youthfu' gilly,
As wild and as skeig as a muirland filly;
Black Madge is far better and fitter for you."

He hem'd and he haw'd, and he drew in his mouth,
And he squeezed the blue bannet his twa hands
between,
For a wooer that comes when the sun 's i' the south
Is mair landward than wooers that come at e'en.

" Black Madge is sae carefu' "—" What's that to
me?"
" She's sober and eydent, has sense in her noddle:
She's douce and respeckit "—" I care na' a bodle:
Love winna be guided, and fancy 's free."

Madge tossed back her head wi' a saucy slight,
And Nanny, loud laughing, ran out to the green;
For a wooer that comes when the sun shines bright
Is no like a wooer that comes at e'en.

Then away flung the laird, and loud mutter'd he,
" A' the daughters of Eve, between Orkney and
Tweed, O !
Black or fair, young or auld, dame or damsel or
widow,
May gang in their pride to the de'il for me !"

But the auld gudewife and her mays sae tight
Cared little for a' his stour banning, I ween;
For a wooer that comes in braid daylight
Is no like a wooer that comes at e'en.

HONORÉ DE BALZAC

HONORÉ DE BALZAC, the greatest of French novelists, born at Tours in 1799; died in Paris in 1850. He began the writing of short stories when still in his teens, and at twenty-five had published about thirty. None were popular. In 1829 he published "Les Derniers Chouans," which established his reputation.

THE GREATNESS AND THE DECLINE OF CÉSAR BIROTTEAU

(Copyright by Little, Brown & Co., Miss Wormeley, translator)

WHEN César came to Paris, he could read, write, and cipher; his education stopped there; his laborious life had hindered him from acquiring any ideas and knowledge foreign to the business of perfumery. Constantly mingling with people who were indifferent to science and letters, whose education did not go beyond specialties; having no time to devote to elevating studies, the perfumer became a practical man. He was forced to adopt the language, errors, opinions of the Parisian bourgeois —the class who admire Molière, Voltaire and Rousseau on faith, who purchase their works without reading them; who maintain that it is proper to say *ormoire*, because ladies lock up in those articles of furniture their *or* (gold) and their dresses which formerly were almost always made of *moire*, and that *armoire* is a corruption. Potier, Talma, Mademoiselle Mars, were, the bourgeois believes, millionaires ten times over, and did not live like other human beings; the great tragedian ate man-flesh; Mademoiselle Mars sometimes made a fricassee of pearls, in imitation of a celebrated Egyptian actress. The Emperor had leather pockets in his waistcoats to enable him to take snuff by the handful, and rode at full gallop up the stairs of the orangery at Versailles. Authors and artists died in the hospital in consequence of their oddities; they were, besides, all atheists, whom it behooved people not to admit into their houses. Joseph Lebas cited, with a shudder, the history of his sister-in-law Augustine's marriage with the painter Sommervieux. Astronomers lived on spiders. These luminous specimens of their knowledge of the French language, of dramatic art, politics, literature, and science, indicate the scope of their intellects. A poet, who passes along the rue des Lombards, and inhales the prevailing perfumes, may dream of Asia there. Breathing the odor of vetyver in a green-house, he may behold the almées of the East. The splendors of cochineal remind him of the poems, the religion, the castes of the Brahmins. Coming in contact with inwrought ivory, he mounts, in imagination, upon the back of an elephant, and there, in a muslin pavilion, makes love like the king of Lahore. But the shop-keeper is ignorant whence come the articles in which he deals, and where they grow. Birotteau knew nothing whatever of natural history or chemistry. In regarding Vauquelin as a great man, he considered him as an exception; he resembled the retired grocer who thus shrewdly summed up a discussion on the way in which tea is brought to France: "Tea comes only in two ways, *by caravan* or *by Havre.*" According to Birotteau, aloes and opium were to be found only in the rue des Lombards. The pretended rose-water of Constantinople was made, like cologne-water, at Paris. These names of places were shams, invented to please the French, who cannot endure the productions of their own country. A French merchant was bound to call his discovery English, in order to make it popular, as in England a druggist attributes his to France. Nevertheless, César could not be quite a dunce and a blockhead; integrity and benevolence gave respectability to the acts of his life, for a good deed obliterates any amount of ignorance. His constant success gave him assurance. At Paris, assurance is accepted for the power of which it is the sign.

Having thoroughly learned the character of César during the first three years of their married life, his wife was in a constant fever of anxiety; she represented, in this union, the part of sagacity and foresight, doubt, hesitation and fear; as César represented that of audacity, ambition, action, and the extraordinary success of fatality. In spite of appearances, the tradesman was timid, whilst his wife possessed real patience and courage. Thus, a narrow-minded and ordinary man, without education, without ideas, without knowledge, without decided character, who, on general principles, could not have succeeded on the most uncertain market in the world, came, by his discreet conduct, by his sentiment of justice, by his truly Christian goodness of heart, by his love for the only woman he had ever possessed, to be regarded as a remarkable man, as one courageous and full of resolution. The public saw the results only. His associates, with the exception of Pillerault and Judge Popinot, saw César but superficially, and could not form an opinion of him. Besides, the twenty or thirty friends who associated with each other were constantly uttering the same stupidities, repeating the same common-places, and all regarded each other as superior beings in their own walks of life. The women vied with each other in dinners and dress; each one of them had said all she knew when she had said a word of contempt for her husband. Madame Birotteau alone had the good sense to treat hers with honor and respect in public; she saw in him a man who in spite of his secret incapacity, had acquired their fortune, and in whose consideration she participated. She sometimes asked herself, however, what the world could be, if all men of pretended superiority resembled her husband. Such conduct contributed not a little to sustain the respectful esteem awarded to a tradesman, in a country where women are so prone to bring their husbands into disrespect and to complain of them in public.

César was now forty years old. The labors which he performed in his laboratory had given him a few premature wrinkles, and had slightly silvered his long bushy hair, around which the pressure of his hat made a glistening circular impression. His heavy eyebrows might have alarmed the beholder, had not his blue eyes, with their clear and honest expression, been in perfect harmony with his open and manly forehead. His nose, broken at its base, and very large at the end, gave him the surprised air of the *quidnuncs* of Paris. His lips were full, and his fat chin hung perpendicularly down. His square and highly colored face indicated, by the disposition of the wrinkles and the general style of his physiognomy, the ingenuous cunning of the peasant. The strength of his body, the heaviness of his limbs, the squareness of his back, and the width of his feet— everything about him in short—denoted the villager transported to Paris. His large and hairy hands, his fat, wrinkled fingers, his big square nails, would have borne witness to his origin, even if there had been no traces of it in his person. He had constantly upon his lips that benevolent smile which shop-keepers assume upon the entrance of a customer; and yet this commercial smile was the faithful image of his internal content, and represented the true state of his tranquil soul. His habitual distrust never went beyond his business; his caution left him when he crossed the threshold of the Exchange or when he closed his ledger. Suspicion was to him what his printed bill-heads were, a necessary and component part of all bargain and sale. His face presented a sort of comic assurance, of fatuity mingled with good-fellowship, which rendered him an original type, as it took away from the resemblance, otherwise perfect, with the flat physiognomy of the Parisian bourgeois. Without this air of guileless admiration and faith in himself, he would have inspired too much respect; he thus maintained his relationship with mankind, by contributing his share of the ridiculous.

When talking, he habitually held his hands behind his back. When he thought he had said something smart or gallant, he raised himself twice upon his toes, and fell back again heavily, as if to emphasize his remark. In the heat of a discussion, he would sometimes turn briskly round, walk a few steps as if he were going to seek for further arguments, and return sharply upon his antagonist. He never interrupted a speaker, and often fell a victim to this exact observance of propriety, for the other cut in whenever they could, and the poor man would be obliged to depart without getting in a word edgewise. His great experience in commercial matters had given him certain peculiar ways which many persons called manias. When a note was not taken up, he sent it to the proper officer, and thought no more of it except to receive the principal, interest and expenses; the officer had instructions to press the matter until the tradesman was bankrupt, and then to stop all proceedings: César put the notes in his pockets and never went to any meetings of the creditors. This system and his implacable detestation of bankrupts, he had derived from Ragon, who, in the course of his mercantile experience, had discovered that so much time was lost in litigation, that the meager and uncertain dividend produced by arrangements and compromises was more than compensated by the time spent in going and coming, and running after the excuses the dishonest are ever so ready to make.

"If the bankrupt is an honest man," said Ragon, "and recovers himself, he will pay you. If he still continues penniless, and is simply unfortunate, why torment him? And if he is a rascal, you'll never get anything any way. Your well-known severity causes you to be regarded as intractable, and as no compromise with you is possible, as long as a man can pay any one, it's you that he pays."

César arrived at an appointment the moment agreed upon, and ten minutes afterward he left with an inflexibility that nothing could conquer; so that his own punctuality rendered those who had business with him punctual themselves.

The costume which he had adopted was in harmony with his manners and his physiognomy. No power on earth could have induced him to give up his white muslin cravats, the ends of which, embroidered by his wife or his daughter, hung down under his neck. His single-breasted white Marseilles waistcoat came very low down upon his somewhat prominent stomach; for César was slightly corpulent. He wore blue pantaloons, black silk stockings, and shoes, the strings of which were constantly coming untied. His olive-green frock-coat, always too large for him, and his broad-brimmed hat, gave him the air of a quaker. When he dressed himself for Sunday evening, he put on a pair of silk smallclothes, shoes with gilt buckles, and his inevitable single-breasted waistcoat, slightly open at the top to show his plaited shirt-frill. His chestnut-colored cloth coat was long in the waist and wide in the skirts. He continued, up to 1819, to wear two watch-chains, hanging parallel to each other, but he only put on the second when he considered himself dressed.

Such was César Birotteau, a worthy creature upon whom the mysterious deities who attend upon the birth of men had refused to confer the power of taking general views either of politics or life, or that of raising himself above the social level of the middling classes. He followed in everything the winding ways of routine; every opinion which he held had been communicated to him by others, and he applied them without examination. Blind but good, not intellectual but profoundly religious, he was a man perfectly pure in heart. In his heart burned one first and only love, the light and strength of his life; for his endeavors to rise, and the little information he had acquired, sprang from his affection for his wife and daughter.

As for Madame César, thirty-seven years old at this time, she resembled the Venus of Milo so closely that all who knew her saw her very portrait in that admirable statue when the Duc de Rivière sent it to Paris. In a few months, however, sorrow and trouble so diffused their yellow tints over her dazzlingly white skin, so cruelly undermined and disclosed the bluish circle within which played her fine sparkling eyes, that she had the appearance of an old madonna; for she still preserved, in the midst of her decay, a pleasing ingenuousness of manner, a pure though melancholy look, and it was impossible not to consider her still a handsome woman, and one singularly reserved and dignified in her demeanor. At the ball contemplated by César, she was destined to enjoy one final and public triumph of beauty.

Every life has its apogee—a period during which the causes which operate are in exact proportion with the results they produce. This high noon of existence, in which every moving force is in equilibrium and is manifested in its highest state, is common, not only to organized beings, but to cities, nations, ideas, institutions, trades, enterprises; all of which, like noble families and dynasties, spring up, come to perfection, and fall. Whence comes the severe impartiality with which this theme of increase and decay is applied to all earthly organizations? For death itself, in times of plague or epidemic, now advances, now slackens its course, now revives and now sleeps. Our globe itself is perhaps a mere rocket, a little more durable than the rest. History, in perpetually repeating the causes of the greatness and decline of everything that has been seen on earth, ought, one would think, to warn mankind of the proper time to arrest the play of their faculties; but neither conquerors nor actors, neither women nor authors, ever listen to its salutary voice.

César Birotteau, who should have regarded himself as having arrived at the apogee of his fortunes, chose to consider this halting-time as a new point of departure. He did not know—and neither nations nor kings have sought to write them in ineffaceable characters—the causes of the downfalls with which history is rife, and of which both mercantile and sovereign houses have furnished such terrible examples. Why should not new pyramids be erected, to keep continually before the world this principle, applicable not only to the politics of nations but to the economy of private individuals, that *whenever the effect produced has ceased to be in direct connection and in equal proportion with its cause, disorganization has begun?* Such movements, however, are everywhere to be seen, in the traditions and stories which speak to us of the past, which embody the caprices of ungovernable destiny, whose hand effaces our dreams and shows us that the greatest events are summed up in an idea. Troy and Napoleon are naught but poems. May this history be the poem of the obscure domestic vicissitudes in behalf of which no voice has been raised, all destitute, as they appear, of greatness; while, on the contrary, and for the same reason, they are immense. We are not now treating of individual woes, but of the sufferings of a people.

* * * * * * *

The ball, like a blazing rocket, died out and came to an end at five o'clock in the morning. At that time, but forty carriages remained of the hundred and odd which had filled the rue St. Honoré. The company were dancing a country dance—dethroned in after years by the German cotillion and the English galop. Du Tillet, Roguin, Cardot, junior, the Count de Grandville, and Jules Desmarets were at the gaming table. Du Tillet had won three thousand francs. The first rays of dawn appeared and paled the light of the candles: the players rose and witnessed the closing dance. In the houses of the bourgeois, the transports of the breaking up rarely pass without the enactment of a few extravagances. The important characters are gone: the intoxication of the motion, the communicative warmth of the atmosphere, the spirit lurking in the most apparently innocent beverages, have by this time softened even the old ladies' stiffest joints, and they complaisantly take part in the dance, and yield to the folly of the moment; the men perspire, their hair comes out of curl and hangs down limp over their faces, giving them a grotesque and laughter-provoking aspect; the young women become giddy, and the wreaths upon their heads begin to rain flowers upon the floor. The Momus of the bourgeois appears, and mirth follows in his train! A burst of laughter welcomes him, and everybody gives himself up to tom-foolery, knowing that on the morrow labor will reclaim their service. Matifat danced with a woman's bonnet on his head; Célestin abandoned himself to buffoonery. A few of the women frantically clapped their hands together when required by the figure of this interminable dance.

"What a good time they are having!" said Birotteau, delighted.

"I only hope they won't break anything," said Constance to her uncle.

"Your ball is the most magnificent I have ever seen, and I have seen a great many," said du Tillet to his former master on bidding him good night.

In that sublime composition—the eight symphonies of Beethoven—there is a fantasia with all the grandeur of an epic poem, which is the burden of the finale to the symphony in C minor. When, after the dallying preparations of the sublime magician so admirably interpreted by Habeneck, the leader of the orchestra, a wave of that enthusiast's hand rolls up the rich curtain of the scene, summoning forth with his baton the dazzling theme in which all the powers of music have been concentrated, poets, whose hearts then beat within them, will comprehend how Birotteau's ball produced, in his simple life, the effect produced upon them by this teeming air, to which, perhaps, the symphony in C owes its supremacy over its brilliant sisters. A radiant fairy darts forward and raises her wand. The listener hears the rustling of the purple curtain, raised by angels' hands. Gates of gold, sculptured like the portals of the Florentine Baptistery, revolve on their diamond hinges. The eye is lost in splendid views; at one glance it embraces a colonnade of marvelous palaces, in which flit beings of heavenly birth. The incense of glory smokes, the altar of happiness flashes, you breathe a perfumed air! Creatures, whose smile is divine, clothed in white tunics edged with blue, pass lightly before your eyes, disclosing faces of superhuman beauty and forms of infinite grace. Cupids hover around, shedding the light of their torches upon the scene. You feel yourself beloved: you are blessed in a happiness which you inhale without comprehending how, bathed in the waves of harmony which flows in living streams, and runs for all, with the nectar they have chosen. The sweet aspirations of your heart are for one instant realized. The enchanter, having convoyed you through the heavens, plunges you back, by the profound and mysterious transition of the violoncellos, into the morass of cold realities, to drag you forth once more, when you thirst anew for his divine melodies, and when your soul cries out, Again! The psychologic analysis of the culminating point of this glorious finale will answer for that of the emotions showered on César and Constance by this wondrous festivity. Collinet, Birotteau's chief musician, had performed the finale of their commercial symphony upon his squeaking three-holed fife.

Weary, but blest, the three Birotteaus fell asleep by daylight, to the dying murmurs of this ball, which, in buildings, repairs, furniture, refreshments, and dress, cost, though César was far from suspecting it, hard upon sixty thousand francs. Such was the issue of the fatal red ribbon fastened by a king to a perfumer's buttonhole. Should César Birotteau meet with misfortune, this absurd expenditure was enough to bring him before the correctional police. A tradesman who goes to expenses considered inordinate in his position, may be found guilty of simple bankruptcy, as distinguished from fraudulent bankruptcy. It is perhaps worse to go before a petty tribunal charged with folly and indiscretion, than to appear at the bar of the court of assizes for one immense imposture. In the eyes of certain people, it is better to be criminal than weak.

EUGÉNIE GRANDET

IN the pure and monotonous life of young girls there comes a delicious hour when the sun sheds its rays into their soul, when the flowers express their thoughts, when the throbbings of the heart send upward to the brain their fertilizing warmth and melt all thoughts into a vague desire—day of innocent melancholy and dulcet joys! When babes begin to see, they smile; when a young girl first perceives the sentiment of nature, she smiles as she smiled when an infant. If light is the first love of life, is not love a light to the heart? The moment to see within the veil of earthly things had come for Eugénie.

An early riser, like all provincial girls, she was up betimes and said her prayers, and then began the business of dressing—a business which henceforth was to have a meaning. First she brushed and smoothed her chestnut hair and twisted its heavy masses to the top of her head with the utmost care, preventing the loose tresses from straying, and giving to her head a symmetry which heightened the timid candor of her face; for the simplicity of these accessories accorded well with the innocent sincerity of its lines. As she washed her hands again and again in the cold water which hardened and reddened the skin, she looked at her handsome round arms and asked herself what her cousin did to make his hands so softly white, his nails so delicately curved. She put on new stockings and her prettiest shoes. She laced her corset straight, without skipping a single eyelet. And then, wishing for the first time in her life to appear to advantage, she felt the joy of having a new gown, well made, which rendered her attractive.

As she finished her toilet the clock of the parish

church struck the hour: to her astonishment, it was only seven. The desire of having plenty of time for dressing carefully had led her to get up too early. Ignorant of the art of retouching every curl and studying every effect, Eugénie simply crossed her arms, sat down by the window, and looked at the court-yard, the narrow garden, and the high terraced walls that overtopped it: a dismal, hedged-in prospect, yet not wholly devoid of those mysterious beauties which belong to solitary or uncultivated nature. Near the kitchen was a well surrounded by a curb, with a pulley fastened to a bent iron rod clasped by a vine whose leaves were withered, reddened, and shriveled by the season. From thence the tortuous shoots straggled to the wall, clutched it, and ran the whole length of the house, ending near the wood-pile, where the logs were ranged with as much precision as the books in a library. The pavement of the court-yard showed the black stains produced in time by lichens, herbage, and the absence of all movement or friction. The thick walls wore a coating of green moss streaked with waving brown lines, and the eight stone steps at the bottom of the court-yard which led up to the gate of the garden were disjoined and hidden beneath tall plants, like the tomb of a knight buried by his widow in the days of the Crusades. Above a foundation of moss-grown, crumbling stones was a trellis of rotten wood, half fallen from decay; over them clambered and intertwined at will a mass of clustering creepers. On each side of the latticed gate stretched the crooked arms of two stunted apple-trees. Three parallel walks, gravelled and separated from each other by square beds, where the earth was held in by box-borders, made the garden, which terminated, beneath a terrace of the old walls, in a group of lindens. At the farther end were raspberry-bushes; at the other, near the house, an immense walnut-tree drooped its branches almost into the window of the miser's sanctum.

A clear day and the beautiful autumnal sun common to the banks of the Loire were beginning to melt the hoar-frost which the night had lain on these picturesque objects, on the walls, and on the plants which swathed the garden and the court-yard. Eugénie found a novel charm in the aspect of things lately so insignificant to her. A thousand confused thoughts came to birth in her mind and grew there, as the sunbeams grew without along the wall. She felt that impulse of delight, vague, inexplicable, which wraps the moral being as a cloud wraps the physical body. Her thoughts were all in keeping with the details of this strange landscape, and the harmonies of her heart blended with the harmonies of nature. When the sun reached an angle of the wall where the "Venus-hair" of southern climes drooped its thick leaves, lit with the changing colors of a pigeon's breast, celestial rays of hope illumined the future to her eyes, and thenceforth she loved to gaze upon that piece of wall, on its pale flowers, its blue harebells, its wilting herbage, with which she mingled memories as tender as those of childhood. The noise made by each leaf as it fell from its twig in the void of that echoing court gave answer to the secret questionings of the young girl, who could have stayed there the livelong day without perceiving the flight of time. Then came tumultuous heavings of the soul. She rose often, went to her glass, and looked at herself, as an author in good faith looks at his work to criticize it and blame it in his own mind.

"I am not beautiful enough for him!" Such was Eugénie's thought,—a humble thought, fertile in suffering. The poor girl did not do herself justice; but modesty, or rather fear, is among the first of love's virtues: Eugénie belonged to the type of children with sturdy constitutions, such as we see among the lesser bourgeoisie, whose beauties always seem a little vulgar; and yet, though she resembled the Venus of Milo, the lines of her figure were ennobled by the softer Christian sentiment which purifies womanhood and gives it a distinction unknown to the sculptors of antiquity. She had an enormous head, with the masculine yet delicate forehead of the Jupiter of Phidias, and gray eyes, to which her chaste life, penetrating fully into them, carried a flood of light. The features of her round face, formerly fresh and rosy, were at one time swollen by the smallpox, which destroyed the velvet texture of her skin, though it kindly left no other traces, and her cheek was still so soft and delicate that her mother's kiss made a momentary red mark upon it. Her nose was somewhat too thick, but it harmonized well with the vermilion mouth, whose lips, creased in many lines, were full of love and kindness. The throat was exquisitely round. The bust, well curved and carefully covered, attracted the eye and inspired revery. It lacked, no doubt, the grace which a fitting dress can bestow; but to a connoisseur the non-flexibility of her figure had its own charm. Eugénie, tall and strongly made, had none of the prettiness which pleases the masses; but she was beautiful with a beauty which the spirit recognizes, and none but artists truly love. A painter seeking here below for a type of Mary's celestial purity, searching womankind for those proud modest eyes which Raphael divined, for those virgin lines, often due to chances of conception, which the modesty of Christian life alone can bestow or keep unchanged,—such a painter, in love with his ideal, would have found in the face of Eugénie the innate nobleness that is ignorant of itself; he would have seen beneath the calmness of that brow a world of love; he would have felt, in the shape of the eyes, in the fall of the eyelids, the presence of the name-less something that we call divine. Her features, the contour of her head, which no expression of pleasure had ever altered or wearied, were like the lines of the horizon softly traced in the far distance across the tranquil lakes. That calm and rosy countenance, margined with light like a lovely full-blown flower, rested the mind, held the eye, and imparted the charm of the conscience that was there reflected. Eugénie was standing on the shore of life where young illusions flower, where daisies are gathered with delights ere long to be unknown; and thus she said, looking at her image in the glass, unconscious as yet of love: " I am too ugly; he will not notice me."

Then she opened the door of her chamber which led to the staircase, and stretched out her neck to listen for the household noises. "He is not up," she thought, hearing Nanon's morning cough as the good soul went and came, sweeping out the halls, lighting the fire, chaining the dog, and speaking to the beasts in the stable. Eugénie at once went down and ran to Nanon, who was milking the cow.

" Nanon, my good Nanon, make a little cream for my cousin's breakfast."

" Why, mademoiselle, you should have thought of that yesterday," said Nanon, bursting into a loud peal of laughter. " I can't make cream. Your cousin is a darling, a darling! oh, that he is! You should have seen him in his dressing gown, all silk and gold! I saw him, I did! He wears linen as fine as the surplice of monsieur lecuré."

" Nanon, please make us a galette."

" And who'll give me wood for the oven, and flour and butter for the cakes ? " said Nanon, who in her function of prime-minister to Grandet assumed at times enormous importance in the eyes of Eugénie and her mother. " Mustn't rob the master to feast the cousin. You ask him for butter and flour and wood: he's your father, perhaps he'll give you some. See! there he is now, coming to give out the provisions."

Eugénie escaped into the garden, quite frightened as she heard the staircase shaking under her father's step. Already she felt the effects of that virgin modesty and that special consciousness of happiness which lead us to fancy, not perhaps without reason, that our thoughts are graven on our foreheads and are open to the eyes of all. Perceiving for the first time the cold nakedness of her father's house, the poor girl felt a sort of rage that she could not put it in harmony with her cousin's elegance. She felt the need of doing something for him,—what, she did not know. Ingenuous and truthful, she followed her angelic nature without mistrusting her impressions or her feelings. The mere sight of her cousin had wakened within her the natural yearnings of a woman,—yearnings that were the more likely to develop ardently because, having reached her twenty-third year, she was in the plenitude of her intelligence and her desires. For the first time in her life her heart was full of terror at the sight of her father; in him she saw the master of her fate, and she fancied herself guilty of wrong-doing in hiding from his knowledge certain thoughts. She walked with hasty steps, surprised to breathe a purer air, to feel the sun's rays quickening her pulses, to absorb from their heat a moral warmth and a new life. As she turned over in her mind some stratagem by which to get the cake, a quarrel—an event as rare as the sight of swallows in winter—broke out between la Grande Nanon and Grandet. Armed with his keys, the master had come to dole out provisions for the day's consumption.

"Is there any bread left from yesterday?" he said to Nanon.

"Not a crumb, monsieur."

Grandet took a large round loaf, well floured and moulded in one of the flat baskets, which they use for baking in Anjou, and was about to cut it, when Nanon said to him,—

"We are five to-day, monsieur."

"That's true," said Grandet, "but your loaves weigh six pounds; there'll be some left. Besides, these young fellows from Paris don't eat bread, you'll see."

"Then they must eat *frippe?*" said Nanon.

Frippe is a word of the local lexicon of Anjou, and means any accompaniment of bread, from butter which is spread upon it, the commonest kind of *frippe,* to peach preserve, the most distinguished of all *frippes;* those who in their childhood have licked the *frippe* and left the bread, will comprehend the meaning of Nanon's speech.

"No," answered Grandet, "they eat neither bread nor *frippe;* they are something like marriageable girls."

After ordering the meals for the day with his usual parsimony, the good man, having locked the closets containing the supplies, was about to go towards the fruit-garden, when Nanon stopped him to say,—

"Monsieur, give me a little flour and some butter, and I'll make a *galette* for the young ones."

"Are you going to pillage the house on account of my nephew?"

"I wasn't thinking any more of your nephew than I was of your dog,—not more than you think yourself; for, look here, you've only forked out six bits of sugar. I want eight."

"What's all this, Nanon? I have never seen you like this before. What have you got in your head? Are you the mistress here? You sha'n't have more than six pieces of sugar."

"Well, then, how is your nephew to sweeten his coffee?"

"With two pieces; I'll go without myself."

"Go without sugar at your age! I'd rather buy you some out of my own pocket."

"Mind your own business."

In spite of the recent fall of prices, sugar was still in Grandet's eyes the most valuable of all the colonial products; to him it was always six francs a pound. The necessity of economizing it. acquired under the Empire, had grown to be the most inveterate of his habits. All women, even the greatest ninnies, knew how to dodge and double to get their ends; Nanon abandoned the sugar for the sake of getting the *galette*.

"Mademoiselle!" she called through the window, "do you want some galette?"

"No, no," answered Eugénie.

"Come, Nanon," said Grandet, hearing his daughter's voice, "see here." He opened the cupboard where the flour was kept, gave her a cupful, and added a few ounces of butter to the piece he had already cut off.

"I shall want wood for the oven," said the implacable Nanon.

"Well, take what you want," he answered sadly; "but in that case you must make us a fruit-tart, and you'll cook the whole dinner in the oven. In that way you won't need two fires."

"Goodness!" cried Nanon, "you needn't tell me that."

Grandet cast a look that was well-nigh paternal upon his faithful deputy.

"Mademoiselle," she cried, when his back was turned, "we shall have the galette."

JAMES MATTHEW BARRIE

James Matthew Barrie, author and dramatist, was born, in 1860, at Kirriemuir, Scotland. He has produced ten novels, of which the most popular have been "A Window in Thrums," "The Little Minister" and "Sentimental Tommy." For the last three years he has devoted the greater part of his time to play-writing.

COURTSHIPS

(From "The Auld Lichts," Charles Scribner's Sons, Publishers of Mr. Barrie's works in America)

WITH the severe Auld Lichts the Sabbath began at six o'clock on Saturday evening. By that time the gleaming shuttle was at rest, Davie Haggart had strolled into the village from his pile of stones on the Whunny road; Hendry Robb, the "dummy," had sold his last barrowful of "rozetty (resiny) roots" for firewood; and the people, having tranquilly supped and soused their faces in their water pails, slowly donned their Sunday clothes. This ceremony was common to all; but here divergence set in. The gray Auld Licht, to whom love was not even a name, sat in his high-backed armchair by the hearth, Bible or "Pilgrim's Progress" in hand, occasionally lapsing into slumber. But—though, when they got the chance, they went willingly three times to the kirk—there were young men in the community so flighty that, instead of dozing at home on Saturday night, they dandered casually into the square, and, forming into knots at the corners, talked solemnly and mysteriously of women.

Not even on the night preceding his wedding was

an Auld Licht ever known to stay out after ten
o'clock. So weekly conclaves at street corners came
to an end at a comparatively early hour, one Cœlebs
after another shuffling silently from the square until
it echoed, deserted, to the townhouse clock. The
last of the gallants, gradually discovering that he
was alone, would look around him musingly, and,
'aking in the situation, slowly wend his way home.
On no other night of the week was frivolous talk
about the softer sex indulged in, the Auld Lichts
being creatures of habit who never thought of smiling on a Monday. Long before they reached their
teens they were earning their keep as herds in the
surrounding glens or filling "pirns" for their
parents; but they were generally on the brink of
twenty before they thought seriously of matrimony.
Up to that time they only trifled with the other
sex's affections at a distance—filling a maid's water
pails, perhaps, when no one was looking, or carrying
her wob; at the recollection of which they would
slap their knees almost jovially on Saturday night.
A wife was expected to assist at the loom as well
as to be cunning in the making of marmalade and
the firing of bannocks, and there was consequently
some heartburning among the lads for maids of
skill and muscle. The Auld Licht, however, who
meant marriage seldom loitered in the streets. By
and by there came a time when the clock looked
down through its cracked glass upon the hemmed-in
square and saw him not. His companions, gazing
at each other's boots, felt that something was going
on, but made no remark.

A month ago, passing through the shabby familiar
square, I brushed against a withered old man totter-
ing down the street under a load of yarn. It was
piled on a wheelbarrow, which his feeble hands
could not have raised but for the rope of yarn that
supported it from his shoulders; and though Auld

Licht was written on his patient eyes, I did not immediately recognize Jamie Whamond. Years ago Jamie was a sturdy weaver and fervent lover whom I had the right to call my friend. Turn back the century a few decades, and we are together on a moonlight night, taking a short cut through the fields from the farm of Craigiebuckle. Buxom were Craigiebuckle's "dochters," and Jamie was Janet's accepted suitor. It was a muddy road through damp grass, and we picked our way silently over its ruts and pools. "I'm thinkin'," Jamie said at last, a little wistfully, "that I micht hae been as weel wi' Chirsty."

Chirsty was Janet's sister, and Jamie had first thought of her. Craigiebuckle, however, strongly advised him to take Janet instead, and he consented. Alack! heavy wobs have taken all the grace from Janet's shoulders this many a year, though she and Jamie go bravely down the hill together. Unless they pass the allotted span of life, the "poors-house" will never know them. As for bonny Chirsty, she proved a flighty thing, and married a deacon in the Established Church. The Auld Lichts groaned over her fall, Craigiebuckle hung his head, and the minister told her sternly to go her way. But a few weeks afterwards Lang Tammas, the chief elder, was observed talking with her for an hour in Gowrie's close; and the very next Sabbath Chirsty pushed her husband in triumph into her father's pew. The minister, though completely taken by surprise, at once referred to the stranger, in a prayer of great length, as a brand that might yet be plucked from the burning. Changing his text, he preached at him; Lang Tammas, the precentor, and the whole congregation (Chirsty included), sang at him; and before he exactly realized his position he had become an Auld Licht for life. Chirsty's triumph was complete when, next week, in broad daylight, too, the minister's wife called, and (in the presence of Betsy Munn, who vouches for the truth of the story) graciously asked her to come up to the manse on Thursday, at 4 p. m., and drink a dish of tea. Chirsty, who knew her position, of course begged modestly to be excused; but a coolness arose over the invitation between her and Janet—who felt slighted—that was only made up at the laying-out of Chirsty's father-in-law, to which Janet was pleasantly invited.

When they had red up the house, the Auld Licht lassies sat in the gloaming at their doors on three-legged stools, patiently knitting stockings. To them came stiff-limbed youths who, with a "Blawy nicht, Jeanie" (to which the inevitable answer was, "It is so, Cha-rles"), rested their shoulders on the door-post and silently followed with their eyes the flashing needles. Thus the courtship began—often to ripen promptly into marriage, at other times to go no further. The smooth-haired maids, neat in their simple wrappers, knew they were on their trial and that it behooved them to be wary. They had not compassed twenty winters without knowing that Marget Todd lost Davie Haggart because she "fittit" a black stocking with brown worsted, and that Finny's grieve turned from Bell Whamond on account of the frivolous flowers in her bonnet: and yet Bell's prospects, as I happen to know, at one time looked bright and promising. Sitting over her father's peat fire one night gossiping with him about fishing flies and tackle, I noticed the grieve, who had dropped in by appointment with some ducks' eggs on which Bell's clockin hen was to sit, performing some slight-of-hand trick with his coat sleeve. Craftily he jerked and twisted it, till his own photograph (a black smudge on white) gradually appeared to view. This he gravely slipped into the hands of the maid of his choice, and then took his departure, apparently much relieved. Had not Bell's light-headedness driven him away, the grieve would have soon followed up his gift with an offer of his hand. Some night Bell would have "seen him to the door," and they would have stared sheepishly at each other before saying good night. The parting salutation given, the grieve would still have stood his ground, and Bell would have waited with him. At last, "Will ye hae 's, Bell?" would have dropped from his half-reluctant lips; and Bell would have mumbled, "Ay," with her thumb in her mouth. "Guid nicht to ye, Bell," would be the next remark—"Guid nicht to ye, Jeames," the answer; the humble door would close softly, and Bell and her lad would have been engaged. But, as it was, their attachment never got beyond the silhouette stage, from which, in the ethics of the Auld Lichts, a man can draw back in certain circumstances without loss of honor. The only really tender thing I ever heard an Auld Licht lover say to his sweetheart was when Gowrie's brother looked softly into Easie Tamson's eyes and whispered, "Do you swite (sweat)?" Even then the effect was produced more by the loving cast in Gowrie's eye than by the tenderness of the words themselves.

The courtships were sometimes of long duration, but as soon as the young man realized that he was courting he proposed. Cases were not wanting in which he realized this for himself, but as a rule he had to be told of it.

There were a few instances of weddings among the Auld Lichts that did not take place on Friday. Betsy Munn's brother thought to assert his two coal carts, about which he was sinfully puffed up, by getting married early in the week; but he was a pragmatical feckless body, Jamie. The foreigner from York that Finny's grieve after disappointing Jinny Whamond, took, sought to sew the seeds of strife by urging that Friday was an unlucky day; and I remember how the minister, who was always great in a crisis, nipped the bickering in the bud by adducing the conclusive fact that he had been married on the sixth day of the week himself. It was a judicious policy on Mr. Dishart's part to take vigorous action at once and insist on the solemnization of the marriage on a Friday or not at all, for he oest kept superstition out of the congregation by branding it as heresy. Perhaps the Auld Lichts were only ignorant of the grieve's lass' theory because they had not thought of it. Friday's claims, too, were incontrovertible; for the Saturday's being a slack day gave the couple an opportunity to put their but and ben in order, and on Sabbath they had a gay day of it, three times at the kirk. The honeymoon over, the racket of the loom began again on the Monday.

The natural politeness of the Allardice family gave me my invitation to Tibbie's wedding. I was taking tea and cheese early one wintry afternoon with the smith and his wife, when little Joey Todd in his Sabbath clothes peered in at the passage, and then knocked primly at the door. Andra forgot himself, and called out to him to come in by; but Jess frowned him into silence, and hastily donning her black mutch, received Willie on the threshold. Both halves of the door were open, and the visitor had looked us over carefully before knocking; but he had come with the compliments of Tibbie's mother, requesting the pleasure of Jess and her man that evening to the lassie's marriage with Sam'l Todd, and the knocking at the door was part of the ceremony. Five minutes afterward Joey returned to beg a moment of me in the passage; when I, too, got my invitation. The lad had just received, with an expression of polite surprise, though he knew he could claim it as his right, a slice of crumbling

shortbread, and taken his staid departure, when Jess
cleared the tea things off the table, remarking
simply that it was a mercy we had not got beyond
the first cup. We then retired to dress.

About six o'clock, the time announced for the
ceremony, I elbowed my way through the expectant
throng of men, women and children that already be-
sieged the smith's door. Shrill demands of " toss,
toss!" rent the air every time Jess' head showed on
the window blind, and Andra hoped, as I pushed
open the door, " that I hadna forgotten my baw-
bees." Weddings were celebrated among the Auld
Lichts by showers of ha-pence, and the guests on
their way to the bride's house had to scatter to
the hungry rabble like housewives feeding poultry.
Willie Todd, the best man, who had never come out
so strong in his life before, slipped through the back
window, while the crowd, led on by Kitty McQueen,
seethed in front, and making a bolt for it to the
" Sosh," was back in a moment with a handful of
small change. " Dinna toss ower lavishly at first,"
the smith whispered me nervously, as we followed
Jess and Willie into the darkening yard.

The guests were packed hot and solemn in Johnny
Allardice' " room ": the men anxious to surrender
their seat to the ladies who happened to be standing
but too bashful to propose it; the ham and the fish
frizzling noisily side by side but the house, and hissing out every now and then to let all whom it might
concern know that Janet Craik was adding more
water to the gravy. A better woman never lived;
but oh! the hypocrisy of the face that beamed
greeting to the guests as if it had nothing to do but
politely show them in, and gasped next moment with
upraised arms, over what was nearly a fall in
crockery. When Janet sped to the door her " spleet
new " merion dress fell, to the pulling of a string,
over her home-made petticoat, like the drop scene

in a theater, and rose as promptly when she returned to slice the bacon. The murmur of admiration that filled the room when she entered with the minister was an involuntary tribute to the spotlessness of her wrapper, and a great triumph for Janet. If there is an impression that the dress of the Auld Lichts was on all occasions as somber as their faces, let it be known that the bride was but one of several in "whites," and that Mag Munn had only at the last moment been dissuaded from wearing flowers. The minister, the Auld Lichts congratulated themselves, disapproved of all such decking of the person and bowing of the head to idols; but on such an occasion he was not expected to observe it. Bell Whamond, however, has reason for knowing that, marriages or no marriages, he drew the line at curls.

By and by Sam'l Todd, looking a little dazed, was pushed into the middle of the room to Tibbie's side, and the minister raised his voice in prayer. All eyes closed reverently, except perhaps the bridegroom's, which seemed glazed and vacant. It was an open question in the community whether Mr. Dishart did not miss his chance at weddings, the men shaking their heads over the compar. tive brevity of the ceremony, the women worshi ping him (though he never hesitated to rebuke them when they showed it too openly) for the urbanity of his manners. At that time, however, only a minister of such experience as Mr. Dishart's predecessor could lead up to a marriage in prayer without inadvertently joining the couple; and the catechizing was mercifully brief. Another prayer followed the union; the minister waived his right to kiss the bride; every one looked at every other one, as if he had for the moment forgotten what he was on the point of saying and found it very annoying; and Janet signed frantically to Willie Todd, who nodded intelligently in reply, but evidently had no idea what she meant. In time Johnny Allardice, our host, who became more and more doited as the night proceeded, remembered his instructions, and led the way to the kitchen, where the guests, having politely informed their hostess that they were not hungry, partook of a hearty tea. Mr. Dishart presided, with the bride and bridegroom near him; but though he tried to give an agreeable turn to the conversation by describing the extensions at the cemetery, his personality oppressed us, and we only breathed freely when he rose to go. Yet we marvelled at his versatility. In shaking hands with the newly married couple the minister reminded them that it was leap year, and wished them " three hundred and sixty-six happy and God-fearing days."

Sam'l station being too high for it, Tibbie did not have a penny wedding, which her thrifty mother bewailed, penny weddings starting a couple in life. I can recall nothing more characteristic of the nation from which the Auld Lichts sprung than the penny wedding, where the only revellers that were not out of pocket by it were the couple who gave the entertainment. The more the guests ate and drank the better, pecuniarily, for their hosts. The charge for admission to the penny wedding (practically to the feast that followed it) varied in different districts, but with us it was generally a shilling. Perhaps the penny extra to the fiddler accounts for the name penny wedding. The ceremony having been gone through in the bride's house, there was an adjournment to a barn or other convenient place of meeting, where was held the nuptial feast. Long white boards from Rob Angus' sawmill, supported on trestles, stood in lieu of tables; and those of the company who could not find a seat waited patiently against the wall for a vacancy. The shilling gave every guest the free run of the groaning board; but though fowls were plentiful, and even white bread, too, little had been spent on them. The farmers of the neighborhood, who looked forward to providing the young people with drills of potatoes for the coming winter, made a bid for their custom by sending them a fowl gratis for the marriage supper. It was popularly understood to be the oldest cock of the farmyard, but for all that it made a brave appearance in a shallow sea of soup. The fowls were always boiled—without exception, so far as my memory carries me—the guidwife never having the heart to roast them, and so lose the broth. One round of whiskey and water was all the drink to which his shilling entitled the guest. If he wanted more he had to pay for it. There was much revelry, with song and dance, that no stranger could have thought those stiff-limbed weavers capable of; and the more they shouted and whirled through the barn, the more their host smiled and rubbed his hands. He presided at the bar improvised for the occasion, and if the thing was conducted with spirit, his bride flung an apron over her gown and helped him. I remember one elderly bridegroom, who, having married a blind woman, had to do double work at his penny wedding. It was a sight to see him flitting about the torch-lit barn, with a kettle of hot water in one hand and a besom to sweep up crumbs in the other.

Though Sam'l had no penny wedding, however, we made a night of it at his marriage.

Wedding chariots were not in those days, though I know of Auld Lichts being conveyed to marriages nowadays by horses with white ears. The tea over, we formed in couples, and—the best man with the bride, the bridegroom with the best maid, leading the way—marched in slow procession in the moonlight night to Tibbie's new home, between lines of hoarse and eager onlookers. An attempt was made by an itinerant musician to head the company with his fiddle; but instrumental music, even in the streets, was abhorrent to sound Auld Lichts, and the minister had spoken privately to Willie Todd on the subject. As a consequence, Peter was driven from the ranks. The last thing I saw that night, as we filed, bare-headed and solemn, into the newly married couple's house, was Kitty McQueen's vigorous arm, in a dishevelled sleeve, pounding a pair of urchins who had got between her and a muddy ha'penny.

That night there was revelry and boisterous mirth (or what the Auld Lichts took for such) in Tibbie's kitchen. At eleven o'clock Davit Lunan cracked a joke. Davie Haggart, in reply to Bell Dundas' request, gave a song of distinctly secular tendencies. The bride (who had carefully taken off her wedding gown on getting home and donned a wrapper) coquettishly let the bridegroom's father hold her hand. In Auld Licht circles, when one of the company was offered whisky and refused it, the others, as if pained at the offer, pushed it from them as a thing abhorred. But Davie Haggart set another example on this occasion, and no one had the courage to refuse to follow it. We sat late round the dying fire, and it was only Willie Todd's scandalous assertion (he was but a boy) about his being able to dance that induced us to think of moving. In the community, I understand, this marriage is still memorable as the occasion on which Bell Whamond laughed in the minister's face.

ELECTION DAY FESTIVITIES

(From " The Auld Lichts ")

WHEN an election day comes round now, it takes me back to the time of 1832. I would be eight or ten year old at that time. James Strachan was at the door by five o'clock in the morning in his Sabbath clothes, by arrangement. We was to go up to the hill to see them building the bonfire. Moreover, there was a word that Mr. Scrimgour was to be there tossing pennies, just like at a marriage. I was wakened before that by my mother at the pans and bowls. I have always associated elections since that time with jelly making; for just as my mother would fill the cups and tankers and bowls with jelly to save cans, she was emptying the pots and pans to make way for the ale and porter. James and me was to help to carry it home from the square—him in the pitcher and me in a flagon, because I was silly for my age and not strong in the arms.

It was a very blowy morning, though the rain kept off, and what part of the bonfire had been built already was found scattered to the winds. Before we rose a great mass of folk was getting the barrels and things together again; but some of them was never recovered, and suspicion pointed to Willitm Geddes, it being well known that William would not hesitate to carry off anything unobserved. More by token Chirsty Lamby had seen him rolling home a barrowful of firewood early in the morning, her having risen to hold cold water in her mouth, being down with the toothache. When we got up to the hill everybody was making for the quarry, which being more sheltered was now thought to be a better place for the bonfire. The masons had struck work, it being a general holiday in the whole country side. There was a great commotion of people, all fine dressed and mostly with glengarry bonnets; and me and James was well acquaint with them, though mostly weavers and the like and not my father's equal. Mr. Scrimgour was not there himself; but there was a small, active body in his room as tossed the money for him fair enough; though not so liberally as was expected, being mostly ha'pence where pennies were looked for. Such was not my fathers' opinion, and him and a few others only had a vote. He considered it was a waste of money giving to them that had no vote and so taking out of other folks' mouths, but the little man said it kept everybody in good humor and made Mr. Scrimgour popular. He was an extraordinary affable man and very spirity, running about to waste no time in walking, and gave me a shilling, saying to me to be a truthful boy and tell my father. He did not give James anything, him being an orphan, but clapped his head and said he was a fine boy.

The Captain was to vote for the Bill if he got in, the which he did. It was the Captain was to give the ale and porter in the square like a true gentleman. My father gave a kind of laugh when I let him see my shilling, and said he would keep care of it for me; and sorry I was I let him get it, me never seeing the face of it again to this day. Me and James was much annoyed with women, especially Kitty Davie, always pushing in when there was tossing, and tearing the very ha'pence out of our hands: us not caring so much about the money, but humiliated to see women mixing up in politics. By the time the topmost barrel was on the bonfire there was a great smell of whisky in the quarry, it being a confined place. My father had been against the bonfire being in the quarry, arguing that the wind on the hill would have carried off the smell of the whisky; but Peter Tosh said they did not want the smell carried off—it would be agreeable to the masons for weeks to come. Except among the women there was no fighting nor wrangling at the quarry but all in fine spirits.

I misremember now whether it was Mr. Scrimgour or the Captain that took the fancy to my father's pigs; but it was this day, at any rate, that the Captain sent them the gamecock. Whichever one it was that fancied the litter of pigs, nothing would content him but to buy them, which he did at thirty shillings each, being the best bargain ever my father made. Nevertheless I'm thinking he was windier of the cock. The Captain, who was a local man when not with his regiment, had the grandest collection of fighting cocks in the county, and sometimes came into the town to try them against the town cocks. I mind well the large wicker cage in which they were conveyed from place to place, and never without the Captain near at hand. My father had a cock that beat all the other town cocks at the cockfight at our school, which was superintended by the elder of the kirk to see fair play; but the which died of its wounds the next day but one. This was a great grief to my father, it having been challenged to fight the Captain's cock. Therefore it was very considerate of the Captain to make my father a present of his bird; father, in compliment to him, changing its name from the "Deil" to the "Captain."

During the forenoon, and I think until well on in the day, James and me was busy with the pitcher and the flagon. The proceedings in the square, however, was not so well conducted as in the quarry, many of the folk there assembled showing a mean and grasping spirit. The Captain had given orders that there was to be no stint of ale and porter, and neither there was; but much of it lost through hastiness. Great barrels was hurled into the middle of the square, where the country wives sat with their eggs and butter on market day, and was quickly stove in with an axe or paving stone or whatever came handy. Sometimes they would break into the barrel at different points; and then, when they tilted it up to get the ale out at one hole, it gushed out at the bottom till the square was flooded. My mother was fair disgusted when told by me and James of the waste of good liquor. It is gospel truth I speak when I say I mind well of seeing Singer Davie catching the porter in a pan as it ran down the sire, and, when the pan was full to overflowing, putting his mouth to the stream and drinking till he was as full as the pan. Most of the men, however, stuck to the barrels. the drink running in the street being ale and porter mixed, and left it to the women and the young folk to do the carrying. Susy McQueen brought as many pans as she could collect on a barrow, and was filling them all with porter, rejecting the ale; but indignation was aroused against her, and as fast as she filled, the others emptied.

My father scorned to go to the square to drink ale and porter with the crowd, having the election on his mind and him to vote. Nevertheless he instructed me and James to keep up a brisk trade with the pans, and run back across the gardens in case we met dishonest folk in the streets who might drink the ale. Also, said my father, we was to let the excesses of our neighbors be a warning in sobriety to us; enough being as good as a feast, except when you can store it up for the winter. By and by my mother thought it was not safe me being in the streets with so many wild men about, and would have sent James himself, him being an orphan and hardier; but this I did not like, but running out, did not come back for long enough. There is no doubt that the music was to blame for firing the men's blood, and the result most disgraceful fighting with no object in view. There was three fiddlers and two at the flute, most of them blind, but not the less dangerous on that account; and they kept the town in a ferment, even playing the country folk home to the farms, followed by bands of townsfolk. They were a quarrelsome set, the ploughmen and others; and it was generally admitted in the town that their overbearing behavior was responsible for the fights. I mind them being driven out of the square, stones flying thick; also some stand-up fights with sticks, and others fair enough with fists. The first fight I did not see. It took place in a field. At first it was only between two who had been miscalling one another; but there was many looking on, and when the town man was like getting the worst of it the others set to, and a most heathenish fray with no sense in it ensued. One man had his arm broken. I mind Hobart the bellman going about ringing his bell and telling all persons to get within doors; but little attention was paid to him, it being notorious that Snecky had had a fight earlier in the day himself.

When James was fighting in the field, according to his own account, I had the honor of dining with the electors who voted for the Captain, him paying all expenses. It was a lucky accident my mother sending me to the townhouse, where the dinner came off, to try to get my father home at a decent hour, me having a remarkable power over him when in liquor, but at no other time. They were very jolly, however, and insisted on my drinking the Captain's health and eating more than was safe. My father got it next day from my mother for this; and so would I myself, but it was several days before I left my bed, completely knocked up as I was with the excitement and one thing or another. The bonfire, which was built to celebrate the election of Mr. Scrimgour, was set ablaze, though I did not see it, in honor of the election of the Captain; it being thought a pity to lose it, as no doubt it would have been. That is about all I remember of the celebrated election of '32 when the Reform Bill was passed.

WET DAYS IN THRUMS

(From "A Window in Thrums")

IN a wet day the rain gathered in blobs on the road that passed our garden. Then it crawled into the cart tracks until the road was streaked with water. Lastly, the water gathered in heavy yellow pools. If the on-ding still continued, clods of earth toppled from the garden dike into the ditch.

On such a day, when even the dulseman had gone into shelter, and the women scudded by with their wrappers over their heads, came Gavin Birse to our door. Gavin, who was the Glen Quharity post, was still young, but had never been quite the same man since some amateurs in the glen ironed his back for rheumatism. I thought he had called to have a crack with me. He sent his compliments up to the attic, however, by Leeby, and would I come and be a witness?

Gavin came up and explained. He had taken off his scarf and thrust into his pocket, lest the rain should take the color out of it. His boots cheeped, and his shoulders had risen to his ears. He stood steaming before my fire.

"If it's no' ower muckle to ask ye," he said, "I would like ye for a witness."

"A witness! But for what do you need a witness, Gavin?"

"I want ye," he said, "to come wi' me to Mag's, and be a witness."

Gavin and Mag Birse had been engaged for a year or more. Mag was the daughter of Janet Ogilvy, who was best remembered as the body that took the hill (that is, wandered about it) for twelve hours on the day Mr. Dishart, the Auld Licht minister, accepted a call to another church.

237

"You don't mean to tell me, Gavin," I asked, "that your marriage is to take place to-day?"

By the twist of his mouth I saw that he was only deferring a smile.

"Far frae that," he said.

"Ah, then, you have quarreled, and I am to speak up for you?"

"Na, na," he said, "I dinna want ye to do that above all things. It would be a favor if ye could gie me a bad character."

This beat me, and I dare say, my face showed it.

"I'm no' juist what ye would call anxious to marry Mag noo," said Gavin, without a tremor.

I told him to go on.

"There's a lassie oot at Craigiebuckle," he explained, "workin' on the farm—Jeanie Luke by name. Ye may hae seen her?"

"What of her?" I asked severely.

"Weel," said Gavin, still unabashed, "I'm thinkin' noo 'at I would rather hae her."

Then he stated his case more fully.

"Ay, I thocht I liked Mag oncommon till I saw Jeanie, an' I like her fine yet, but I prefer the other ane. That state o' matters canna gang on forever, so I came into Thrums the day to settle 't one wy or another."

"And how," I asked, "do you propose going about it? It is a somewhat delicate business."

"Ou, I see nae great difficulty in 't. I'll speir at Mag, blunt oot, if she 'll let me aff. Yes, I'll put it to her plain."

"You're sure Jeanie would take you?"

"Ay; oh, there's nae fear o' that."

"But if Mag keeps you to your bargain?"

"Weel, in that case there's nae harm done."

"You are in a great hurry, Gavin?"

"Ye may say that; but I want to be married. The

wifie I lodge wi' canna last lang, an' I would like to
settle doon in some place."

"So you are on your way to Mag's now?"

"Ay, we'll get her in atween twal' and ane."

"Oh, yes; but why do you want me to go with
you?"

"I want ye for a witness. If she winna let me
aff, weel and guid; and if she will, it's better to hae
a witness in case she should go back on her word."

Gavin gave his proposal briskly, and as coolly as
if he were only asking me to go fishing; but I did
not accompany him to Mags. He left the house to
look for another witness, and about an hour afterward Jess saw him pass with Tammas Haggart.
Tammas cried in during the evening to tell us how
the mission prospered.

"Mind ye," said Tammas, a drop of water hanging to the point of his nose, "I disclaim all respon-
sibility in the business. I ken Mag weel for a
thrifty, respectable woman, as her mither was afore
her, and so I said to Gavin when he came to speir
me."

"Ay, mony a pirn has 'Lisbeth filled to me," said
Hendry, settling down to a reminiscence.

"No to be ower hard on Gavin," continued Tammas, forestalling Hendry, "he took what I said in
guid part; but aye when I stopped speakin' to draw
breath, he says, 'The queistion is, will ye come wi'
me?' He was michty made up in 's mind."

"Weel, ye went wi' him," suggested Jess, who
wanted to bring Tammas to the point.

"Ay," said the stone breaker, "but no in sic a
hurry as that."

He worked his mouth round and round, to clear
the course, as it were, for a sarcasm.

"Fowk often say," he continued, "'at 'am quick
beyond the ordinar' in seein' the humorous side o'
things."

Here Tammas paused, and looked at us.

"So ye are, Tammas,' said Hendry. "Losh, ye mind hoo ye saw the humorous side o' me wearin' a pair o' boots 'at wisna marrows! No, the ane had a toe piece on, an' the other hadna."

"Ye juist wore them sometimes when ye was delvin'," broke in Jess; "ye have as guid a pair o' boots as ony in Thrums."

"Ay, but I had worn them," said Hendry, "at odd times for mair than a year, an' I had never seen the humorous side o' them. Weel, as fac as death" (here he addressed me), "Tammas had just seen them twa or three times when he saw the humorous side o' them. Syne I saw their humorous side, too, but no till Tammas pointed it oot."

"That was naething," said Tammas, "naething ava to some things I've done."

"But what aboot Mag?" said Leeby.

"We wasna' that length, was we?" said Tammas.

"Na, we was speakin' aboot the humorous side. Ay, wait a wee."

"Na, I didna mention the humorous side for naething."

He paused to reflect. "Oh, yes," he said at last, brightening up, "I was sayin' to ye hoo quick I was to see the humorous side o' onything. Ay, then, what made me say that was, 'at in a clink (flash) I saw the humorous side o' Gavin's position."

"Man, man," said Hendry, admiringly, "and what is 't?"

"Oh, it's this, there's something humorous in speirin' a woman to let ye aff so as ye can be married to another woman."

"I daur say there is," said Hendry, doubtfully.

"Did she let him aff?" asked Jess, taking the words out of Leeby's mouth.

"I'm comin' to that," said Tammas. "Gavin proposes to me after I had haen my laugh——"

"Yes," cried Hendry, banging the table with his fist, "it has a humorous side. Ye 're richt again, Tammas."

"I wish ye wadna blatter (beat) the table," said Jess, and then Tammas proceeded—

"Gavin wanted me to tak' paper an' ink an' a pen wi' me, to write the proceedin's doon, but I said, 'Na, na, I'll tak' paper, but nae ink nor nae pen, for ther 'll be ink an' a pen there.' That was what I said."

"An' did she let him aff?" asked Leeby.

"Weel," said Tammas, "aff we goes to Mag's hoose, an' sure enough Mag was in. She was alane, too: so Gavin, no to waste time, juist sat doon for politeness' sake, an' sune rises up again; an' says he, 'Marget Lownie, I hae a solemn question to speir at ye, namely this, Will you, Marget Lownie, let me, Gavin Birse, aff?'"

"Mag would start at that?"

"Sal, she was braw an' cool. I thocht she maun hae got wind o' his intentions aforehand, for she juist replies, quiet-like, "Hoo do ye want aff, Gavin?"

"'Because,' says he, like a book, 'my affections has undergone a change.'"

"'Ye mean Jean Luke,' says Mag."

"'That is wha I mean,' says Gavin, very straitforrard."

"But she didna let him aff, did she?"

"Na, she wasna the kind. Says she, 'I wonder to hear ye, Gavin, but 'am no goin' to agree to naething o' that sort.'"

"'Think it ower,' says Gavin."

"'Nae, my mind's made up,' said she."

"'Ye would sune get anither man,' he says earnestly."

"'Hoo do I ken that?' she spiers, rale sensibly, I thocht, for men's no sae easy to get."

"'An sure o' 't,' Gavin says, wi' mighty conviction in his voice, 'for ye 're bonny to look at, an' weel-kent for bein' a guid body.'

"'Ay,' says Mag, 'I'm glad ye like me, Gavin, for ye have to tak' me.'"

"That put a clincher on him," interrupted Hendry.

"He was loth to gie in," replied Tammas, "so he says, 'Ye think 'am a fine character, Marget Lownie, but ye 're very far mista'en. I wouldna wonder but what I was lossin' my place some o' thae days, an' syne whaur would ye be?—Marget Lownie,' he goes on, ''am nat'rally lazy an' fond o' the drink. As sure as ye stand there, 'am a reg'lar deevil!'"

"That was strong language," said Hendry, "but he would be wantin' to fleg (frighten) her?"

"Juist so, but he didna manage 't; for Mag says, 'We a' hae oor faults, Gavin, an' deevil or no deevil, ye 're the man for me!'"

"Gavin thocht a bit," continued Tammas, "an' syne he tries her on a new tack. 'Marget Lownie,' he says, 'yer father's an aul man noo, an' he has naebody but yersel' to look after him. I'm thinkin' it would be kind o' cruel o' me to tak' ye awa frae him.'"

"Mag wouldna be ta'en in wi' that; she wasna born on a Sawbath," said Jess, using one of her favorite sayings.

"She wasna," answered Tammas. "Says she, 'Hae nae fear on that score, Gavin; my father's fine willin' to spare me!'"

"An' that ended it?"

"Ay, that ended it."

"Did ye tak' it doon in writin'?" asked Hendry.

"There was nae need," said Tammas. "No, I never touched paper. When I saw the thing was settled, I left them to their coortin'. They're to tak' a look at Snecky Hobarts' auld hoose. It's to let."

LORD BEACONSFIELD

BENJAMIN DISRAELI, Earl of Beaconsfield, states-
man and novelist, born in London, in 1804; died
there 1881. His father, Israel Disraeli, was a lover
of literature and a writer of note. Young Disraeli
at the age of twenty-two wrote "Vivian Grey." It
caused a great sensation, as it caricatured broadly
many leading men of the day. "The Young Duke"
and "Contarini Fleming" added to the author's
fame. The latter was highly praised by Goethe.

LADY CORISANDE

ONE'S life changes in a moment. Half a month
ago Lothair, without an acquaince, was
meditating his return to Oxford. Now he seemed
to know everybody who was anybody. His table was
overflowing with invitations to all the fine houses in
town. First came the routs and the balls; then,
when he had been presented to the husbands, came
the dinners. His kind friends the Duchess and Lady
St. Jerome were the fairies who had worked this
sudden scene of enchantment. A single word from
them, and London was at Lothair's feet.

He liked it amazingly. He quite forgot the conclusion at which he had arrived respecting society a
year ago, drawn from his vast experience of the single party which he had then attended. Feelings are
different when you know a great many persons, and
every person is trying to please you; above all, when
there are individuals whom you want to meet, and
whom, if you do not meet, you become restless.

Town was beginning to blaze. Broughams whirled
and bright barouches glanced, troops of social cav-

alry cantered and caracolled in morning rides, and
the bells of prancing ponies, lashed by delicate
hands, gingled in the laughing air. There were
stoppages in Bond Street, which seems to cap the
climax of civilization, after crowded clubs and
swarming parks.

But the great event of the season was the presen-
tation of Lady Corisande. Truly our bright maiden
of Brentham woke and found herself famous. There
are families whom everybody praises, and families
who are treated in a different way. Either will do;
all the sons and daughters of the first succeed, all
the sons and daughters of the last are encouraged in
perverseness by the prophetic determination of society. Half a dozen married sisters, who were the
delight and ornament of their circles, in the case of
Lady Corisande were good precursors of popularity;
but the world would not be content with that; they
credited her with all their charms and winning
qualities, but also with something grander and beyond comparison; and from the moment her fair
cheek was sealed by the gracious approbation of
Majesty, all the critics of the Court at once recognized her as the cynosure of the Empyrean.

Monsignor Catesby, who looked after Lothair,
and was always breakfasting with him without the
necessity of an invitation (a fascinating man, and
who talked upon all subjects except High Mass),
knew everything that took place at Court without
being present there himself. He led the conversation
to the majestic theme, and while he seemed to be
busied in breaking an egg with delicate precision,
and hardly listening to the frank expression of opinions which he carelessly encouraged, obtained a not
insufficient share of Lothair's views and impressions
of human beings and affairs in general during the
last few days, which had witnessed a Levée and a
Drawing-room.

"Ah, then you were so fortunate as to know the beauty before her début," said the Monsignore.

"Intimately; her brother is my friend. I was at Brentham last summer. Delicious place! and the most agreeable visit I ever made in my life, at least, one of the most agreeable."

"Ah! ah!" said the Monsignore. "Let me ring for some toast."

On the night of the Drawing-room, a great ball was given at Crecy House to celebrate the entrance of Corisande into the world. It was a sumptuous festival. The palace, resonant with fantastic music, blazed amid illumined gardens rich with summer warmth.

A prince of the blood was dancing with Lady Corisande. Lothair was there, vis-à-vis with Miss Arundel.

"I delight in this hall," she said to Lothair; "but how superior the pictured scene to the reality!"

"What! would you like, then, to be in a battle?"

"I should like to be with heroes, wherever they might be. What a fine character was the Black Prince! And they call those days the days of superstition!"

The silver horns sounded a brave flourish. Lothair had to advance and meet Lady Corisande. Her approaching mien was full of grace and majesty, but Lothair thought there was a kind expression in her glance, which seemed to remember Brentham, and that he was her brothers' friend.

A little later in the evening he was her partner. He could not refrain from congratulating her on the beauty and the success of the festival.

"I am glad you are pleased, and I am glad you think it successful; but, you know, I am no judge, for this is my first ball!"

"Ah! to be sure; and yet it seems impossible," he continued, in a tone of murmuring admiration.

"Oh! I have been at little dances at my sisters'; half behind the door," she added, with a slight smile. "But to-night I am present at a scene of which I have only read."

"And how do you like balls?" said Lothair.

"I think I shall like them very much," said Lady Corisande; "but to-night, I will confess, I am a little nervous."

"You do not look so."

"I am glad of that."

"Why?"

"Is it not a sign of weakness?"

"Can feeling be weakness?"

"Feeling without sufficient cause is, I should think." And then, and in a tone of some archness, she said, "And how do you like balls?"

"Well, I like them amazingly," said Lothair. "They seem to me to have every quality which can render an entertainment agreeable: music, light, flowers, beautiful faces, graceful forms, and occasionally charming conversation."

"Yes; and that never lingers," said Lady Corisande, "for see, I am wanted."

When they were again undisturbed, Lothair regretted the absence of Bertram, who was kept at the House.

"It is a great disappointment," said Lady Corisande; "but he will yet arrive, though late. I should be most unhappy though, if he were absent from his post on such an occasion. I am sure if he were here I could not dance."

"You are a most ardent politician," said Lothair.

"Oh! I do not care in the least about common politics, parties and office, and all that; I neither regard nor understand them," replied Lady Corisande. "But when wicked men try to destroy the country, then I like my family to be in the front."

As the destruction of the country meditated this

night by wicked men was some change in the status of the Church of England, which Monsignore Catesby in the morning had suggested to Lothair as both just and expedient and highly conciliatory, Lothair did not pursue the theme, for he had a greater degree of tact than usually falls to the lot of the ingenuous.

The bright moments flew on. Suddenly there was a mysterious silence in the hall, followed by a kind of suppressed stir. Every one seemed to be speaking with bated breath, or, if moving, walking on tiptoe. It was the supper hour:

"Soft hour which wakes the wish and melts the heart."

Royalty, followed by the imperial presence of ambassadors, and escorted by a group of dazzling duchess and paladins of high degree, was ushered with courteous pomp by the host and hostess into a choice saloon, hung with rose-colored tapestry and illumined by chandeliers of crystal, where they were served from gold plate. But the thousand less favored were not badly off, when they found themselves in the more capacious chambers, into which they rushed with an eagerness hardly in keeping with the splendid nonchalance of the preceding hours.

"What a perfect family," exclaimed Hugo Bohun, as he extracted a couple of fat little birds from their bed of aspic jelly; "everything they do in such perfect taste. How safe you were here to have ortolans for supper!"

All the little round tables, though their number was infinite, were full. Male groups hung about; some in attendance on fair dames, some foraging for themselves, some thoughtful and more patient and awaiting a satisfactory future. Never was such an elegant clatter.

"I wonder where Carisbrooke is," said Hugo Bohun. "They say he is wonderfully taken with the beauteous daughter of the house."

"I will back the Duke of Brecon against him," said one of his companions. "He raved about her at White's yesterday."

"Hem!"

"The end is not so near as all that," said a third wassailer.

"I do not know that," said Hugo Bohun. "It is a family that marries off quickly. If a fellow is obliged to marry, he always likes to marry one of them."

"What of this new star?" said his friend, and he mentioned Lothair.

"O! he is too young; not launched. Besides he is going to turn Catholic, and I doubt whether that would do in that quarter."

"But he has a greater fortune than any of them."

"Immense! A man I know, who knows another man——" and then he began a long statistical story about Lothair's resources.

"Have you got any room here, Hugo?" drawled out Lord St. Aldegonde.

"Plenty, and here is my chair."

"On no account; half of it and some soup will satisfy me."

"I should have thought you would have been with the swells," said Hugo Bohun.

"That does not exactly suit me," said St. Aldegonde. "I was ticketed to the Duchess of Salop, but I got a first-rate substitute with the charm of novelty for her Grace, and sent her in with Lothair."

St. Aldegonde was the heir apparent of the wealthiest, if not the most ancient, dukedom in the Kingdom. He was spoiled, but he knew it. Had he been an ordinary being, he would have merely subsided into selfishness and caprice, but having good abilities and a good disposition, he was eccentric, adventurous, and sentimental. Notwithstanding the apathy which had been engendered by premature experience, St. Aldegonde held extreme opinions, especially on political affairs, being a republican of the reddest dye. He was opposed to all privilege, and indeed to all orders of men, except dukes, who were a necessity. He was also strongly in favor of the equal division of all property, except land. Liberty depended on land, and the greater the land-owners, the greater the liberty of a country. He would hold forth on this topic even with energy, amazed at any one differing from him; "as if a fellow could have too much land," he would urge with a voice and glance which defied contradiction. St. Aldegonde had married for love and he loved his wife, but he was strongly in favor of woman's rights and their extremest consequences. It was thought that he had originally adopted these latter views with the amiable intention of piquing Lady St. Aldegonde; but if so, he had not succeeded. Beaming with brightness, with the voice and airiness of a bird, and a cloudless temper, Albertha St. Aldegonde had, from the first hour of her marriage, concentrated her intelligence, which was not mean, on one object; and that was never to cross her husband on any conceivable topic. They had been married several years, and she treated him as a darling spoiled child. When he cried for the moon, it was promised him immediately; however irrational his proposition, she always assented to it, though generally by tact and vigilance she guided him in the right direction. Nevertheless, St. Aldegonde was sometimes in scrapes; but then he always went and told his best friend, whose greatest delight was to extricate him from his perplexities and embarrassments.

* * * * *

It was agreed that after breakfast they should go and see Corisande's garden. And a party did go:

all the Phœbus family, and Lord and Lady St. Aldegonde, and Lady Corisande, and Bertram and Lothair.

In the pleasure-grounds of Brentham were the remains of an ancient garden of the ancient house that had long ago been pulled down. When the modern pleasure-grounds were planned and created, notwithstanding the protests of the artists in landscape, the father of the present Duke would not allow this ancient garden to be entirely destroyed, and you came upon its quaint appearance in the dissimilar world in which it was placed, as you might in some festival of romantic costume upon a person habited in the courtly dress of the last century. It was formed upon a gentle southern slope, with turfen terraces walled in on three sides, the fourth consisting of arches of golden yew. The Duke had given this garden to Lady Corisande, in order that she might practise her theory, that flower-gardens should be sweet and luxuriant, and not hard and scentless imitations of works of art. Here, in their season, flourished abundantly all those productions of nature which are now banished from our once delighted senses: huge bushes of honeysuckle, and bowers of sweet-pea and sweet-briar, and jessamine clustering over the walls, and gillyflowers scenting with their sweet breath the ancient bricks from which they seemed to spring. There were banks of violets which the southern breeze always stirred, and mignonette filled every vacant nook. As they entered now, it seemed a blaze of roses and carnations, though one recognized in a moment the presence of the lily, the heliotrope, and the stock. Some white peacocks were basking on the southern wall, and one of them, as their visitors entered, moved and displayed its plumage with scornful pride. The bees were busy in the air, but their homes were near, and you might watch them laboring in their glassy hives.

" Now, is not Corisande quite right?" said Lord St. Aldegonde, as he presented Madame Phœbus with a garland of woodbine, with which she said she would dress her head at dinner. All agreed with him, and Bertram and Euphrosyne adorned each other with carnations, and Mr. Phœbus placed a flower on the uncovered head of Lady St. Aldegonde, according to the principles of high art, and they sauntered and rambled in the sweet and sunny air amid a blaze of butterflies and the ceaseless hum of bees.

Bertram and Euphrosyne had disappeared, and the rest were lingering about the hives while Mr. Phœbus gave them a lecture on the apiary and its marvelous life. The bees understood Mr. Phœbus at least he said so, and thus his friends had considerable advantage in this lesson in entomology. Lady Corisande and Lothair were in a distant corner of the garden, and she was explaining to him her plans; what she had done and what she meant to do.

" I wish I had a garden like this at Muriel," said Lothair.

" You could easily make one."

" If you helped me."

" I have told you all my plans," said Lady Corisande.

" Yes; but I was thinking of something else when you spoke," said Lothair.

" This is not very complimentary."

" I do not wish to be complimentary," said Lothair, " if compliments mean less than they declare. I was not thinking of your garden, but of you."

" Where can they have all gone?" said Lady Corisande, looking round. " We must find them."

" And leave this garden?" said Lothair. " And I without a flower, the only one without a flower? I am afraid that is significant of my lot."

" You shall choose a rose," said Lady Corisande.

"Nay; the charm is that it should be your choice."

But choosing the rose lost more time, and when Corisande and Lothair reached the arches of golden yew, there were no friends in sight.

"I think I hear sounds this way," said Lothair, and he led his companion farther from home.

"I see no one," said Lady Corisande, distressed, and when they had advanced a little way.

"We are sure to find them in good time," said Lothair. "Besides, I wanted to speak to you about the garden at Muriel. I wanted to induce you to go there and help me to make it. Yes," he added, after some hesitation, "on this spot, I believe on this very spot, I asked the permission of your mother two years ago to express to you my love. She thought me a boy, and she treated me as a boy. She said I knew nothing of the world, and both our characters were unformed. I know the world now. I have committed many mistakes, doubtless many follies, have formed many opinions, and have changed many opinions; but to one I have been constant, in one I am unchanged, and that is my adoring love for you."

She turned pale, she stopped, then gently taking his arm, she hid her face in his breast.

VENERABLE BEDE

The Venerable Bede, an English monk, born in Northumberland about A.D. 672; died 735. He was a noted scholar and was acquainted with all that his day could teach. His great work was "The Ecclesiastical History of England."

DESCRIPTION OF BRITAIN

BRITAIN, an island in the ocean, formerly called Albion, is situated between the north and west, facing, though at a considerable distance, the coasts of Germany, France, and Spain, which form the greatest part of Europe. It extends 800 miles in length toward the north, and is 200 miles in breadth, except where several promontories extend further in breadth, by which its compass is made to be 3,675 miles. To the south, as you pass along the nearest shore of the Belgic Gaul, the first place in Britain which opens to the eye, is the city of Rutubi Portus, by the English corrupted into Reptacestir. The distance from hence across the sea to Gessoriacum, the nearest shore of the Marini, is fifty miles, or as some writers say, 450 furlings. On the back of the island, where it opens upon the boundless ocean, it has the islands called Orcades. Britain excels for grain and trees, and is well adapted for feeding cattle and beasts of burden. It also produces vines in some places, and has plenty of land and water-fowls of several sorts; it is remarkable also for rivers abounding in fish, and plentiful springs. It has the greatest plenty of salmon and eels; seals are also frequently taken, and dolphins, as also whales; besides many sorts of shellfish, such as mussels, in which are often found excellent pearls of all colors, red, purple, violet, and green, but mostly white. There is also a great abundance of cockles, of which the scarlet dye is made; a most beautiful color, which never fades with the heat of the sun, or the washing of the rain; but the older it is, the more beautiful it becomes. It has both salt and hot springs, and from them flow rivers which furnish hot baths, proper for all ages and sexes, and arranged accordingly. For water, as St. Basil says, receives the heating quality when it runs along certain metals, and becomes not only hot but scalding. Britain has also many veins of metal, as copper, iron, lead, and silver; it has much and excellent jet, which is black and sparkling, glittering at the fire, and when heated, drives away serpents; being warmed with rubbing, it holds fast whatever is applied to it, like amber. The island was formerly embellished with twenty-eight noble cities, besides innumerable castles, which were all strongly secured with walls, towers, gates, and locks. And, from its lying almost under the North Pole, the nights are light in summer, so at midnight the beholders are often in doubt whether the evening twilight still continues, or that the morning is coming on; for the sun, in the night, returns under the earth, through the northern regions at no great distance from them. For this reason the days are of a great length in summer, as, on the contrary, the nights are in winter, for the sun then withdraws into the southern parts, so that the nights are eighteeen hours long. Thus the nights are extraordinarily short in summer, and the days in winter, that is, of only six equinoctial hours. Whereas in Armenia, Macedonia, Italy, and other countries of the same latitude, the longest day or night extends but to fifteen hours, and the shortest to nine.

This island at present, following the number of the books in which the Divine law was written, contains five nations, the English, Britons, Scots, Picts and Latins, each in its own peculiar dialect cultivating the sublime study of Divine truth. The Latin tongue is, by the study of the Scriptures, become common to all the rest. At first the island had no other inhabitants but the Britons, from whom it derived its name, and who coming over into Britain, as is reported, from Armorica, possessed themselves of the southern parts thereof. When they, beginning at the south, had made themselves masters of the greatest part of the island, it happened, that the nation of the Picts from Scythia, as is reported, putting to sea in a few long ships, were driven by the winds beyond the shores of Britain and arrived on the northern coasts of Ireland, where, finding the nation of the Scots, they begged to be allowed to settle among them, but could not succeed in obtaining their request. Ireland is the greater island next to Britain, and lies to the west of it; but as it is shorter than Britain to the north, so, on the other hand, it runs out far beyond it to the south, opposite to the northern parts of Spain, though a spacious sea lies between them. The Picts, as has been said, arriving in this island by sea, desired to have a place granted them in which they might settle. The Scots answered that the island could not contain them both; but "We can give you good advice," said they, "what to do; we know there is another island, not far from ours, to the eastward, which we often see at a distance when the days are clear. If you will go thither, you will obtain settlement; or, if they should oppose you, you shall have our assistance." The Picts, accordingly, sailing over into Britain, began to inhabit the northern parts thereof, for the Britons were possessed of the southern. Now the Picts had no wives, and asked them of the

Scots; who would not consent to grant them under
any other terms, than that when any difficulty should
arise, they should choose a king from the female
royal race rather than from the male: which custom as is well known, is observed among the Picts
to this day. In process of time, Britain, besides the
Britons and the Picts, received a third nation, the
Scots, who, migrating from Ireland under their
leader, Renda, either by fair means, or by force of
arms, secured to themselves some settlements among
the Picts which they still possess. From the name
of their commander, they are to this day called
Dalrendians; for, in their language, Dal signifies a
part.

Ireland, in breadth, and for wholesomeness and
serenity of climate, far surpasses Britain; for the
snow scarcely ever lies there above three days: no
man makes hay in the summer for winter's provision,
or builds stables for his beasts of burden. No rep-
tiles are found there, and no snakes can live there;
for though often carried thither out of Britain, as
soon as the ship comes near the shore, and the scent
of the air reaches them, they die. On the contrary,
almost all things in the island are good against
poison. In short, we have known that when some
persons have been bitten by serpents, the scrapings
of leaves of books that were brought out of Ireland,
being put into water, and given them to drink, have
immediately expelled the spreading poison, and as-
suaged the swelling. The island abounds in milk
and honey, nor is there any want of vines, fish, or
fowl; and it is remarkable for deer and goats. It
is properly the country of the Scots, who, migrating from thence, as has been said, added a third
nation in Britain to the Britons and the Picts. There
is a very large gulf of the sea, which formerly divided the nation of the Picts from the Britons,
which gulf runs from the west very far into the

land, where, to this day, stands the strong city of the Britons, called Aleluith. The Scots, arriving on the north side of this bay, settled themselves there.

EGBERT, THE PRIEST

At that time the venerable servant of Christ, and priest, Egbert, whom I cannot name but with the greatest respect, and who, as was said before, lived a stranger in Ireland to obtain hereafter a residence in heaven, proposed to himself to do good to many, by taking upon him the apostolical work, and preaching the word of God to some of those nations that had not yet heard it; many of which nations he knew there were in Germany, from whom the Angles, or Saxons, who now inhabit Britain, are known to have derived their origin; for which reason they are still corruptly called Garmans by the neighboring nations of the Britons. Such are the Frisons, the Rugins, the Danes, the Huns, the Ancient Saxons, and the Boructuars (or Bructers). There are also in the same parts many other nations still following pagan rites, to whom the aforesaid soldier of Christ designed to repair, sailing round Britain, and to try whether he could deliver any of them from Satan, and bring them over to Christ; or if this could not be done, to go to Rome, to see and adore the hallowed thresholds of the holy apostles and martyrs of Christ.

However, Wictbert, one of his companions, being famous for his contempt of the world and for his knowledge, for he had lived many years a stranger in Ireland, living an eremitical life in great purity, went abroad, and arriving in Frisland, preached the word of salvation for the space of two years successively to that nation and to its king, Rathbed; but reaped no fruit of all his great labor among his barbarous auditors. Returning then to the beloved place of his peregrination, he gave himself up to our Lord in his wonted repose, and since he could not be profitable to strangers by teaching them the faith, he took care to be the more useful to his own people by the example of his virtue.

PIERRE JEAN DE BÉRANGER

PIERRE JEAN DE BÉRANGER, one of the most popular of French poets, born in 1780, in Paris; died
there in 1857. He composed many stirring songs
during the Napoleonic period, but he did not begin
to write them down until 1812. While an enthusi-
astic republican, he was at the same time a most
devoted follower of Napoleon, a combination that
endeared him to the populace. He runs the whole
scale in his work, from some couplets sparkling with
wit to powerful pieces that could be used as literary weapons by the faction with which he allied
himself.

LISETTE IN ATTIC CELL

O, IT was here that Love his gifts bestowed
    On youth's wild age.
Gladly once more I seek my youth's abode,
    In pilgrimage!
Here my young mistress with her poet dared
    Reckless to dwell;
She was sixteen, I twenty, and we shared
    This attic cell.

Yes, 'twas a garret, be it known to all,
    Here was Love's shrine;
Here read, in charcoal traced along the wall,
    The unfinished line,
Here was the board where kindred hearts would
      blend.
    The Jew can tell
How oft I pawned my watch to feast a friend
    In attic cell!

O, my Lisette's fair form could I recall
    With fairy wand!
There she would blind the window with her shawl,
    Bashful, yet fond!
What though from whom she got her dress I've
      since
    Learned but too well?
Still, in those days I envied not a prince
    In attic cell.

Here the glad tidings on our banquet burst,
    'Mid the bright bowls.
Yes, it was here Marengo's triumph first
    Kindled our souls!
Bronze cannon roared; France, with redoubled
      might,
    Felt her heart swell!
Proudly we drank our Consul's health that night
    In attic cell.

Dreams of my youthful days! I'd freely give,
    Ere my life's close,
All the dull days I'm destined yet to live,
    For one of those!
Where shall I now find raptures that were felt,
    Joys that befell,
And hopes that dawned at twenty, when I dwelt
    In attic cell!

THE OLD VAGABOND

(Translation in Tait's Magazine)

HERE in the ditch my bones I'll lay;
    Weak, wearied, old, the world I'll leave.
"He's drunk," the passing crowd will say:
    'Tis well, for none will need to grieve.

THE OLD VAGABOND

Some turn their scornful heads away,
 Some fling an alms in passing by;
 Haste—'tis the village holiday,
The aged beggar needs no help to die.

Yes! here, alone, of sheer old age
 I die; for hunger slays me not at all.
I hoped my misery's closing page
 To fold within some hospital;
But crowded thick is each retreat,
 Such numbers now in misery lie;
 Alas; my cradle was the street!
As he was born the aged wretch must die.

In youth, of workmen o'er and o'er,
 I've asked, "Instruct me in your trade."
"Begone! our business is not more
 Than keeps ourselves; go, beg," they said—
Ye rich, who bade me toil for bread,
 Of bones your tables gave me store,
 Your straw has often made my bed:—
In death I lay no curses at your door.

Thus poor, I might have turned to theft;
 No!—better still for alms to pray!
At most, I've plucked some apples left
 To ripen near the public way.
Yet weeks and weeks in dungeons laid,
 In the King's name, they let me pine;
 They stole the only wealth I had:
Though poor and old, the sun at least was mine.

What country has the poor to claim?
 What boots to me your corn and wine,
Your busy toil, your vaunted fame,
 The Senate where your speakers shine?

Once when your homes by war o'er swept,
  Saw strangers battling on your land,
  Like any paltry fool I wept,
The aged fool was nourished by their hand.

Mankind! why trod you now the worm,
  The noxious thing beneath your heel?
Ah! had you taught me to perform
  Due labor for the common weal!
Then sheltered from the adverse wind,
  The worm and ant had time to grow;
  Aye, then I might have loved my kind;
The aged beggar dies your bitter foe.

WALTER BESANT

WALTER BESANT, novelist, born at Portsmouth, England, 1838; died 1901. He intended to become a clergyman and was educated at Cambridge University. He became professor in Royal College, Mauritius, but returned home to take up a literary career. He was knighted in 1895. In addition to producing numerous stories he wrote constantly for a large number of magazines. Among his best novels are "All Sorts and Conditions of Men," "Armorel of Lyonesse," and "Beyond the Dreams of Avarice."

THE CHILD OF SAMSON

(Harper & Bros., Publishers)

IT was the evening of a fine September day. Through the square window, built out so as to form another room almost as large as that which had been thus enlarged, the autumn sun, now fast declining to the west, poured in warm and strong, but not too warm or strong for the girl on whose head it fell as she sat leaning back in the low chair, her face turned toward the window. The sun of Scilly is never too fierce or too burning in summer, nor in winter does it ever lose its force; in July, when the people of the adjacent islands of Great Britain and Ireland venture not forth into the glare of the sun, here the soft sea mists and the strong sea air temper the heat; and in December the sun still shines with a lingering warmth, as if he loved the place. This girl lived in the sunshine all the year round; rowed in it; lay in it; basked in it, bareheaded, summer and winter; in the winter she would

263

sit sheltered from the wind in some warm
corner of the rocks; in summer she would lie on the
hillside or stand upon the high headlands of the
sea-beat crags while the breezes, which in the Land
of Lyonesse do never cease, played with her long
tresses and kept her soft cheek cool.

The window was wide open on all three sides; the
girl had been doing some kind of work, but it had
dropped from her hands, and now lay unregarded on
the floor; she was gazing upon the scene before her,
but with the accustomed eyes which looked out
upon it every day. A girl who has such a picture
continually before her all day long, never tires of
it, though she may not be always consciously considering it and praising it. The stranger, for his
part, cannot choose but cry aloud for admiration;
but the native, who knows it as no stranger can, is
silent. The house, half-way up the low hill, looked
out upon the south—to be exact; its aspect was S.W.
by S.—so that from this window the girl saw always,
stretched out at her feet, the ocean, now glowing in
the golden sunshine of September. Had she been
tall enough she might even have seen the coast of
South America, the nearest land in the far distance.
Looking S.W. that is, she would have seen the broad
mouth of Oroonooque and the shores of El Dorado.
This broad seascape was broken exactly in the middle
by the Bishop's Rock and its stately light-house rising tall and straight out of the water; on the left
hand the low hill of Annet shut out the sea; and on
the right Great Minalto, rugged and black, the white
foam always playing round its foot or flying over its
great black northern headland, bounded and framed
the picture. Almost in the middle of the water, not
more than two miles distant, a sailing ship, all sails
set, made swift way, bound outward one knows not
whither. Lovely at all times is a ship in full sail,
but doubly lovely when she is seen from afar, sailing

on a smooth sea, under a cloudless sky, the sun of afternoon lighting up her white sails. No other ships were in sight; there was not even the long line of smoke which proclaims the steamer below the horizon; there was not even a Penzance fishing-boat tacking slowly homeward with brown sails and its two masts: in this direction there was no other sign of man.

The girl, I say, saw this sight every day; she never tired of it, partly because no one ever tires of the place in which he was born and has lived—not even an Arab of the Great Sandy Desert; partly because the sea, which has been called, by unobservant poets, unchanging, does, in fact, change—face, color, mood, even shape—every day, and is never the same, except, perhaps, when the east wind of March covers the sky with a monotony of gray and takes the color out of the face of ocean as it takes the color from the granite rocks, last year's brown and yellow fern, and the purple heath. To this girl, who lived with the sea around her, it always formed a setting, a background, a frame for her thoughts and dreams. Wherever she went, whatever she said or sung, or thought or did, there was always in her ears the lapping or the lashing of the waves; always before her eyes was the white surge flying over the rocks; always the tumbling waves. But as for what she actually thought, or what she dreamed, seeing how ignorant of the world she was, and how innocent and how young, and as for what was passing in her mind this afternoon as she sat at the window, I know not. On the first consideration of the thing, one would be inclined to ask how, without knowledge, can a girl think or imagine or dream anything? On further thought, one understands that knowledge has very little to do with dreams or fancies. Yet, with or without knowledge, no poet, sacred bard, or prophet has ever been able to divine the thoughts of a girl or to interpret them, or even to set them down, in consecutive language. I suppose they are not, in truth, thoughts. Thought implies reasoning, and the connection of facts, and the experience of life as far as it has gone. A young maiden's mind is full of dimly seen shadows and pallid ghosts which flit across the brain and disappear. These shadows have the semblance of shape, but it is dim and uncertain; they have the pretense of color, but it changes every moment; if they seem to show a face, it vanishes immediately and is forgotten. Yet these shadows smile upon the young with kindly eyes; they beckon with their fingers, and point to where, low down on the horizon, with cloudy outline, lies the Purple Island—to such a girl as this the future is always a small island girt by the sea, far off and lonely. The shadows whisper to her; they sing to her; but no girl has ever yet told us—even if she understands—what it is they tell her.

She had been lying there, quiet and motionless, for an hour or more, ever since the tea-things had been taken away—at Holy Hill they have tea at half past four. The ancient lady who was in the room with her had fallen back again into the slumber which held her nearly all day long as well as all the night. The house seemed thoroughly wrapped and lapped in the softest peace and stillness; and in one corner a high clock, wooden cased, swung its brass pendulum behind a pane of glass with solemn and sonorous chronicle of the moments, so that they seemed to march rather than to fly. A clock ought not to tick as if Father Time were hurried and driven along without dignity by a scourge. This clock, for one, was not in a hurry. Its tick showed that Time rests not—but hastens not. There is admonition in such a clock. When it has no one to admonish but a girl whose work depends on her own sweet will, its voice might seem thrown away;

yet one never knows the worth of an admonition, besides, the clock suited the place and the room. Where should time march, with solemn step and slow, if not on the quiet island of Samson, in the Archipelago of Scilly? On its face was written the name of its maker, plain for all the world to see— "Peter Trevellick, Penzance, A. D. 1741."

The room was not ceiled, but showed the dark joists and beams above, once painted, but a long time ago. The walls were wainscoted and painted drab, after an old fashion now gone out; within the panels hung colored prints, which must have been there since the beginning of this century. They represented rural subjects—the farmer sitting before a sirloin of beef, while his wife, a cheerful nymph, brought him Brown George, foaming with her best home-brewed; the children hung about his knees expectant of morsels. Or the rustic bade farewell to his sweetheart, the recruiting-sergeant waiting for him, and the villagers, to a woman, bathed in tears. There were half a dozen of those compositions simply colored. I believe they are now worth much money. But there were many other things in this room worth money. Opposite the fire-place stood a cabinet of carved oak, black with age, precious beyond price. Behind its glass windows one could see a collection of things once strange and rare—things which used to be brought home by sailors long before steamers plowed every ocean, and globe-trotters trotted over every land. There were wonderful things in coral, white and red and pink; Venus's fingers from the Philippines; fans from the Seychelles, stuffed birds of wondrous hue, daggers and knives, carven tomahawks, ivory toys, and many of her wonders from the far East and fabulous Cathay. Beside the cabinet was a wooden desk, carved in mahogany, with a date of 1645, said to have been brought to the islands by one of the Royallst prisoners whom Cromwell hanged upon the highest cairn of Hangman's Island. There was no escaping Cromwell—not even in Scilly any more than in Jamaica. In one corner was a cupboard, the door standing open. No collector ever came here to gaze upon the treasures unspeakable of cups and saucers, plates and punchbowls. On the mantel-shelf were brass candlesticks and silver candlesticks, side by side with "ornaments" of china, pink and gild, belonging to the artistic reign of good King George the Fourth. On the hearth-rug before the fire, which was always burning in this room, all the year round, lay an old dog sleeping.

Everybody knows the feeling of a room or a house belonging to the old. Even if the windows are kept open, the air is always close. Rest, a gentle, elderly angel, sits in the least frequented room with folded wings. Sleep is always coming to the doors at all hours: for the sake of Rest and Sleep the house must be kept very quiet; nobody must ever laugh in the house, there is none of the litter that children make, nothing is out of its place, nothing is disturbed; the furniture is old-fashioned and formal, the curtains are old and faded, the carpets are old, faded, and worn: it is always evening; everything belonging to the house has done its work; all together, like the tenant, are sitting still—solemn, hushed, at rest, waiting for the approaching end.

The only young thing at Holy Hill was the girl at the window. Everything else was old—the servants, the farm laborers, the house, and the furniture. In the great hooded arm-chair beside the fire reposed the proprietor, tenant, or owner of all. She was the oldest and most venerable dame ever seen. At this time she was asleep; and her head had dropped forward a little, but not much; her eyes were closed; her hands were folded in her lap. She was now so very ancient that she never left her chair except for the bed; also, by reason of her great antiquity, she now passed most of the day in sleep, partly awake in the morning, when she gazed about and asked questions of the day. But sometimes, as you will presently see, she revived again in the evening, became lively and talkative, and suffered her memory to return to the ancient days.

By the assistance of her handmaidens, this venerable lady was enabled to present an appearance both picturesque and pleasing, chiefly because it carried the imagination back to a period so very remote. To begin with, she wore her bonnet all day long. Forty years ago it was not uncommon in country places to find very old ladies who wore their bonnets all day long. Ursula Rosevean, however, was the last who still preserved that ancient custom. It was a large bonnet that she wore, a kind of bonnet calculated to impress very deeply the imagination of one —whether male or female—who saw it for the first time; it was of bold design, as capacious as a storeship, as flowing in its lines as an old man-of-war; inspired to a certain extent by the fashions of the Waterloo period. Yet, in great part, of independent design. Those few who were permitted to gaze upon the bonnet beheld it reverently. Within the bonnet an adroit arrangement of cap and ribbons concealed whatever of baldness or exiguity as to locks—but what does one know? Venus Calva has never been worshipped by men; and women only pay their tribute at her shrine from fear, never from love. The face of the sleeping lady reminded one— at first, vaguely—of history. Presently one perceived that it was the identical face which that dread Occidental star, Queen Elizabeth herself, would have assumed had she lived to the age of ninety-five, which was Ursula's time of life in the year 1884. For it was an aquiline face, thin and sharp; and if her eyes had been open you would have remarked that they were bright and piercing, almost like those of the Tudor Queen. Her cheek still preserved something of the color which had once made it beautiful; but cheek and forehead alike were covered with lines innumerable, and her withered hands seemed to have grown too small for their natural glove. She was dressed in black silk, and wore a gold chain about her neck.

The clock struck half past five melodiously. Then the girl started and sat upright—as awakened out of her dream. "Armorel," it seemed to say—nay, since it seemed to say, it actually did say—"Child Armorel, I am old and wise. For a hundred and forty-three years, ever since I left the hands of the ingenious Peter Trevellick, of Penzance, in the year 1741, I have been counting the moments, never ceasing save at those periods when surgical operations have been necessary. In each year there are thirty-one million five hundred and thirty-six thousand moments. Judge, therefore, for yourself how many moments in all I have counted. I must, you will own, be very wise indeed. I am older even than your great-great-grandmother. I remember her a baby first, and then a pretty child, and then a beautiful woman, for all she is now so worn and wizened. I remember her father and her grandfather. Also her brothers, and her son and her grandson—and your own father, dear Armorel. The moments pass; they never cease; I tell them as they go. You have but short space to do all you wish to do. You, child, have done nothing at all yet. But the moments pass. Patience. For you, too, work will be found. Youth passes. You can hear it pass. I tell the moments in which it melts away and vanishes. Age itself shall pass. You may listen if you please. I tell the moments in which it slowly passes."

Armorel looked at the clock with serious eyes during the delivery of this fine sermon, the whole bearing of which she did not perhaps comprehend. Then she started up suddenly and sprung to her feet, stung by a sudden pang of restlessness, with a quick breath and a sigh. We who have passed the noon of life are apt to forget the disease of restlessness to which youth is prone; it is an affection which greatly troubles that period of life, though it should be the happiest and most contented; it is a disorder due to anticipation, impatience, and inexperience. The voyage is all before; youth is eager to be sailing on that unknown ocean full of strange islands; who would not be restless with such a journey before one and such discoveries to make?

Armorel opened the door noiselessly, and slipped out. At the same moment the old dog awoke and crept out with her, going delicately and on tiptoe lest he should awaken the ancient lady. In the hall outside, the girl stood listening. The house was quite silent, save from the kitchen there was wafted on the air a soft droning—gentle, melodious, and murmurous, like the contented booming of a bumble-bee among the figwort. Armorel laughed gently. "Oh!" she murmured; "they are all asleep. Grandmother is asleep in the parlor; Dorcas and Chessun are asleep in the kitchen; Justinian is asleep in the cottage, and I suppose the boy is asleep somewhere in the farmyard."

The girl led the way, and the dog followed.

She passed through the door into the garden of the front. It was not exactly a well-ordered garden, because everything seemed to grow as it pleased; but then in Samson you have not to coax flowers and plants into growing: they grow because it pleases them to grow: this is the reason why they grow so tall and so fast. The garden faced the south-west, and was protected from the north and east by the house itself and by a high stone wall. There is not anywhere on the island a warmer and sunnier corner than this little front garden of Holy Hill. The geranium clambered up the walls beside and among the branches of the tree-fuchsia, both together covering the front of the house with the rich coloring of their flowers. On either side of the door grew a great tree, with gnarled trunk and twisted branches, of lemon verbena, fragrant and sweet, perfuming the air; the myrtles were like unto trees for size; the very marguerites ran to timber of the smaller kind; the pampas-grass in the warmest corner rose eight feet high, waving its long silver plumes; the tall stalk still stood which had borne the flowers of an aloe that very summer; the leaves of the plant itself were slowly dying away, their life work, which is nothing at all but the production of that one flowering stem, finished. That done, the world has no more attractions for the aloe; it is content; it slowly dies away. And in the front of the garden was a row of tall dracæna palms. An old ship's figure-head, thrown ashore after a wreck, representing the head and bust of a beautiful maiden, gilded, but with a good deal of the gilt rubbed off, stood in the left hand of the garden, half hidden by another fuchsia-tree in flower; and a huge old-fashioned ship's lantern hung from an iron bar projecting over the door of the house.

The house itself was of stone, with a roof of small slates. Impossible to say how old it was, because in this land, stone-work ages rapidly, and soon becomes covered with yellow and orange lichen, while in the interstices there soon grows the gray sandwort; and in the soft sea air and the damp sea mists the sharp edges of granite are quickly rounded off and crumbled. But it was a very old house, save for the square projecting window, which had been added recently—say thirty or forty years ago—a long, low house of two stories, simply built; it stands half-way up the hill which slopes down to the water's edge;

it is protected from the north and north-east winds, which are the deadliest enemies to Scilly, partly by the hill behind and partly by a spur of gray rock running like an ancient Cyclopean wall down the whole face of the hill into the sea, where for many a fathom it sticks out black teeth, round which the white surge rises and tumbles, even in the calmest time.

Beyond the garden wall—why they wanted a garden wall I know not, except for the pride and dignity of the thing—was a narrow green, with a little —a very little—pond; in the pond there were ducks; and beside the green was a small farm-yard, containing everything that a farm-yard should contain except a stable. It had no stable, because there are no horses or carts upon the island. Pigs there are, and cows; fowls there are, and ducks and geese, and a single donkey for the purpose of carrying the flower baskets from the farm to the landing-place. But neither horse nor cart.

Beyond the farm-yard was a cottage, exactly like the house, but smaller. It was thatched, and on the thatch grew clumps of samphire. This was the abode of Justinian Tryeth, bailiff, head man, or foreman, who managed the farm. When you have named Ursula Rosevean and Armorel, her great-great-granddaughter, and Justinian Tryeth, and Dorcas his wife—she was a native of St. Agnes, and therefore a Hicks by birth—Peter his son, and Chessun his daughter, you have a complete directory of the island, because nobody else now lives on Samson. Formerly, however, and almost within the memory of the oldest inhabitant, according to the computation of antiquaries and the voice of tradition, this island maintained a population of over two score.

The hill which rises behind the house is the southern hill of the two which, with the broad valley between them, make up the Island of Samson. This hill slopes steeply seaward to south and west. It is not a lofty hill, by any means. In Scilly there are no lofty hills. When nature addressed herself to the construction of this archipelago she brought to the task a light touch; at the moment she happened to be full of feeling for the great and artistic effects which may be produced by small elevations, especially in those places where the material is granite. Therefore, though she raised no Alpine peak in Scilly, she provided great abundance and any variety of bold coastline with rugged cliffs, lofty cairns, and headlines piled with rocks. And her success as an artist in this *genre* has been undoubtedly wonderful. The actual measurement of Holy Hill, Samson—but why should we measure— has been taken, for the admiration of the world, by the Ordnance Survey. It is really no more than a hundred and thirty-two feet—not a foot more or less. But then one knows hills ten times that height —the Herefordshire Beacon for example—which are not half so mountainous in the effect produced. Only a hundred and thirty-two feet—yet on its summit one feels the exhilaration of spirits caused by the air elsewhere of five thousand feet at least. On its southern and western slopes lie the fields which form the Flower Farm of Holy Hill.

Below the farm-yard the ground sloped more steeply to the water; the slope was covered with short heather fern, now brown and yellow, and long trailing branches of bramble, now laden with ripe blackberries, the leaves enriched with blazon of gold and purple and crimson.

Armorel ran across the green and plunged among the fern, tossing her arms and singing aloud, the old dog trotting and jumping, but with less elasticity, beside her. She was bareheaded; the sunshine made her dark cheeks ruddy and caused her black eyes to glow. Hebe, young and strong, loves Phœbus and fears not any freckles. When she came to the water's edge, where the boulders lie piled in a broken mass among and above the water, she stood still and looked across the sea, silent for a moment. Then she began to sing in a strong contralto; but no one could hear her, not even the coastguard on Telegraph Hill, or he of the Star Fort; the song she sung was one taught her by the old lady, who had sung it herself in the old, old days, when the road was always filled with merchantmen waiting for convoy up the Channel, and when the islands were rich with the trade of the ships, and their piloting, and their wrecks—to say nothing of the free trade which went on gallantly without break or stop. As she sung she lifted her arms and swung them in a slow cadence, as a Nautch girl sometimes swings her arms. What she sung was nothing other than the old song:

" Early one morning, just as the sun was rising,
    I heard a maid sing in the valley below:
        ' Oh! don't deceive me. Oh! never leave me,
            How could you use a poor maiden so? ' "

In the year of grace 1884, Armorel was fifteen years of age. But she looked nineteen or twenty, because she was so tall and well-grown. She was dressed simply in a blue flannel; the straw hat which she carried in her hand was trimmed with red ribbons; at her throat she had stuck a red verbena— she naturally took to red, because her complexion was so dark. Black hair; black eyes; a strongly marked brow; a dark cheek of warm and ruddy hue; the lips full, but the mouth finely curved; features large but regular—she was already, though so young, a tall and handsome woman. Those able to understand things would recognize in her dark complexion, in her carriage, in her eyes, and in her upright

figure the true Castilian touch. The gypsy is
swarthy; the negro is black, the mulatto is dusky;
it is not the color alone, but the figure and the carriage also, which mark the Spanish blood. A noble
Spanish lady; yet how could she get to Samson?

She wore no gloves—you cannot buy gloves in
Samson—and her hands were brown with exposure
to sea and sun, to wind and rain; they were by no
means tiny hands, but strong and capable hands;
her arms—no one ever saw them, but for shape and
whiteness they could not be matched—would have
disgraced no young fellow of her own age for
strength and muscle. That was fairly to be expected
in one who continually sailed and rowed across the
inland seas of this archipelago; who went to church
by boat and to market by boat; who paid her visits
by boat, and transacted her business by boat, and
went by boat to do her shopping. She who rows
every day upon the salt water, and knows how to
manage a sail when the breeze is strong and the Atlantic surge rolls over the rocks and roughens the
still water of the road, must needs be strong and
sound. For my own part, I admire not the fragile
maiden so much as her who rejoices in her strength.
Youth in woman, as well as in man, should be brave
and lusty; clean of limb as well as of heart; strong
of arm as well as of will; enduring hardness of voluntary labor as well as hardness of involuntary
pain; with feet that can walk, run, and climb, and
with hands that can hold on. Such a girl as Armorel,
so tall, so strong, so healthy, offers, methinks, a
home ready-made for all the virtues, and especially
the virtues feminine, to house themselves therein.
Here they will remain, growing stronger every day,
until at last they have become part and parcel of
the very girl herself, and cannot be parted from her.
Whereas, when they visit the puny creature, weak,
timid, delicate—but no—'tis better to remain **silent**.

How many times had the girl wandered, morning or afternoon, down the rough face of the hill, and stood looking vaguely out to sea, and presently returned home again? How many such walks had she taken and forgotten? For a hundred times? yea, a thousand times—we do over and over again the old familiar action, the little piece of the day's routine, and forget it when we lie down to sleep. But there comes the thousandth time when the same thing is done again in the same way, yet is never to be forgotten. For on that day happens the thing which changes and charges a whole life. It is the first of many days. It is the beginning of new days. From it, whatever may have happened before, everything shall now be dated until the end. Mohammed lived many years, but all the things that happened unto him or his successors are dated from the Flight. Is it for nothing that it has been told what things Armorel did and how she looked on this day? Not so, but for the sake of what happened afterward, and because the history of Armorel begins with this restless fit, which drove her out of the quiet room down the hill-side to the sea. Her history begins, like every history of a woman worth relating, with the man cast by the sea upon the shores of her island. The maiden always lives upon an island, and whether the man is cast upon the shore by the sea of society, or the sea of travel, or the sea of accident, or the sea of adventure, or the sea of briny waves and roaring winds and jagged rocks, matters little. To Armorel it was the last. To you, dear Dorothy or Violet, it will doubtless be by the sea of society. And the day that casts him before your feet will ever after begin a new period in your reckoning.

BJÖRNSTJERNE BJÖRNSON

BJÖRNSTJERNE BJÖRNSON, poet and novelist, was born at Kvikne, Norway, in 1832. He became a student at the University of Christiania in 1852, and almost immediately became a writer for periodicals. Later he managed a theater, edited two papers and traveled extensively. While on his tours he was a voluminous writer of poems, plays and novels. His most important works include "Magnhild," "Arne," "Flags are Flying." The best dramas from his pen are "Mary Stuart," "A Glove" and "Leonardo."

THE PRINCESS

THE Princess sat alone in her maiden bower,
The lad blew his horn at the foot of the tower.
"Why playest thou alway? Be silent, I pray,
It fetters my thoughts that would flee far away,
　　As the sun goes down."

In her maiden bower sat the Princess forlorn,
The lad had ceased to play on his horn.
"Oh, why art thou silent? I beg thee to play!
It gives wing to my thoughts that would flee away,
　　As the sun goes down."

In her maiden bower sat the Princess forlorn,
Once more with delight played the lad on his horn.
She wept as the shadows grew long, and she sighed:
"Oh, tell me, my God, what my heart doth betide,
　　Now the sun has gone down."

THE NORTH LAND

MY land will I defend,
   My land will I befriend,
And my son to help its fortunes and be faithful
      I will train;
   Its weal shall be my prayer,
   And its want shall be my care,
From the rugged old snow mountains to the cabins
      by the main.

   We have sun enough and rain,
   We have fields of golden grain;
But love is more than fortune, or the best of sunny
      weather;
   And we have many a Child of Song,
   And Sons of Labor strong,
We have hearts to raise the North Land, if they only
      beat together.

   In many a gallant fight
   We have shown the world our might,
And reared the Norseman's banner on a vanquished
      stranger's shore;
   But fresh combats we will brave,
   And a nobler flag shall wave,
With more of health and beauty than it ever had
      before!

ARNE

[The following extracts from "Arne" are taken from a translation made by a Norwegian, and published in English at Bergen by
H. J. Geelmuydens]

(A Tale of Peasant Life in Norway)

[Arne is the son of Margit Kampen, the owner
of a small farm; his father Nils, the tailor and fid-

279

dler, a drunken ne'er-do-well, who had been the idol of the lasses at all rural gatherings, is dead. Arne has grown up an industrious lad, but a maker of songs, and possessed with strange longings to see other lands beyond the hills of snow. Besides managing his mother's land he works at seasons at neighbors' farms, and he falls in love with Eli, the daughter of Birgit Boen, who had been one of his father's many admirers, and had hoped to be his wife.]

As Arne with his hand-saw on his shoulder walked over the ice and approached the farm of Boen, it seemed to him a very nice one. The house looked as if it were newly painted. He felt somewhat cold, and perhaps that was why the house looked so comfortable. He did not go straight in, but went first to the cow-house. There a flock of thick-haired goats were standing in the snow, gnawing the bark of some sprigs. A chained dog was running to and fro by its kennel barking as if the fiend himself had been coming, but wagged his tail as soon as Arne stopped, and then allowed himself to be patted. The kitchen door on the upper side of the house was often opened, and, every time, Arne looked that way: but it was either the dairy-maid who came with her milk-pans, or the cook-maid, who emptied some vessels for the goats. In the barn they were threshing; to the left before the wood-house a boy was standing, cutting wood, and behind him there was a great quantity of wood piled together. Arne put down his hand-saw and went into the kitchen; there was white sand on the floor and juniper cut in very small pieces strewn over. Copper kettles were shining on the walls, and jugs and plates standing in long rows. They were preparing dinner, and he asked to speak to Bard. "Go into the room," said somebody, pointing to the door. He went. There was no latch to the door, but the handle was of brass. Inside it was light and painted, the ceiling ornamented with many roses; the cupboards red, with the name of the proprietor in black; the bedstead red likewise, but with blue stripes on all the edges. Near the stove there was a broad-shouldered man sitting with a mild face and long yellow hair. He was putting some hoops round some little tubs. At the long table a tall and slender woman was sitting with a handkerchief on her head and with a tight-sleeved gown. She was dividing some corn into two heaps. There was no one else in the room.

"Good day, and blessing to your work!" said Arne, taking off his cap. Both looked up, the man smiling, and asked who he was.

"He who is to cut with a hand-saw." The man then smiled more and said, whilst bending his head down and again beginning his work, "Oh! Arne Kampen?"

"Arne Kampen!" cried out the woman, staring with all her eyes.

Her husband looked up, smiling anew. "Son of Nils the tailor;" and he set to work again.

Some while afterwards the woman rose, went up to a shelf, turned round, went to the cupboard, turned again, and whilst at last standing and looking at something in the drawer of the table she asked without looking up, "Is he going to work here?"

"Yes, he is," replied the man, also without looking up. "I am afraid nobody has asked you to sit down," continued he, turning towards Arne. He went to take a seat; the woman went out, the man went on working, so Arne asked if he should also begin. "We must dine first."

The woman did not come in any more, but the next time the kitchen door was opened it was Eli who entered. She pretended at first not to see him; when he rose to go to her she stopped, half turning to offer him her hand, but she did not look at him.

They then spoke a couple of words to each other, the father going on working. She had her hair plaited, was dressed in a high-bodied gown with narrow sleeves; she was slender and straight, round about the waist, and had very small hands. She laid the table, as the working men dined in the other room, but Arne with the family in this room. "Will not your mother come?" asked the man.

"No, she is upstairs weighing some wool."

"Have you asked her?"

"Yes, but she says she wants nothing." There was some silence.

"But it is cold upstairs."

"She did not wish that I should light a fire."

After dinner Arne worked; in the evening he was again in the room with the family. Then Eli's mother was also there. The women were sewing, the husband doing some little jobs, Arne assisting him, and there was a silence of some hours, for Eli, who always seemed to be the spokeswoman, was also silent now. It pained Arne to think that so it was also often in his home, but he did not seem to think of it before now. At length Eli once drew a deep breath, as if she had kept silence long enough, and then she began to laugh. Then her father also laughed, and Arne also thought it very ridiculous, and began to laugh too. From this time they talked a little, especially Eli and Arne, the father occasionally joining in with a word. But once, as Arne had happened to talk a long time, he looked up. He then saw that the mother had let her work fall and sat looking eagerly at him. She now began to work again, but at the first words he happened to say she looked up.

It was now bedtime, and every one went to rest. Arne would try to remember the dream he had the first night he slept in a new place, but there was no sense in it. The whole day he had spoken little or nothing with Eli's father, but all night long it was of him he was dreaming. The last thing he dreamed was, that Bard was sitting playing cards with Nils the tailor, who was very angry and pale in the face, whilst Bard was smiling and dragging all the cards over to him.

Arne remained there several days, during which little was spoken, but a great deal of work was done. Not only the family in their own room were silent, but even the servants, the workmen, and the women. There was an old dog in the yard, which was always barking whenever there came any stranger to the farm; but the people said "Hush!" and then he went away growling to lie down again. At home at Kampen there was a great weathercock on the top of the house, that turned with the wind. Here there was a still larger one that Arne could not but take notice of, because it did not turn at all. When the wind was strong the weather-cock always worked hard to get loose, and Arne looked at this so long that he was induced to go up on the roof to loosen it. It was not frozen fast, as he thought, but a stick was put in to make it stand still. This Arne took out and threw down. The stick hit Bard, who was walking underneath. He looked up: "What are you doing there?"

"I am loosening the weather-cock."

"Do not do that, it creaks when it goes."

Arne was sitting astride on the ridge of the house. "I am sure that it is better than to let it be silent."

Bard looked up at Arne and Arne looked down on Bard. Then Bard smiled and called up to him, "If I must shriek when I am to talk then I had better be silent."

Now it may happen so that a word is remembered a long time after it has been said, and especially when it is the last word said. These words followed Arne when in the cold weather he crept down from the roof, and they were in his mind when he entered the room in the evening. There stood Eli in the dusk of the evening near a window looking across the ice, which was lying as smooth as a mirror in the moonlight. He went to the other window and looked out as she did. Inside it was warm and quiet, outside cold; and a sharp evening breeze rushed through the valley, shaking the trees so much that the shadows which they threw in the moonlight did not lie still, but groped about and crept on the surface of the snow. In the parsonage a light could be seen that came ever opening and shutting itself, taking many shapes and colors as it always appears when one is looking too long at it. The dark mountain stood overhead, with many marvelous fairy stories in the bottom, but with moonlight on the snowy plains of its summit. In the sky could be seen the stars and some little flickering aurora borealis yonder in one corner; but it did not increase all over the sky. Some distance from the window down towards the water several trees were standing, and they seemed stealing over to each other through their shadows; but the great ash stood by itself writing on the snow.

It was quite silent everywhere; only occasionally there was something that gave a long and yelling shriek that sounded quite plaintive. "What is that?" asked Arne.

"It is the weather-cock," replied Eli, afterwards adding more slowly, as if to herself, "It must have been loosened." Arne had felt as if he had been wanting to talk and was not able; but now he said:

"Do you remember the story of the thrushes; that song?"

"Yes, I do."

"Well, I remember it was you who told it us That was a nice story."

She now said in so soft a voice that it seemed to him the first time he heard it, "I often think there is something that sings when it is quite still."

"That is what is good in us."

She looked towards him as if there was something too much in that answer. They were both silent afterwards. Then she asked him while she was writing with her finger on the glass-pane, "Have you lately made any song?"

He turned red, but she did not see it. She therefore asked again, "How do you manage to make songs?"

"Would you like to know?"

"Yes, I should."

"I take care of such thoughts as others allow to pass." She was now silent a long time. I dare say she was trying to compose a song of some sort or other, as if she had had some thoughts, but allowed them to pass. "That was strange," said she, as if to herself, and began writing again on the glass-pane.

"I was making a song the first time I saw you."

"Where was that?"

"Near the parsonage that evening you left it. I saw you in the water."

She laughed, stood quiet a little, and said, "Let me hear that song."

Arne had never before done anything of the kind, but now he commenced saying the song:

My Thora jumped so light on her feet
  Her lover to meet.
He sang. It was heard over roof and way—
  Good day! good day!
And all little birds sang merry and gay:
  "Till midsummer-eve
  Laughter and dancing they never leave;
Later but little I know, if she does her garland
   weave."

Eli stood very attentive a long time after he had done. At last she burst out, "Well, how I do pity her!"

"It appears to me as if I had not made that song," said he, and remained standing as if looking after the song.

Then she said, "But I hope it will not go so with me."

"No, I thought more of myself."

"Will it go so with you then?"

"I do not know, but I have felt so at times."

"That is strange," and she wrote on the glass-pane again.

The next day when Arne came in to dine he went up to the window. Outside it was gray and thick, inside it was warm and comfortable. But on the window-pane was written with a finger, Arne, Arne, Arne, and continually Arne. It was near this window that Eli had been standing the preceding night.

[His mother dreads that Arne will go away, and is glad to discover that he has fallen in love; but, knowing his shyness, she schemes to bring about the match, and the kindly pastor of the village aids her.

"Good-bye," said Margit, in the door up at the clergyman's. It was a Sunday evening later in the summer; he was come from church, and she had been sitting there till now—it was almost seven. "Good-bye, Margit," said the clergyman. She made haste down the stairs and out into the yard, for there she had just seen Eli Boen playing with the clergyman's son and her own brother.

"Good evening," said Margit, and remained standing. "God bless the party!" "Good evening," said Eli. She was burning red in the face, and would leave off, though the boys pressed her to go on; but she begged to be excused, and was permitted to leave off for to-night.

"I almost think I should know you," said Margit.

"That may be so," said the other.

"It could not be Eli Boen?" Yes, it was she.

286

'Why to be sure, so you are Eli Boen? Yes, now I see how like you are to your mother."

Eli's tawny hair was torn out, so it hung long and loose down; she was as hot and red in the face as a berry; her breath came heavily, so much so that she could not talk and laugh. "Well, now, that belongs to youth, that does," said Margit, and looked at the girl till she grew quite fond of her. "I suppose you do not know me, do you?" Eli wished to ask, but did not do so on account of the other being elder, so she said that she did not recollect ever having seen her before. "Why, no, it could not be expected that you knew me; old people seldom get out. My son you know perhaps a little—Arne Kampen? I am his mother." She stole a glance at Eli, whose breath directly came slowly, and her face became serious, and eyes staring. "I almost think he has been at work once yonder at Boen." Yes, he had. "It is beautiful weather to-night. We threw about the hay during the day and took it in before I left, it is such blessed weather."

"It will certainly be a good hay harvest this year," said Eli.

"Yes, you may say so. At Boen I suppose it is beautiful?"

"They have done there now."

"I dare say they have; great help, active people. Are you going home to-night?" No, she should not do so. "Could not you go with me part of the road? It is so seldom I find any one to talk with, and I dare say it does not matter much for you." Eli excused herself that she had not her jacket on. "Why, yes. I am almost ashamed to ask such a thing the first time I see a person, but one must bear with old people." Eli said she might go with her; she would only run in for her jacket.

It was a very close jacket. When it was hooked, it looked as if it were a body of a dress that she had on; but now she only hooked the two lowest hooks, she was so hot. Her fine linen had a little collar, that was turned over and kept together in the front by a silver button in the form of a bird with wings spread out. Such a button Nils the tailor had worn the first time Margit Kampen danced with him.

"A nice button," said she, looking at it.

"I got it from mother," said Eli.

"Yes, I suppose you have," and she was helping her and putting her in order.

Now they walked on. The grass was mowed down, and was lying in little heaps, to which Margit went up, and found when smelling it that it was good hay. She asked about the cattle they had on this farm, and then got the opportunity to ask about the cattle they had at Boen and told how much cattle they had at Kampen. "Our farm has improved much in the later years, and it may be more than twice as large. There are now twelve milch cows, and there might be more, but Arne has so many books he reads in and manages after, therefore he will have them fed in such a grand style." Eli said nothing to all this, as might be expected, but Margit asked her how old she was. She was a little more than twenty years. "Have you tried your hand in house-keeping? You look such a lady I suppose it has not been much." Yes, she had helped somewhat, especially in the later time. "Well, it is good to be used to everything. When one gets a large house much may be wanted. But certainly that one who finds good help before her has no reason to complain." Eli would like to return, for now they were a long way past the parsonage. "It will be a couple of hours before the sun goes down; it would be kind of you to go on talking with me a little longer." And Eli went with her.

Margit now began to talk of Arne. "I do not

know if you know much of him. He might be able to teach you something. Good Lord, what a deal he has read!" Eli confessed she knew he had read much. "But that is the least good in him, that is. So good as he has been towards his mother all his days, that is something more. If the old adage be true that the person who is kind to his mother is sure to make a good husband, then that one he chooses will not have much to complain of." Eli asked why they had painted the house yonder with gray colors. "I suppose they have not had any other," thought Margit. "I am sure I should wish with all my heart that my Arne got a reward for all the good he has been doing to his mother. The woman he ought to have for a wife ought to be well instructed and of good heart. What is it you are looking after, my child?"

"I only lost a little sprig I was carrying."

"Well, I have many thoughts, I can tell you, whilst I am sitting yonder in the forest by myself. If he should happen to carry one home who took a blessing with her both to the house and to her husband, then I know that many a poor one would be glad on that day." They were both silent, and walked on without looking at each other. "He is so strange," began again the mother, "he has been so much frightened as a child, and therefore he has been used to keep all his thoughts quite to himself, and such people do not generally get on." Now Eli insisted on returning, but Margit said it was only about a mile to Kampen—not so much even—and therefore she must see Kampen as she had come so far. But Eli thought it was too late for her. "Oh! there are always those who will go home with you," said Margit.

"No, no!" answered Eli quickly, and wanted to return.

"Well, Arne is not at home." said Margit, "so

it will not be he; but I dare say we shall find somebody else."

Eli had now no longer so great an objection. "If it only will not be too late," said she.

"Well, if we stand here long talking it may soon be too late;" and they walked on. "I suppose you have read much, you who have been educated at the clergyman's?" Yes, she had. "That will be of good service to you when you get one for your husband who knows somewhat less." No; such a one Eli said she would not have. "I dare say that would not be the best either; but here in the parish people generally know very little." Eli now asked if it was Kampen that she could see right before her. "No; that is Gransetren, the last farm before you come into the wood; when you come a little further up you will see Kampen. It is easy to live at Kampen I can tell you. It certainly seems to be a little aside, but happiness does not depend upon that."

Eli now asked what it was she saw smoking yonder in the wood. "It is from the house of a tenant who has got a place under Kampen. There lives a man from Uplands whose name is Canute. He went about quite alone, and then Arne gave him this spot to clear. Poor Arne knows what it is to be alone." In a little while they came so high up that they could see the farm.

"Is that Kampen?" said Eli, stopping and pointing.

"It is," said Margit. She stopped also.

The sun now looked them right in the face; they put their hands up to shade their eyes and looked downwards. In the middle of the plain lay the farmhouse, painted red, with white window-frames; round about, the grass was mowed down; some hay was standing in heaps; the corn-fields lay green beyond the pale meadow; yonder, near the cow-house, they were very busy—cows, sheep, and goats coming home.

the dogs barking, the dairy-maids calling; but over it all the loud noise of the waterfall of the glen. The longer Eli looked the more she heard this sound, which at last grew so frightful that her heart began to palpitate. It kept on thundering and roaring through her head till she felt as if quite wild, but afterwards so timid, that without perceiving it she walked cautiously with small steps, so Margit asked her to go on a little faster. This quite frightened her. "I have never heard anything like that water-fall before," said she. "I am getting frightened.." "You will soon get used to it," said the mother.

"Dear me! Do you think so?" asked Eli.

"Well, that you will soon see," said Margit, smiling. "Come now, and let us first look at the cattle," continued she, turning away a little from the road. "These trees Nils planted on both sides, for Nils wanted to have it nice; and so does Arne also. Look, there is the garden he has laid out."

"Only look!" cried out Eli, running fast up to the fence.

"Yes; by-and-by we shall look at that also," said Margit. Eli now looked quickly through the windows as she passed them; nobody was inside.

Both halted on the bridge going up to the barn and looked at the cows as they passed them bellowing and going into the cow-house. Margit named them all by names, told Eli how much milk each of them had yielded, what time some should be calving, and which of them not. The sheep were counted and allowed to come in; they were all of a large foreign species, for Arne had been able to get hold of two lambs of that species from the southern parts of the country. "He is always applying himself to all such things, though we should not think it of him." They now went into the barn to have a look at the hay that was just taken in, and Eli must smell it, "for such hay is not found everywhere'

Through an opening in the wall of the barn they looked out on the corn-fields, Margit telling Eli how much each field bore, and how much was sown of every sort. "Yes, I am sure she will be comfortable, that one who comes here." They went out of the barn and walked towards the house, but Eli, who had not answered anything to all the rest, when passing the garden now asked if she might be allowed to go in. And when she entered she asked if she might be allowed to take a flower or two. There was a little bench in the corner on which she sat down only just to try it, for she immediately rose.

"We must make haste now, lest it should be too late," said Margit, standing at the door of the house, and they walked in. Margit asked if she should not treat her with anything as this was her first visit; but Eli blushed, answering shortly, "No." She looked about the room: it was not very large, but comfortable, and contained a clock and a stove. Here Nils's fiddle was hanging, now old and dark but with new strings. Here also a couple of guns that belonged to Arne, English fishing tackle, and other strange things that his mother took down and showed her. Eli looked, but did not touch anything. The room was not painted, for Arne liked it so. Nor was there need of any painting in the room, for the window overlooked the glen, that had the high mountain right opposite to it and the beautiful blue in the back-ground; this room was larger and nicer than the others; but in two smaller rooms in the wing the walls were painted, for there the mother was to live when she grew old, and when he had got a wife in the house. They went to the kitchen, to the pantry and larder, to the drying-houses, and it now only remained to go up to the second story.

Here, also, were rooms well fitted up and exactly corresponding to those downstairs, but they were new, and not taken into use with the excep-

tion of one overlooking the glen. In these rooms up
stairs all sorts of furniture was placed, that was not
used every day. Here were hanging a great many
fur-coverlets and other bed-clothes. The mother took
hold of them; lifting them; Eli did the same. All
these things she was very fond of looking at; returned to some of them, asked many questions, and
was more and more amused. Then said the mother,
"Now we shall find the key to Arne's own room."
They found it under a chest, and went into the room
that overlooked the glen. The dreadful noise of the
waterfall was again close to them, for the window
was open. Here they could see the water lashing up
between the rocks, but not the waterfall itself except higher up where a piece of rock had fallen into
it, just as it came with all its might to its last plunge
down into the deep. On the upper part of this rock
fresh turf was lying; a couple of fir-cones had
found place here, and were growing up again with
the roots in the crevices of the rock. The wind had
been wearing and tearing these trees, the waterfall
continually washed them, so there was not a twig four
ells from the root; on their knees they seemed bent,
their branches crooked, but yet they stood there rising high between the rocks. These were the first
things Eli saw from the window, then the white
snowy mountain higher up than the green. She
looked back; over the fields there was peace and fer-
tility; she then looked about in the room, and the
first object she saw was a great book-shelf. There
were so many books that she did not think the clergyman had more. A cupboard was standing near to
the shelf, and down here he had his money. Twice
they had inherited, said the mother, and they ought
also to take a third inheritance if everything went
on as it ought to do. "But money is not the best
thing in the world. He might get what was much
better." There were many little things interesting to

look at in this cupboard, and Eli looked at them all as joyfully as a child. Then the mother showed her a big chest where all his gear was lying. This chest they also opened and looked at. Margit patted her on her shoulder, saying, "I have not seen you before to-day, but I love you already so much, my child," and she looked kindly into her eyes. Before Eli had time to be a little abashed Margit pulled her dress, saying quite slowly, "There you see a little red-painted box; you may be sure there is something strange in it." Eli looked at it: it was a little square box, that she should like very much to have. "He does not want me to know what is in it," whispered the mother, "and he hides away the key every time." She went to some clothes that were hanging on the wall, took down a velvet waistcoat, looked in the watchpocket, and there was the key lying. "Come now, and you shall see," whispered she. They went quite slowly and placed themselves on their knees before the box. At the same time as the mother opened the lid a delightful perfume arose out of it, so Eli beat her hands together before she had yet seen anything. Uppermost there lay a hand-kerchief spread out, which the mother took aside. "Look here," whispered she, taking up a fine black silk handkerchief, not such a one as men wear. "It looks just as if it were for a girl," said the mother. Eli spread it out over her lap, looking at it, but did not say a word. "Here is one more," said the mother. Eli took it,—she could not help herself; but the mother must try it on her, though Eli did not like it, and bent her head. She did not know what she would give for such a handkerchief, but yet it was not this she was thinking of. They put them together again, but slowly. "Here you shall see," said the mother, taking up some nice silk ribbands. "It all looks as if it were for a girl." Eli turned fiery red, but was silent. "Here is something

more;" the mother now took up a nice black dress.
"I'm sure that's fine," said she, holding it up
towards daylight. Eli's hands trembled a little,
her chest was rising, she felt the blood rushing up
to her head, she would like to turn away, but that
would not do. "He has bought something every
time he has been to town," said the mother. Eli was
scarcely able to stand it any longer, her eyes ran
from one thing to another in the box and turned
again to the dress. She was burning hot in the face.
The last thing the mother took up was lying in a
paper, which they removed; it was a pair of small
shoes. They had never seen anything like these
shoes, any of them. The mother said she did not
think they could be worked. Eli did not say a
word, but when she took the shoes in her hand all
her five fingers were seen marked on them. "I am
in a perspiration, I see," whispered she, drying herself. The mother laid the things to rights again.
"Does it not look quite as if he had bought these all
little by little for one he dared not give them to?"
said she, looking at Eli; "in the meantime he seems
to have put them here in the box." She replaced
everything carefully. "Now we shall see what there
is here in this small compartment at the end of the
box." She opened it very slowly, as if she should
see something very nice. There was lying a buckle
wide and broad as if for a waistband. This was the
first think Eli saw; then she saw a couple of gold
rings tied together, and then a psalm-book bound in
velvet with silver clasps, but she could not see any
more, for she had seen pricked in on the silver of
the psalm-book with very fine letters, "Eli Boen."
The mother wanted her to look again, but got no answer, and presently saw tears rolling down her
cheeks. Then the mother laid down the buckle she
had been keeping in her hand, shut again this little
compartment, turned to Eli, and took her to her

bosom. Then the daughter wept, and the mother cried over her without any of them saying anything more.

Some while after this Eli walked by herself in the garden; the mother was busy in the kitchen, as she had something nice to prepare, for now Arne would be coming. Afterwards she went out to look at Eli in the garden; she was sitting cowering down there writing names in the sand with a stick. She was sweeping it out when Margit came; she looked up and smiled; she had been crying. "Nothing to cry for, my child," said Margit, patting her cheek. "Now supper is ready, and Arne will be coming." They saw something black between the bushes up on the road. Eli stole in, the mother following her. Here was a great laying out of the table with cream pudding, smoked bacon, and fancy bread, but Eli did not look at it; she sat down on a chair yonder near the clock, trembling if she only heard a cat move. The mother stood at the table. Quick and manly steps were heard outside on the stone-flags, a short and easy step in the passage, the door opened, and Arne entered. The first thing he saw was Eli yonder near the clock. He let go the handle of the door and stood still. This made Eli still more embarrassed. She rose, repented it immediately, and turned towards the wall. "Are you here?" said Arne, and became fiery red as soon as he had said these words. She lifted up one of her hands, as when the sun shines too strong in the eyes. "How are you come here?" said he, making a step or two. She dropped the hand, turned a little towards him, but bent her head, and burst into violent tears. "Why do you cry, Eli?" asked he, going up to her. She did not answer, but cried more. "God bless you, Eli!" said he, putting his hand round her waist. She leaned upon him. He whispered something into her ear; she did not answer, but took him round his neck with both her hands.

A long time did they remain thus; not a sound was heard save from the waterfall, that sang its eternal song, distant and quiet. Then there was somebody who cried near the table. Arne looked up; it was his mother, whom he had not seen before. "Now I am sure you will not leave me, Arne!" said she, going towards him; she cried much, but it did her good, she said.

RICHARD D. BLACKMORE

RICHARD DODDRIDGE BLACKMORE, novelist, born at Longworth, England, in 1825; died 1900. He began the practice of law in 1852. He devoted himself to writing in 1862. Although he wrote many poems and translated much from the classics, it is on his novels, especially that of "Lorna Doone," on which his fame rests. This novel is one of the greatest produced in the nineteenth century, and the Exmoor country owes its fascination to thousands of visitors from the glamor of romance thrown over it by his pen. "Cripps the Carrier," "Springhaven" and "Perlycross" perhaps rank next in importance.

IN THE DOONE VALLEY

(From "Lorna Doone")

WHEN I started on my road across the hills and valleys (which now were pretty much alike), the utmost I could hope to do was to gain the crest of hills, and look into the Doone Glen. Hence I might at least descry whether Lorna still was safe, by the six nests still remaining (a signal arranged by the lovers), and the view of the Captain's house. When I was come to the open country, far beyond the sheltered homestead, and in the full brunt of the wind, the keen blast of the cold broke on me, and the mighty breadth of snow. Moor and highland, field and common, cliff and vale, and watercourse, over all the rolling folds of misty white were flung. There was nothing square or jagged left, there was nothing perpendicular; all the rugged lines were eased, and all the breaches smoothly filled.

Curves, and mounds, and rounded heavings took the place of rock and stump; and all the country looked as if a woman's hand had been on it.

Through the sparkling breadth of white, which seemed to glance my eyes away, and past the humps of laden trees, bowing their backs like a woodman, I contrived to get along, half sliding and half walking, in places where a plain-shodden man must have sunk, and waited, freezing, till the thaw should come to him. For although there had been such violent frost every night upon the snow, the snow itself having never thawed even for an hour, had never coated over. Hence it was as soft and light as if all had fallen yesterday. In places where no drift had been, but rather off than on to them, three feet was the least of depth; but where the wind had chased it round, or any draught led like a funnel, or anything opposed it, there you might very safely say that it ran up to twenty feet, or thirty, or even fifty, and I believe sometimes a hundred.

At last I got to my spy-hill (as I had begun to call it), although I never should have known it but for what it looked on. And even to now this last again required all the eyes of love, soever sharp and vigilant. For all the beautiful Glen Doone (shaped from out the mountains, as if on purpose for the Doones, and looking in the summer-time like a sharp-cut vase of green now was besnowed half up the sides, and at either end, so that it was more like the white basins wherein we boil plum-puddings. Not a patch of grass was there, not a black branch of a tree; all was white; and the little river flowed beneath an arch of snow, if it managed to flow at all.

Now this was a great surprise to me; not only because I believed Glen Doone to be a place outside all frost, but also because I thought perhaps that it was quite impossible to be cold near Lorna.

And now it struck me all at once that perhaps her ewer was frozen (as mine had been for the last three weeks, requiring embers around it), and perhaps her window would not shut, any more than mine would; and perhaps she wanted blankets. This idea worked me up to such a chill of sympathy, that seeing no Doones now about, and doubting if any guns would go off in this state of the weather, and knowing that no man could catch me up (except with shoes like mine), I even resolved to slide the cliffs, and bravely go to Lorna.

It helped me much in this resolve, that the snow came on again, thick enough to blind a man who had not spent his time among it, as I had done now for days and days. Therefore I took my neatsfoot oil, which now was clogged like honey, and rubbed it hard into my leg-joints, so far as I could reach them. And then I set my back and elbows well against a snow-drift, hanging far adown the cliff, and saying some of the Lord's Prayer, threw myself on Providence. Before there was time to think or dream, I landed very beautifully upon a ridge of run-up snow in a quiet corner. My good shoes, or boots, preserved me from going far beneath it; though one of them was sadly strained, where a grub had gnawed the ash, in the early summer time. Having set myself aright, and being in good spirits, I made boldly across the valley (where the snow was furrowed hard), being now afraid of nobody.

If Lorna had looked out of the window, she would not have known me, with those boots upon my feet, and a well-cleaned sheepskin over me, bearing my own (J. R.) in red, just between my shoulders, but covered now in snowflakes. The house was partly drifted up, though not so much as ours was; and I crossed the little stream almost without knowing that it was under me. At first, being pretty safe against interference from the other huts, by virtue of the blinding snow and the difficulty of walking, I examined all the windows, but these were coated so with ice, like ferns and flowers and dazzling stars, that no one could so much as guess what might be inside of them. Moreover I was afraid of prying narrowly into them, as it was not a proper thing where a maiden might be: only I wanted to know just this, whether she were there or not.

Taking nothing by this movement, I was forced, much against my will, to venture to the door and knock, in a hesitating manner, not being sure but what my answer might be the mouth of a carbine. However, it was not so, for I heard a pattering of feet and a whispering going on, and then a shrill voice through the keyhole, asking, "Who's there?"

"Only me, John Ridd," I answered; upon which I heard a little laughter, and a little sobbing, or something that was like it; and then the door was opened about a couple of inches, with a bar behind it still; and then the little voice went on:

"Put thy finger in, young man, with the old ring on it. But mind thee, if it be the wrong one, thou shalt never draw it back again."

Laughing at Gwenny's mighty threat, I showed my finger in the opening: upon which she let me in, and barred the door again like lightning.

"What is the meaning of all this, Gwenny" I asked, as I slipped about on the floor, for I could not stand there firmly with my great snow-shoes on.

"Maning enough, and bad maning, too," the Cornish girl made answer. "Us be shut in here, and starving, and dursn't let anybody in upon us. I wish thou wer't good to ate, young man: I could manage most of thee."

I was so frightened by her eyes, full of wolfish hunger, that I could only say, "Good God!" having never seen the like before. Then drew I forth a large piece of bread, which I had brought in case of accidents, and placed it in her hands. She leaped at it, as a starving dog leaps at sight of his supper, and she set her teeth in it, and then withheld it from her lips, with something very like an oath at her own vile greediness; and then away round the corner with it, no doubt for her young mistress. I meanwhile was occupied, to the best of my ability, in taking my snow-shoes off, yet wondering much within myself why Lorna did not come to me.

But presently I knew the cause, for Gwenny called me, and I ran, and found my darling quite unable to say so much as, "John, how are you?" Between the hunger, and the cold, and the excitement of my coming, she had fainted away, and lay back on a chair, as white as the snow around us. In betwixt her delicate lips, Gwenny was thrusting with all her strength the hard brown crust of the rye-bread, which she had snatched from me so.

"Get water, or get snow," I said; "don't you know what fainting is, you very stupid child?"

"Never heered on it, in Carnwall," she answered, trusting still to the bread: "be un the same as bleeding?"

"It will be directly, if you go on squeezing away with that crust so. Eat a piece; I have got some more. Leave my darling now to me."

Hearing that I had some more, the starving girl could resist no longer, but tore it in two, and had swallowed half before I had coaxed my Lorna back to sense, and hope, and joy, and love.

"I never expected to see you again. I had made up my mind to die, John; and to die without your knowing it."

As I repelled this fearful thought in a manner highly fortifying, the tender hue flowed back again into her famished cheeks and lips, and a softer brilliance glistened from the depth of her dark eyes.

She gave me one little shrunken hand, and I could not help a tear for it.

"After all, Mistress Lorna," I said, pretending to be gay, for a smile might do her good; "you do not love me as Gwenny does; for she even wanted to eat me."

"And shall, afore I have done, young man," Gwenny answered, laughing; "you come in here with they red chakes, and make us think o' sirloin."

"Eat up your bit of brown bread, Gwenny. It is not good enough for your mistress. Bless her heart! I have something here such as she never tasted the like of, being in such appetite. Look here, Lorna; smell it, first. I have had it ever since Twelfth-day, and kept it all the time for you. Annie made it. That is enough to warrant it good cooking."

And then I showed my great mince pie in a bag of tissue paper, and I told them how the mince-meat was made of golden pippins finely shred, with the undercut of the sirloin, and spice and fruit accordingly and far beyond my knowledge. But Lorna would not touch a morsel until she had thanked God for it, and given me the kindest kiss, and put a piece in Gwenny's mouth.

I have eaten many things myself, with very great enjoyment, and keen perception of their merits, and some thanks to God for them. But I never did enjoy a thing that had found its way between my own lips, half or even a quarter as much as I now enjoyed beholding Lorna, sitting proudly upwards (to show that she was faint no more) entering into that mince pie, and moving all her pearls of teeth (inside her little mouth-place) exactly as I told her. For I was afraid lest she should be too fast in going through it, and cause herself more damage so, than she got of nourishment. But I had no need to fear at all, and Lorna could not help laughing at me for thinking that she had no self-control.

303

Some creatures require a deal of food (I myself among the number), and some can do with a very little; making, no doubt, the best of it. And I have often noticed that the plumpest and most perfect women never eat so hard and fast as the skinny and three-cornered ones. These last be often ashamed of it, and eat most when the men be absent. Hence it came to pass that Lorna, being the loveliest of all maidens, had as much as she could do to finish her own half of pie; whereas Gwenny Carfax (though generous more than greedy) ate up hers without winking, after finishing the brown loaf; and then I begged to know the meaning of this state of things.

"The meaning is sad enough," said Lorna; "and I see no way out of it. We are both to be starved until I let them do what they like with me."

"That is to say, until you choose to marry Carver Doone, and be slowly killed by him."

"Slowly! No, John, quickly. I hate him so intensely, that less than a week would kill me."

"Not a doubt of that," said Gwenny; oh, she hates him nicely then: but not half so much as I do."

I told them both that this state of things could be endured no longer; on which point they agreed with me, but saw no means to help it. For even if Lorna could make up her mind to come away with me and live at Plover's Barrows farm, under my good mother's care, as I had urged so often, behold the snow was all around us, heaped as high as mountains, and how could any delicate maiden ever get across it?

Then I spoke, with a strange tingle upon both sides of my heart, knowing that this undertaking was a serious one for all, and might burn our farm down,—

If I warrant to take you safe, and without much

fright or hardship, Lorna, will you come with me?"

"To be sure I will, dear," said my beauty with a smile, and a glance to follow it, "I have small alternative, to starve, or go with you, John."

"Gwenny, have you courage for it? Will you come with your young mistress?"

"Will I stay behind?" cried Gwenny, in a voice that settled it. And so we began to arrange about it; and I was much excited. It was useless now to leave it longer; if it could be done at all, it could not be too quickly done. It was the Counsellor who had ordered, after all other schemes had failed, that his niece should have no food until she would obey him. He had strictly watched the house, taking turns with Carver, to insure that none came nigh it bearing food or comfort. But this evening, they had thought it needless to remain on guard; and it would have been impossible, because themselves were busy offering high festival to all the valley, in right of their own commandership. And Gwenny said that nothing made her so nearly mad with appetite as the account she received from a woman of all the dishes preparing. Nevertheless she had answered bravely,—

"Go and tell the Counsellor, and go and tell the Carver, who sent you to spy upon us, that we shall have a finer dish than any set before them." And so in truth they did, although so little dreaming it; for no Doone that was ever born, however much of a Carver, might vie with our Annie for mince-meat.

Now while we sat, reflecting much, and talking a good deal more, in spite of all the cold,—for I never was in a hurry to go, when I had Lorna with me,— she said, in her silvery voice, which always led me so along, as if I were slave to a beautiful bell,—

"Now, John, we are wasting time, dear. You have praised my hair, till it curls with pride, and my eyes till you cannot see them, even if they are brown diamonds, which I have heard for the fiftieth time at least; though I never saw such a jewel. Don't you think that it is high time to put on your snow-shoes, John?"

"Certainly not," I answered, "till we have settled something more. I was so cold, when I came in; and now I am as warm as a cricket. And so are you, you lively soul; though you are not upon my hearth yet."

"Remember, John," said Lorna, nestling for a moment to me; "the severity of the weather makes a great difference between us. And you must never take advantage."

"I quite understand all that, dear. And the harder it freezes the better, while that understanding continues. Now do try to be serious."

"I try to be serious! And I have been trying fifty times, and could not bring you to it, John. Although I am sure the situation, as the Counsellor always says, at the beginning of a speech, the situation, to say the least, is serious enough for anything. Come, Gwenny, imitate him."

Gwenny was famed for her imitation of the Counsellor making a speech; and she began to shake her hair, and mount upon a foot-stool; but I really could not have this, though even Lorna ordered it. The truth was that my darling maiden was in such wild spirits at seeing me so unexpected, and at the prospect of release, and of what she had never known, quiet life and happiness, that, like all warm and loving natures, she could scarce control herself.

"Come to this frozen window, John, and see them light the stack fire. They will little know who looks at them. Now be very good, John. You stay in that corner, dear, and I will stand on this side; and try to breathe yourself a peep-hole through the lovely spears and banners. Oh, you don't know how to do it. I must do it for you. Breathe three times, like

that, and that; and then you rub it with your fingers,
before it has time to freeze again."

All this she did so beautifully, with her lips put up
like cherries and her fingers bent half back, as only
girls can bend them, and her little waist thrown out
against the white of the snowed-up window, that I
made her do it three times over; and I stopped her
every time, and let it freeze again, that so she might
be the longer. Now I knew that all her love was
mine, every bit as much as mine was hers; yet I
must have her to show it, dwelling upon every proof,
lengthening out all certainty. Perhaps the jealous
heart is loth to own a life worth twice its own. Be
that as it may, I know that we thawed the window
nicely.

And then I saw, far down the stream (or rather
down the bed of it, for there was no stream visible),
a little form of fire arising, red, and dark, and
flickering. Presently it caught on something and
went upward boldly; and then it struck into many
forks, and then it fell and rose again.

"Do you know what all that is, John?" asked
Lorna, smiling cleverly at the manner of my staring.

"How on earth should I know? Papists burn
Protestants in the flesh; and Protestants burn Papists in effigy, as we mock them. Lorna, are they
going to burn any one to-night?"

"No, you dear. I must rid you of these things.
I see that you are bigoted. The Doones are firing
Dunkery beacon to celebrate their new captain."

"But how could they bring it here through the
snow? If they have sledges, I can do nothing."

"They brought it before the snow began. The
moment poor grandfather was gone, even before his
funeral, the young men, having none to check them,
began at once upon it. They had always borne a
grudge against it: not that it ever did them harm,
but because it seemed so insolent. 'Can't a gentle-

man go home without a smoke behind him?' I have often heard them saying. And though they have done it no serious harm, since they threw the firemen on the fire, many, many years ago they have often promised to bring it here for their candle, and now they have done it. Ah, now look! The tar is kindled."

Though Lorna took it so in joke, I looked upon it very gravely, knowing that this heavy outrage to the feelings of the neighborhood would cause more stir than a hundred sheep stolen, or a score of houses sacked. Not of course that the beacon was of the smallest use to any one, neither stopped anybody from stealing: nay, rather it was like the parish-knell, which begins when all is over, and depresses all the survivors; yet I knew that we valued it, and were proud, and spoke of it as a mighty institution; and even more than that, our vestry had voted, within the last two years, seven shillings and sixpence to pay for it, in proportion with other parishes. And one of the men who attended to it, or at least who was paid for doing so, was our Jem Slocombe's grandfather.

However, in spite of all my regrets, the fire went up very merrily, blazing red, and white, and yellow, as it leaped on different things. And the light danced on the snowdrifts with a misty lilac hue. I was astonished at its burning in such depths of snow; but Gwenny said that the wicked men had been three days hard at work, clearing, as it were, a cock-pit, for their fire to have its way. And now they had a mighty pile, which must have covered five landyards square, heaped up to a goodly height and eager to take fire.

In this I saw a great obstacle to what I wished to manage. For when this pyramid should be kindled thoroughly, and pouring light and blazes round, would not all the valley be like a white room full of candles? Thinking thus, I was half inclined to abide my time for another night; and then my second thoughts convinced me that I would be a fool in this. For lo, what an opportunity! All the Doones would be drunk of course, in about three hours time, and getting more and more in drink as the night went on. As for the fire, it must sink in about three hours or more, and only cast uncertain shadows friendly to my purpose. And then the outlaws must cower round it, as the cold increased on them, helping the weight of the liquor; and in their jollity any noise would be cheered as a false alarm. Most of all, and which decided once for all my action, when these wild and reckless villains should be hot with ardent spirits, what was door, or wall, to stand betwixt them and my Lorna?

This thought quickened me so much that I touched my darling reverently, and told her in a few short words how I hoped to manage it.

"Sweetest, in two hours' time I shall be again with you. Keep the bar up and have Gwenny ready to answer any one. You are safe while they are dining, dear, and drinking healths, and all that stuff; and before they have done with that I shall be again with you. Have everything you care to take in a very little compass; and Gwenny must have no baggage. I shall knock loud, and then wait a little; and then knock twice, very softly."

With this I folded her in my arms; and she looked frightened at me, not having perceived her danger; and then I told Gwenny over again what I had told her mistress; but she only nodded her head and said, "Young man, go and teach thy grandmother."

To my great delight I found that the weather, so often friendly to lovers, and lately seeming so hostile, had in the most important matter done me a signal service. For when I had promised to take my love from the power of those wretches, the only

309

way of escape apparently lay through the main Doone-gate. For though I might climb the cliffs myself, especially with the snow to aid me, I durst not try to fetch Lorna up them, even if she were not half-starved as well as partly frozen; and as for Gwenny's door, as we called it (that is to say, the little entrance from the wooded hollow), it was snowed up long ago to the level of the hills around. Therefore I was at my wit's end how to get them out; the passage by the Doone-gate being long, and dark, and difficult, and leading to such a weary circuit among the snowy moors and hills.

But now, being homeward-bound by the shortest possible track, I slipped along between the bonfire and the boundary cliffs, where I found a caved way of snow behind a sort of avalanche: so that if the Doones had been keeping watch (which they were not doing, but reveling), they could scarcely have discovered me. And when I came to my old ascent, where I had often scaled the cliff and made across the mountains, it struck me that I would just have a look at my first and painful entrance, to wit, the water-slide. I never for a moment imagined that this could help me now; for I never had dared to descend it, even in the finest weather; still I had a curiosity to know what my old friend was like with so much snow upon him. But to my very great surprise, there was scarcely any snow there at all, though plenty curling high over head from the cliff like bolsters over it. Probably the sweeping of the northeast wind up the narrow chasm had kept the showers from blocking it, although the water had no power under the bitter grip of frost. All my water-slide was now less a slide than path of ice; furrowed where the waters ran over fluted ridges; seamed where wind had tossed and combed them, even while congealing; and crossed with little steps wherever the freezing torrent lingered. And here and there the ice was fibred with the trail of sludge-weed, slanting from the side, and matted, so as to make resting place.

Lo it was easy track and channel, as if for the very purpose made, down which I could guide my sledge with Lorna sitting in it. There were only two things to be feared: one lest the rolls of snow above should fall in and bury us; the other lest we should rush too fast, and so be carried headlong into the black whirlpool at the bottom, the middle of which was still unfrozen, and looking more horrible by the contrast. Against this danger I made provision, by fixing a stout bar across; but of the other we must take our chance, and trust ourselves to Providence.

I hastened home at my utmost speed, and told my mother for God's sake to keep the house up till my return, and to have plenty of fire blazing, and plenty of water boiling, and food enough hot for a dozen people, and the best bed aired with the warming-pan. Dear mother smiled softly at my excitement, though her own was not much less, I am sure, and enhanced by sore anxiety. Then I gave very strict directions to Annie, and praised her a little, and kissed her; and I even endeavored to flatter Eliza, lest she should be disagreeable.

After this I took some brandy, both within and about me; the former, because I had sharp work to do; and the latter in fear of whatever might happen, in such great cold, to my comrades. Also I carried some other provisions, grieving much at their coldness; and then I went to the upper linhay and took our new light pony-sled, which had been made almost as much for pleasure as for business; though God only knows how our girls could have found any pleasure in bumping along so. On the snow, however, it ran as sweetly as if it had been made for it; yet I durst not take the pony with it; in the first place, because his hoofs would break through the ever-shifting surface of the light and piling snow; and secondly, because those ponies, coming from the forest, have a dreadful trick of neighing, and most of all in frosty weather.

Therefore I girded my own body with a dozen turns of hay-rope, twisting both the ends in under at the bottom of my breast, and winding the hay on the skew a little, that the hempen thong might not slip between, and so cut me in the drawing. I put a good piece of spare rope in the sled, and the cross seat with the back to it, which was stuffed with our own wool, as well as two or three fur coats: and then just as I was starting, out came Annie, in spite of the cold, panting for fear of missing me, and with nothing on her head, but a lantern in one hand.

"Oh, John, here is the most wonderful thing! Mother has never shown it before; and I can't think how she could make up her mind. She had gotten it in a great well of a cupboard, with camphor, and spirits, and lavender. Lizzie says it is a most magnificent sealskin cloak, worthy fifty pounds, or a farthing."

"At any rate it is soft and warm," said I. very calmly flinging it into the bottom of the sled. "Tell mother I will put it over Lorna's feet."

"Lorna's feet! Oh, you great fool," cried Annie, for the first time reviling me. "Over her shoulders; and be proud, you very stupid John."

"It is not good enough for her feet," I answered, with strong emphasis; "but don't tell mother I said so, Annie. Only thank her very kindly."

With that I drew my traces hard, and set my ashen staff into the snow, and struck out with my best foot foremost (the best one at snow-shoes, I mean), and the sled came after me as lightly as a dog might follow; and Annie with the lantern seemed to be left behind and waiting, like a pretty lamp-post.

The full moon rose as bright behind me as a patin of pure silver, casting on the snow long shadows of the few things left above, burdened rock, and shaggy foreland, and the laboring trees. In the great white desolation, distance was a mocking vision: hills looked nigh and valleys far; when hills were far and valleys nigh. And the misty breath of frost, piercing through the ribs of rock, striking to the pith of trees, creeping to the heart of man, lay along the hollow places, like a serpent sloughing. Even as my own gaunt shadow (travestied as if I were the moonlight's daddy-long-legs) went before me down the slope; even I, the shadow's master, who had tried in vain to cough, when coughing brought good liquorice, felt a pressure on my bosom and a husking in my throat.

However, I went on quietly and at a very tidy speed; being only too thankful that the snow had ceased and no wind as yet arisen. And from the ring of low white vapor girding all the verge of sky, and from the rosy blue above, and the shafts of starlight set upon a quivering bow, as well as from the moon itself and the light behind it, having learned the signs of frost from its bitter twinges, I knew that we should have a night as keen as ever England felt. Nevertheless, I had work enough to keep me warm if I managed it. The question was, Could I contrive to save my darling from it?

Daring not to risk my sled by any fall from the valley-cliffs, I dragged it very carefully up the steep incline of ice, through the narrow chasm, and so to the very brink and verge where first I had seen my Lorna, in the fishing days of boyhood. As then I had a trident fork, for sticking of the loaches, so now I had a strong ash stake, to lay across from rock to rock and break the speed of descending. With this I moored the sled quite safe, at the very lip of the chasm, where all was now substantial ice, green and black in the moonlight; and then I set off up the valley, skirting along one side of it.

The stack fire still was burning strongly, but with more of heat than blaze; and many of the younger Doones were playing on the verge of it, the children making rings of fire and their mothers watching them. All the grave and reverend warriors, having heard of rheumatism, were inside of log and stone, in the two lowest houses, with enough of candles burning to make our list of sheep come short.

All these I passed without the smallest risk or difficulty, walking up the channel of drift which I spoke of once before. And then I crossed, with more of care, and to the door of Lorna's house, and made the sign, and listened, after taking my snow-shoes off.

But no one came, as I expected, neither could I espy a light. And I seemed to hear a faint low sound, like the moaning of the snow-wind. Then I knocked again more loudly, with a knocking at my heart; and receiving no answer, set all my power at once against the door. In a moment it flew inwards and I glided along the passage with my feet still slippery. There in Lorna's room I saw, by the moonlight flowing in, a sight which drove me beyond sense.

Lorna was behind a chair, crouching in the corner, with her hands up, and a crucifix or something that looked like it. In the middle of the room lay Gwenny Carfax, stupid, yet with one hand clutching the ankle of a struggling man. Another man stood above my Lorna, trying to draw the chair away. In a moment I had him around the waist, and he went out of the window with a mighty crash of glass; luckily for him that window had no bars like some of them. Then I took the other man by the neck, and he could not plead for mercy. I bore him out of the house as lightly as I would bear a baby, yet squeezing his throat a little more than I fain would do to an infant. By the bright moonlight I saw that I carried Marwood de Whichehalse. For his father's sake I spared him, and because he had been my schoolfellow; but with every muscle of my body strung with indignation, I cast him, like a skittle, from me into a snowdrift, which closed over him. Then I looked for the other fellow, tossed through Lorna's window; and found him lying stunned and bleeding, neither able to groan yet. Charleworth Doone, if his gushing blood did not much mislead me.

It was no time to linger now: I fastened my shoes in a moment, and caught up my own darling with her head upon my shoulder, where she whispered faintly; and telling Gwenny to follow me, or else I would come back for her if she could not walk the snow, I ran the whole distance to my sled, caring not who might follow me. Then by the time I had set up Lorna, beautiful and smiling, with the sealskin cloak all over her, sturdy Gwenny came along, having trudged in the track of my snow-shoes, although with two bags on her back. I set her in beside her mistress, to support her and keep warm; and then with one look back at the glen, which had been so long my home of heart, I hung behind the sled, and launched it down the steep and dangerous way.

Though the cliffs were black above us, and the road unseen in front, and a great white grave of snow might at a single word come down, Lorna was as calm and happy as an infant in its bed. She knew that I was with her; and when I told her not to speak she touched my hand in silence. Gwenny was in a much greater fright, having never seen such a thing before, neither knowing what it is to yield to pure love's confidence. I could hardly keep her quiet without making a noise myself. With my staff from rock to rock, and my weight thrown backward, I broke the sled's too rapid way, and brought my grown love safely out, by the selfsame road which first had led me to her girlish fancy and my boyish slavery.

Unpursued, yet looking back as if some one must be after us, we skirted round the black whirling pool and gained the meadows beyond it. Here there was hard collar work, the track being all uphill and rough; and Gwenny wanted to jump out to lighten the sled and to push behind. But I would not hear of it; because it was now so deadly cold and I feared that Lorna might get frozen, without having Gwenny to keep her warm. And after all, it was the sweetest labor I had ever known in all my life, to be sure that I was pulling Lorna, and pulling her to our own farmhouse.

Gwenny's nose was touched with frost before we had gone much further, because she would not keep it quiet and snug beneath the sealskin. And here I had to stop in the moonlight (which was very dangerous) and rub it with a clove of snow, as Eliza had taught me; and Gwenny scolding all the time, as if myself had frozen it. Lorna was now so far oppressed with all the troubles of the evening and the joy that followed them, as well as by the piercing cold and difficulty of breathing, that she lay quite motionless, like fairest wax in the moonlight—when we stole a glance at her beneath the dark folds of the cloak; and I thought that she was falling into the heavy snow-sleep whence there is no awaking.

Therefore I drew my traces tight, and set my whole strength to the business; and we slipped along at a merry pace, although with many joltings, which must have sent my darling out into the cold snowdrifts but for the short strong arm of Gwenny. And so in about an hour's time, in spite of many hindrances, we came home to the old courtyard, and all the dogs saluted us. My heart was quivering and my cheeks as hot as the Doones's bonfire, with wondering both what Lorna would think of our farmyard and what my mother would think of her. Upon the former subject my anxiety was wasted, for Lorna neither saw a thing nor even opened her heavy eyes. And as to what mother would think of her, she was certain not to think at all, until she had cried over her.

And so indeed it came to pass. Even at this length of time I can hardly tell it, although so bright before my mind, because it moves my heart so. The sled was at the open door with only Lorna in it; for Gwenny Carfax had jumped out and hung back in the clearing, giving any reason rather than the only true one—that she would not be intruding. At the door were all our people; first of course Betty Muxworthy, teaching me how to draw the sled, as if she had been born in it, and flourishing with a great broom wherever a speck of snow lay. Then dear Annie, and old Molly (who was very quiet and counted almost for nobody), and behind them mother, looking as if she wanted to come first, but doubted how the manners lay. In the distance Lizzie stood, fearful of encouraging, but unable to keep out of it.

Betty was going to poke her broom right in under the sealskin cloak, where Lorna lay unconscious, and where her precious breath hung frozen, like a silver cobweb! but I caught up Betty's broom an? flung it clean away over the corn-chamber; a? then I put the others by and fetched my m? forward.

"You shall see her first," I said; "is she not your daughter? Hold the light there, Annie."

Dear mother's hands were quick and trembling as she opened the shining folds; and there she saw my Lorna sleeping, with her black hair all disheveled, and she bent and kissed her forehead, and only said, "God bless her, John!" And then she was taken with violent weeping and I was forced to hold her.

"Us may tich of her now, I rackon," said Betty in her most jealous way: "Annie, tak her by the head and I'll tak her by the toesen. No taime to stand here like girt gawks. Don'ee tak on zo, missus. Ther be vainer vish in the zea—Lor, but her be a booty!"

With this they carried her into the house, Betty chattering all the while, and going on now about Lorna's hands, and the others crowding round her, so that I thought I was not wanted among so many women, and should only get the worst of it and perhaps do harm to my darling. Therefore I went and brought Gwenny in, and gave her a potful of bacon and pease, and an iron spoon to eat it with, which she did right heartily.

Then I asked her how she could have been such a fool as to let those two vile fellows enter the house where Lorna was; and she accounted for it so naturally, that I could only blame myself. For my agreement had been to give one loud knock (if you happen to remember), and after that two little knocks. Well, these two drunken rogues had come; and one, being very drunk indeed, had given a great thump; and then nothing more to do it; and the other, being three-quarters drunk, had followed his ꟷader (as one might say) but feebly, and making ꟷ of it. Whereupon up jumped Lorna, and de- ꟷ that her John was there.

ꟷhis Gwenny told me shortly, between the

318